Ken Duncum was awarded the 2010 New Zealand Post Katherine Mansfield Prize and is recognised as one of New Zealand's leading playwrights.

His plays include a loose trilogy looking at the impact of music on New Zealand—from 50s rock 'n' roll versus Beatles-era British Invasion (*Blue Sky Boys*) to 70s glam (*John, I'm Only Dancing*) and punk (*Waterloo Sunset*). He has also written plays about men lost at sea (*Flipside*), surrogacy disputes (*Cherish*), unsolved murders (*Trick of the Light*) and dark goings-on in smalltown New Zealand (*Horseplay*).

Ken's most recent plays include *The Great Gatsby*, *West End Girls* and *White Cloud.*

He is currently co-writing a musical with Tim Finn—*The Nightdress.*

After studying theatre, film and English at Victoria University in the 1980s, **Rebecca Rodden** wrote and performed in plays and film projects around Wellington.

Acting roles include the Fool in Simon Bennett's *King Lear*, the Queen in *Salve Regina*, and Polythene Pam and Nadine in various productions of *Polythene Pam* and *Flybaby.*

In 1994 Rebecca played the lead role of Anna Bowman in short film *The Terrorist*, directed by Shane Loader, which was selected to compete at the prestigious Clermont-Ferrand short film festival.

In her parallel career as a playwright, Rebecca co-wrote *Polythene Pam, Truelove, Flybaby, JISM* and *Panic!*, and is also sole writer of *Stigma.*

BATS Plays

Ken Duncum &
Rebecca Rodden

Victoria University Press

VICTORIA UNIVERSITY PRESS
Victoria University of Wellington
PO Box 600 Wellington
vuw.ac.nz/vup

Copyright © Ken Duncum and Rebecca Rodden 2016
First published 2016

With notes by Simon Bennett, Emma Kinane, Gary Henderson and Petra Massey

National Library of New Zealand Cataloguing-in-Publication Data
Duncum, Ken, 1959-
BATS plays / Ken Duncum and Rebecca Rodden.
ISBN 978-1-77656-089-9
1. Duncum, Ken, 1959- 2. Rodden, Rebecca.
3. New Zealand drama—20th century. I. Rodden, Rebecca. II. Title.
NZ822.2—dc 23

Printed by Ligare, Auckland

Contents

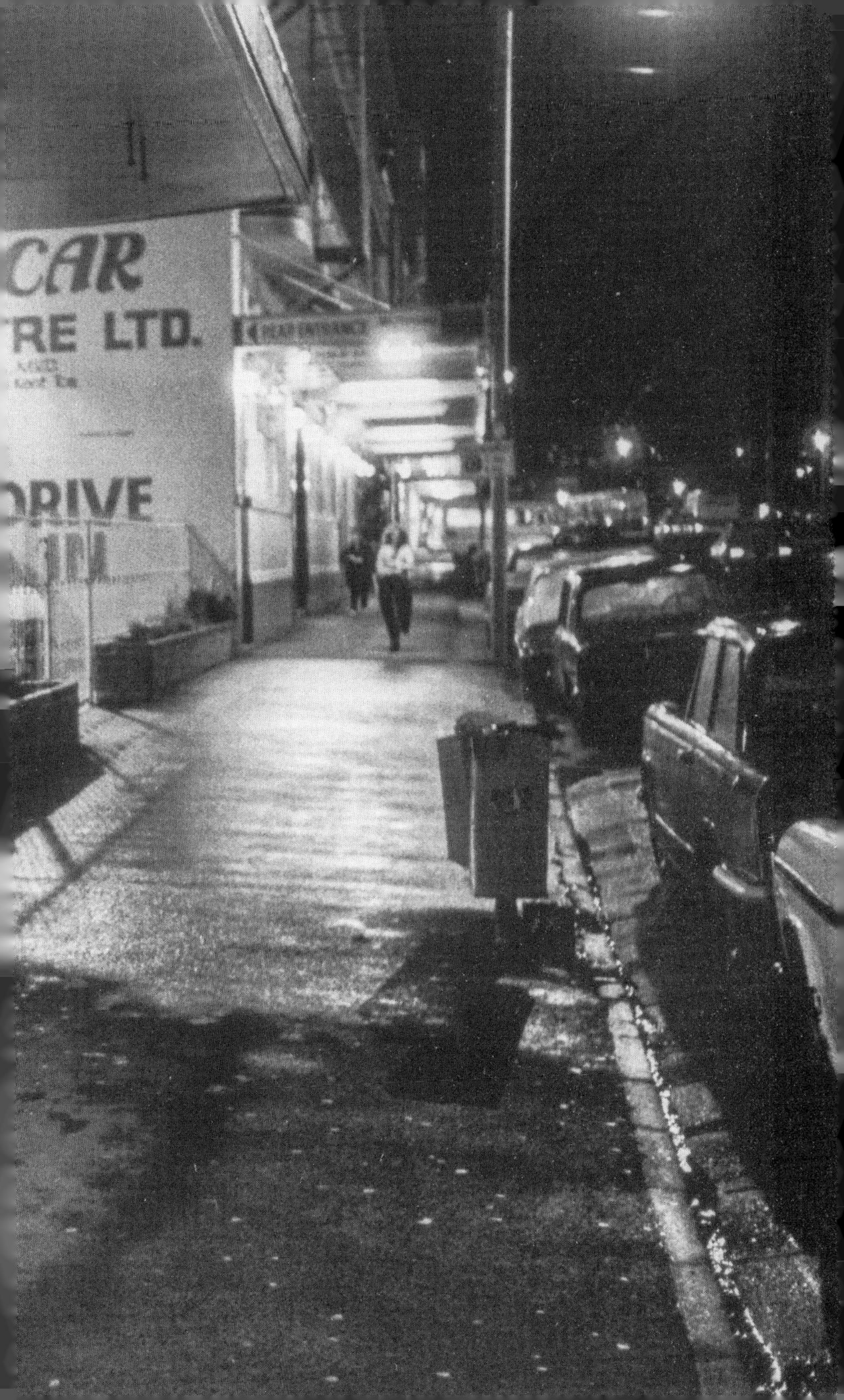
CAR
RE LTD.
DRIVE

authorised capital

1 million shares of 1 cent each

certificate of shares

no: 33......

register page no:.1.....

no of shares: 10.000.

bats theatre

registered office 1 kent terrace, wellington city

given under the common seal of the company at wellington on:

limited

(incorporated under the companies act, 1955)

this is to certify that

......KEN DUNCUM........

is the registered holder of fully paid share numbered: 940001-950000 ....

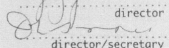

....13./.10.../1993...

....
director

....
director/secretary

this certificate is issued on the condition that no transfer of any of the shares comprised therein will be registered unless and until this certificate has been deposite in the office of the company

Fly by Night:
Memories of BATS

Ken:

Wellington was dark then—next to nobody lived in the city and by 6pm there were only stragglers on the rain-blasted streets. The urine-coloured streetlights were on but the shops were out, and an emptiness consumed block after block. Old Wellington was dying—under the reign of the architect–mayor, buildings disappeared over the weekend, leaving rubble then empty sockets. Nothing seemed to be being built. Three-day southerlies descended like judgement. Scattered around were a few hardy cafés—Suzy's if you were cultured; Kenny's if you drove a taxi—and Roy's Burger Bar on Kent Terrace was perennially the last port of call after 10pm closing time at the Clarendon and Cambridge Hotels, or the Duke's. The light was shining at Roy's when all was dark around. Minuscule premises steeped in sweat and grease, the two heavies behind the counter looked like old sailors gone to seed. With the clientele composed almost exclusively of drunks, bonhomie was in short supply and everyone seemed to have one eye on the door, not sure what might come through it at any moment.

Immediately to the left of Roy's was the entrance to BATS Theatre—where the steps up to the door provided the ideal semi-shelter to eat your chunky chips or disintegrating egg-burger if your drunk legs would carry you no further. Consequently, getting in or out of BATS late at night often required running a gauntlet. It was best to do it quick, using the element of surprise—particularly if leaving. Take a breath, whip the door open (not too far), squeeze through, slam it shut, don't fumble with the lock too long, then off down the street—before whatever glazed-eyed patrons of Roy's you'd surprised mid-chew had time to collect enough consciousness between them to see you as a potential plaything. 'What . . .' they'd be left saying to each other, squinting behind them at the now sealed door, 'What is this place, anyway?'

The approach to BATS for me was always, and still is, along Kent Terrace. I'd be parked along there—say, by the Greek–New Zealand Memorial or up by Clyde Quay School—and would have to make the dash along the three or four blocks, past the brick College of Australasian Surgeons, past the KFC car park in its heyday full of a brief blooming subculture of Indian boy racers, past E. Morris Jnr Ltd funeral directors, which later became a dessert restaurant, past Halswell Lodge with its buzzing Vacancy/No Vacancy sign, past Deluxe and the pre-Peter Jackson Embassy Theatre, across Majoribanks Street, past the pub on the corner and finally swinging in the door of BATS to the secret world within. Sometimes this approach might be jet-powered by a freezing southerly, more often greatly impeded by an in-your-face northerly accompanied by shotgun rain which, with a true sense of dramatic arc, increased in power and aggression the closer I struggled towards my goal. This still happens to me and I always marvel how this is one of the most unpleasant weather experiences you can have in a city that truly excels in this area. What kind of philistine wind is this that must have had many a BATS-goer besides myself on the verge of allowing themselves to be blown home again before finally falling through the door exhausted, frozen, soaked and with crazy hair? Supporting local theatre should not involve a risk of dying from exposure— but with BATS that seems to have been part of the deal from the beginning.

I don't remember the first time I went into BATS—but I know at that time it was a venue for hire, at the not inconsiderable sum of $60 a day. Charlie Harter did shows there—I remember particularly *Life Ain't No Dress Rehearsal*—and I think the New Zealand Drama School (then situated above a liquor store at the other end of Kent Terrace) used it sometimes for graduation shows. It was also theatre-of-choice for Conrad Newport's Famous Door Theatre Company. I've still got vivid memories of Conrad's adaptation of *Frankenstein*, which seemed to have a hundred scenes, each accompanied by elaborately painted backdrops and sliding panels representing everything from foliage to a castle. The curtain would drop, there would be the sound of furious activity behind it for five minutes or so, and then the curtain would rise on a completely transformed scene—at which point the capacity audience would applaud wildly. As the play went on, scenes seemed to get shorter and scene changes longer until things reached an apogee when the curtain went up on an intricately painted meadow where a young girl sat happily threading a daisy chain. The monster entered; the girl screamed; he picked her up under his arm and staggered off . . . curtain down. During the particularly extended scene change which followed, Wellington's premiere theatre couple, Peter and Kate Harcourt, picked their way down the stairs from the back row. As they passed in front of me on the way to the exit Peter observed to me in his resonant tone, 'There is only so much one can suffer in the name of art.' Conrad was delighted when I relayed this back to him.

The first time I hired BATS was for a season of *Truelove/Polythene Pam* in December of 1986. I remember coming in on our first day and finding Andrew Foster up a ladder unrigging lights. He must have been all of 17 but, for some reason, was my contact for the hiring of the theatre. Andrew was up and down ladders in BATS Theatre for many a year afterwards. Gradually I learnt the history of the place. The RAOB—Royal Antediluvian Order of Buffaloes—still gathered on the mysterious top floor. The Buffs—as hard-drinking and un-arty a bunch of crusty old guys as you could imagine—owned the building and leased out the downstairs to Roy's Burger Bar, as well as to a bonsai insurance firm who occupied a rabbit-hutch of space on the other side and to the Bane and Austin Touring Society, otherwise known as BATS. Previously the theatre space had been the Savage Club, a frisky dance hall (particularly during WWII, when American GIs trotting out local girls made it a site rich in romance, misbehaviour and tensions with the hometown boys)—then centre of operations for Unity Theatre, a gallant and talented bunch of actors and directors who didn't shirk from labels such as intellectual or communist. (It's a toss-up in 1950s New Zealand as to which was considered worst.) Then Mr Bane and Mr

Austin took over with a vision for touring theatre, which thrived for its due time and after which, still holding the lease, they made BATS available to any young, thrusting or deluded theatre aficionados prepared to stump up the rent in order to strut and fret their hour under the dim glow of the six included-in-the-price theatre lights. Reader, that was all the invite I needed.

The Buffaloes in full rut would stamp their feet and sing—what were they doing up there? I climbed the stairs one day to ask about something. I knocked on a rippled-glass door for some time before a figure swam into view. He was wearing a bloodstained apron and carrying a cleaver. He squinted at me suspiciously, grunted at whatever message I was trying to convey, shut the door and faded back into the dim interior and whatever preparations for the night's festivities I had interrupted. A couple of actors told me they had penetrated the Holy of Holies and seen a board with horns mounted on it and a bare blue lightbulb at each end. This image has remained with me ever since—simple, crude, homemade but all the more disturbing for that, like the stick 'sharpened at both ends' the boys whisper about in *Lord of the Flies*.

In those days a corridor led from the Kent Terrace front door down to double doors to the theatre. Going through these, you turned right and entered on that side of the auditorium. A door off the stage on the other side opened directly into the alley and the wall of the fire station next door—which proved irresistible in terms of entrances and exits, resulting in actors running round the outside of the building in whatever costume in order to appear from somewhere else (and often as someone else) the audience didn't expect. There were originally only two doors on the upstage wall, but they steadily proliferated through the years until you had a choice of left, right or middle for both the downstairs and upstairs level. Open them all at once and the building might fall down . . .

After a couple of years of shows there—a revolution. Simon Bennett and Simon Elson took over the lease and modern BATS was born. No longer a space for hire, it was a programming, constantly running theatre set up with the intention of providing an outlet for emerging writers, actors and directors. There was a great uprush of plays and theatre activity—Wellington-written plays abounded, along with quirky other stuff from overseas; late-night shows appeared, including a regular devised soap serial (*Lainghaven*—part of the *Lewd and the Ludicrous* late-night show). Innovations in the building included a liquor licence and a nibble nook selling, amongst other things, flashback-to-childhood bags of 'dolly mixture', which have since become the worst BATS tradition ever. (Why would a theatre—a *theatre*—sell lollies in little paper bags? I take the same view as in the Old West—rustlers should be lynched.) It was agreed that all co-ops who performed there would purchase a share in BATS—so I've still got an original share, though I haven't attended a shareholders' meeting in twenty years.

After the two Simons, BATS was run by people like Liz Penny, Jeremy Grogan, Guy Boyce, Steve Marshall, Helen Searancke and many others. In those years it was not unusual for there to be seven mainbill shows on at the same time in Wellington—at Downstage, the Depot, BATS, Circa, Repertory and Stagecraft—and BATS carved out its niche within that line-up. I remember one night sitting beside foundation Circa Theatre member Ross Jolly, who had come to check out what the opposition was doing right. The show might have been *Sunset Café* by Gary Henderson. As music pumped and the young audience chattered before the lights went down, Ross glanced around and announced, 'See? We're already having fun.'

BATS has been like home to a lot of people—and was like home to me for a while. One night during the run of *Truelove/Polythene Pam*, it seemed too late to bother going home, so I slept in the bed on stage . . . When I wrote *Blue Sky Boys* it gave me great pleasure to set the play in the same place it was being performed (albeit in an earlier 60s incarnation)—as a tribute to 1 Kent Terrace and its history, a link to those arty Kiwi battlers who'd gone before and also as a measure of my affection for the place.

I still go to BATS. Roy's closed and became office space for the theatre, the tiny insurance company became the tiny Pit Bar for pre- and post-show refreshment. Both, and the corridor between, are now part of the expanded bar and foyer. The entrance to the theatre is not on the right but where Simon and Simon cut it through the centre of the seating block some twenty-seven years ago now. Upstairs there's a whole other theatre (where the Buffaloes' last secret is revealed in the stained-glass ceiling dome), plus office and rehearsal space—and the whole thing is earthquake safe no matter how many doors you open, all thanks to Fran Walsh and Peter Jackson coming to save the day (and the building) like the eagles do in *The Hobbit*, perhaps wanting to maintain the conduit for up-and-coming actors which BATS has served as over the last decades.

The lights are on now in Wellington; Courtenay Place is lit up like the world's fair at all hours; and warm light spills out the big new windows of BATS Theatre, inviting everyone in. It's a better town to live in and the seats are more comfortable, but, crucially, the black box is the same.

Regardless of ownership and leases, BATS belongs to anyone who's splashed up a coat of black paint there—covering the layers and accretions and ideas of all those who've been there before. And it belongs to the audience; which is not one audience but thousands. In the old VHS videos I shot of my plays there, I would always leave the camera running after the last bow. Now if I watch the digital transfers of those tapes, I lean forward at the end, picking out faces, couples, haircuts and smiles as the audience rises and files slowly out into another time. I keep watching and see myself go past, down the stairs and out into the foyer. The camera whirs on alone, pointed at an empty stage. I lean closer . . . BATS Theatre breathes . . .

Emma Kinane:

The usual agreed-upon formula for cancelling a performance because of a small audience is 'cast and crew, plus two'. Any less in the audience means it's reasonable to cancel. One night—I can't remember which show—there were two people in the audience. We quoted the saying and offered them the option; we could do the show for the two of them (we were already there, in costume and ready to go) or we could rebook them for another night. I think it was winter, nice and warm in the black box, and surprisingly they opted to stay. Also surprisingly, we had the best show ever. It was intimate and special and wonderfully free of any of the bad stuff. No nerves. No sense of artifice in reaching the back row. It was direct: from us to them, about a distance of two metres. It was personal, like reading a story to your kid in bed. One of the best nights of my life. I have no idea what the play was, or my part in it. I bet I had two lines or something, and I've turned it into this huge (potentially not-real) moment in my memory.

I was there when Simon Elson took a chainsaw (or was it a Skilsaw? I'm an actor, what do I know?) to the old seating block and cut a new aisle in the centre of BATS. Even at the time, it felt like this was the real start of BATS' new life. It was shocking and liberating; a no-turning-back moment. I don't think I realised at the time how brave Simon and Simon were. Perhaps they didn't either. When you're in your early 20s you just get on with it.

Making a living from co-op theatre has always been an oxymoron, but in the early days of new BATS there was some relatively well-paid (compared to now) commercial work to be had in Wellington, and most actors tried to get the odd day of extra work during a season to tide them over until the co-op payout. There was even a technique to be learned; actors who went before us passed down a now-lost skill set of ways to be unrecognisable on camera so you wouldn't miss out on other work due to being associated with one product. These included getting the costumier to let you wear a hat, hiding in the background of shots, angling your body and facing away from the camera wherever possible. I'm amazed we got away with any of it. (Maybe we didn't, and it was all talk.)

One BATS co-op I was part of (actually, it might have been *JISM*) decided it was well worth missing a day's rehearsal when we were all cast as extras in a TV ad for a sound system. The entire cast were dressed up in posh clothes, sitting in the stalls of the State Opera House, listening to the apparently awesome sounds coming from a tiny speaker in the orchestra pit. The footage is probably sitting in a vault somewhere.

Gary Henderson:

The BATS website has a fairly comprehensive history of the theatre. The time covered by the plays from *Truelove/Polythene Pam* to *Panic!* starts just before the 'Building a new BATS' heading. My memories won't be too different from anyone else's. Between 1989 and 1996

I directed five of my own plays there, helped out with many others, and watched everything I could. Like most of us who worked there, I have memories of all-nighters in the theatre hammering and drilling, eating bad food from the nearest takeaway bar, having or avoiding arguments, becoming so fatigued it was hard to make good choices, and getting the first bus home for a couple of hours' sleep before returning. Hard, sometimes dispiriting, always exciting.

The most important and lasting effects of that time are the relationships. In the cast and crew lists from that period, the same names keep appearing. The director of this show acted in the previous one and will be set building for the next. Today many of those people are still my closest friends and professional colleagues.

The best thing of all is that it's still happening. New practitioners are still working at BATS, having experiences that are the same and different and equally formative. While they do their work, they too are making connections and relationships that will last throughout their lives.

Polythene Pam

Finalists in the 1985 Shell One Act Play Contest:

The Bit Players Present...

Jonesco's
The Chairs

Polythene Pam
by Ken Duncum and Rebecca Rodden
A fundraising venture.

BATS THEATRE SUNDAY 8th SEPTEMBER
(1 Kent Tce.)   7:30p.m. $5.00

Ken:

We were not lovers.

I did write Rebecca a poem. And then we wrote some plays together.

But we were not, as some assumed, lovers.

I don't remember our first meeting—except that I mention it in that poem, written half-my-lifetime ago—but I know it happened in a 1984 theatre studies course at Victoria University. To be precise, at a stripped-out chemistry lab in the old Hunter Building—because the Kelburn arsonist had burnt out the usual theatre space.

Rebecca was a punk with a limp—quick-witted, overactive and shamelessly manipulative. I was an ex-computer programmer and not-yet-poet at 25, looking for a moment of change, a pivot in my life that might save me from living in my head for all time. I appreciated her constant comic turn of punctured princess, and she enjoyed having a poem written about her (regardless of the picture of her it offered to the world), so we became friends.

As part of that theatre course, taught by Phil Mann and David Carnegie, there was a playwriting stream; a small group of maybe eight. Our first exercise was to write something short based on the story of Jonah and his difficulties getting to the city of Nineveh. I overthought it and came up with a fairly forced piece about travellers in a dystopian future trying to cross a border, who ended up scapegoating each other and were swallowed by the whale of the authoritarian state—get it? By contrast, Rebecca decided it was too much trouble and inveigled a guy who was susceptible to her charm to write the exercise under her name. She was quite open with me about this and I was predictably withering. When we came to read the scenes out in class I had to admit, however, that the guy had done a pretty good job—it was sharp and funny. When I told Rebecca this, she said what the stand-in writer had produced was so lame that at the last minute she'd been forced to write something herself. So it was her writing that was sharp and funny. Hmmm . . .

Rebecca faded out the following year—probably something to do with her hip—while I went on to do more theatre and film courses. At the end of that second year she materialised in the small audience for an excerpt of *Equus* that I directed as part of my last theatre course. I seem to remember she was draped in some kind of gold mesh that made her look like a punk Cleopatra. Her reappearance was staged as carefully as my little 25-minute, 36-lighting-cue play.

Not having known how to get hold of her before, I pounced. I told her we were going to write something together and she was going to act in it. I don't think it was phrased as a question.

That 'something' became *Polythene Pam*.

I should mention that my time in those theatre courses—while it had ignited a passion for plays and playwriting—had by this time also convinced me (and everyone else) that I could not act. The first-person outlet for my theatre writing was closed to me. The usual training-wheels for a playwright are monologues, a medium that makes for an intimate relationship with an audience. My awkwardly wooden, forced and uncharismatic stage presence loudly proclaimed the fact that I needed someone to front for me. Hello Rebecca, wanna do a show?

So we started to meet, tell each other stories, scribble them down, shape them, put punchlines on the other one's setups. It was no easier to corral Rebecca, get writing out of her, than it had been in the theatre course, but the deal was always that what we wrote was for her to perform; that if she went through the aggravation of inventing and shaping a script, then her moment on stage would come, the truly important moment for her.

I organised everything, I kept all the drafts, I created structure, I kept things moving forward. But neither of us could have done it without the other. Everything was conceived and built off Rebecca's unique persona—which she had composed all by herself before she met me: a charm (in both senses of the word) that could hold a room. If I was the bottle she was the lightning.

Polythene Pam was the alter ego I came up with so we wouldn't just call the character Rebecca—and maybe to create elbow room for some of my outlook on life to slip in unnoticed. The name comes from the Beatles song—something in John Lennon's eponymous, androgynous character (who was likely to be splashed across the scandal rags) put me in mind of Rebecca.

We collaged stuff together. I might have given Rebecca writing assignments or just created deadlines that squeezed out whatever was on her mind, or on mine. We formed it into a rambling monologue which entwined both our voices, skating on humorous evasion, circling down into the pit of something serious. I've still got the jigsaw pieces we started with—both mine and Rebecca's carefully typed (how official!) page after page of *On the Road* screeds and rants. I glimpse all sorts of things in them. Rebecca's confessions that were not true and at the same time hardly made up. I quickly learnt that it was fatal to assume these were in any way the facts of her experience, but that they served to sketch out a roundedness, a shape that was true to her life. In my own contributions I can read the headlines of my ongoing struggle to negotiate boundaries between myself and the world. I see myself thinking and writing back to when I was nineteen and appeared to be tumbling into a manic state, obsessing about the Killing Fields of Cambodia as they were rolled back and revealed by a Vietnamese incursion, while our Muldoon government threatened to send troops to support Pol Pot. In the words of a psychology textbook I consulted at the time, I seemed 'unable to screen out irrelevant stimuli'. Or were the stimuli all too relevant? I still don't know. Was Polythene Pam's retreat into resignation my own?

Once we had a version of the script, we started to rehearse. The writer–writer relationship became a director–actor relationship. Rebecca would act; I'd sit there watching her—usually in the basement of the theatre space at 93 Kelburn Parade. I can't now remember what the plan was for taking our genius to the world—I suspect there wasn't one. I was working shift as a postal sorter, and

Rebecca might have been wearing a wig to do bar work. Life had no point if we weren't meeting in a dank basement with a bag of dummies.

I'm pretty sure that the first words I wrote for the play were 'Polythene Pam shoves a dummy's head through a paper wall.' So I knew from the beginning that Rebecca would have co-stars—a couple of life-sized blank canvases that any relationship could be projected onto. The dummies were created by my partner Jill and her sister Norma—they designed, sewed and stuffed them. I lay on the floor to create the outline for the vaguely male one. Jill's sister Norma was the model for the slightly smaller one.

The dummies were generally compliant, occasionally prone to doing something annoying like slipping comically off a chair during a serious bit. Rebecca had to learn how to wrangle them, and I became expert at folding and packing them into a black plastic (polythene) rubbish bag so they could be extracted in the right way at the right time.

I think the first showing of the play was in the basement at 93 Kelburn Parade for a gaggle of theatre studies people who were hanging around there or could be induced to come and watch a 'thing' on a Sunday afternoon. Some of them were no doubt just curious about what we'd been doing behind that closed door . . .

Then I've got a memory of doing *Polythene Pam* in the Student Union building as part of a short season of one-act plays collectively titled *Apocalypso*, but was that before or after our one-night stand at BATS?

So this is where BATS Theatre enters the story . . . briefly.

It was a fundraiser for another production I was associated with. In the theatre course where I had directed that excerpt of *Equus*, a classmate, Colleen Foss, directed Ionesco's *The Chairs*. She and the cast enjoyed it so much that Colleen decided to enter it in the Shell Community Drama Festival. It won at the local (Wellington) and regional (held in Hawera) levels and was invited to the national final in Whangarei. To raise funds for the trip, *The Chairs* was performed on a Sunday evening at BATS. I was part of the crew for *The Chairs*—I think I was operating sound. It was suggested that to make more of an evening of it for what was (for the first time) a paying audience, Rebecca and I did *Polythene Pam* as a curtain-raiser. A black box and flat lighting suited us fine—as did the overflowing audience sitting on the stairs and the floor across the front of the stage and in the exit, all in fine contravention of the fire regulations.

The Chairs didn't win in Whangarei—but we had a good time, and decided to carry on as a theatre company. For the sake of the Shell Community Drama Festival we had been called the Bit Players but now mutated into the more sharply titled *Stiletto Theatre*. Besides Colleen and myself, members included the cast of *The Chairs*—Maria Buchanan, Jonathon Hendry, Simon Bennett—plus Jennifer Major and Sarah Pomeroy. The idea was to help each other realise our theatre ambitions as actors, directors and writers. Simon directed some short Beckett pieces, I remember, which we hoped to be able to perform at Downstage Theatre in their bar space. Nothing came of it and morale was starting to flag. I remember Maria suggesting to me that we should wind up *Stiletto*—and my retort that everything I'd done for the company was so in return I could get everybody's support for the show I had planned for the end of that year. I'd obviously been a bit reticent about my intentions but once the others realised I was serious about an actual production in a proper theatre they all threw their energies behind it.

'It' was a pre-Christmas ten-night season of two plays by Rebecca and me—one being *Polythene Pam*. We wanted more people to see *Pam*, but I also realised that to make it a decent night out we needed another play to put against the 50-minute show. This was (or became) *Truelove*, a step up the ladder in terms of writing something requiring set, design, costumes, special effects and—hold the front page—more than one actor!

More on that later. But to conclude the story of *Polythene Pam*; it was in preparation for the season at BATS that I think we finally shaped the script so that it was bookended by the 'Two weeks . . .' speech—that is, that the overarching concept settled into the form of Pam coming on to make her resignation speech, losing her nerve and diverting, diverting, diverting until she works her way back to the emotional matter at hand. This felt right. What had been a skipping montage now found an intention that ran from beginning to end. The pieces were beads on a string that might remain invisible to the audience but nevertheless united everything.

We rehearsed for months in the run-up to the BATS season—*Truelove* one night, *Polythene Pam* the next. More time with just me and Rebecca in a black room working, working to give it new life, make it solid all the way down to the bone. I was doing too much and pushing too hard. Rebecca just wanted to get to that audience away off in the distance. When it came to dress rehearsal—late at night after a fraught run-through of a not-ready *Truelove*—Rebecca and I very much alone in BATS theatre, her down there on stage talking at a hundred empty seats, going through it for the umpteenth time while I slumped in the back row supposedly gauging her projection . . . I slept through it. Imagine what that was like for Rebecca: her co-writer—her director—couldn't even stay awake, both of us weighed down with a sense of hopelessness and the tedium of our own inventions.

But then along came the audience (not a moment too soon) and Rebecca's muscle memory was married to the live spark of watch-me-watch-me-watch-me, and all was well. She amused; she entranced. It worked. Rebecca had kept the faith and I'd made good on my promise to her. To us—and a few scattered others—*Polythene Pam* was and would always be special.

It also achieved the goal of setting us on our way—even if, in the long term, only one of us would stay on that road.

Our first actual review said, 'Rebecca Rodden holds the audience with the story of Pam's life from her fat childhood to her chillingly dismissive account of a life slipping away, devoid of purpose or desire,' and concluded with, 'There is a raw, unusual talent evident in the writing team of Ken Duncum and Rebecca Rodden. We will be seeing and hearing more from them.' Cheers, Laurie!

September of the following year, we took *Polythene Pam* down to Dunedin and performed it late-night (11pm!) for three nights at Allen Hall, ending on my 28th birthday. I remember that while we were tidying up and packing out, a young couple came back into the theatre. They'd been walking home and had had a disagreement about what the end of the play meant—so they'd turned around and come back to ask us.

Some years later Simon Bennett directed Rebecca in *Polythene Pam* in Auckland and also back at BATS. I think that was post-Rebecca's first hip-replacement, because they managed to get a story into *Truth* about how Rebecca's dog ran away with her removed hipbone. I must have seen that version of the play, but all my memories are of the head-to-head collaboration of Rebecca and I writing and producing *Polythene Pam*. A tight connection? A claustrophobic one? We would carry on writing together, but we'd never quite be in a room or a theatre the way we had been. There'd be more people, a little more space and separation in the process. And I never directed Rebecca again.

If you ask me now, what I liked most was there was no bullshit. In other areas of our lives both Rebecca and I can dissemble with the best of them, but working together I think we were direct and honest. We felt we could say anything to each other and we did.

At least, that's my story. You'd have to ask her. Or maybe the dummies . . .

Rebecca:

Rehearsing *Polythene Pam*, I learnt I couldn't pronounce 'else' correctly. I would put a 't' in it after the 'l'—'eltse'. When I tried to say it proper-like, there was a distinct pause and then a hissed 's' sound. Uplift on the 'el', then a slow, sibilant 'elsse'.

I also learnt I couldn't bloody laugh realistically. Pam does a striptease of her wrist bandage, looks at the watch underneath (no scars) and drops to her knees, laughing in delight at her playing the audience. Unfortunately I sounded more frenetically unhinged than belly laughing.

Ken and I remember some things differently, but our first meeting and his consequent poem are spot on (and yes, you psychologising people-watcher, I also loved the poem about being upstaged by my dead boyfriends). I wasn't a narcissist (surely, please) but I will own to exhibitionist, manipulative and what a swaggering wench I was. I still remember the words the notice-me witch threw out in front of a small group: 'I hear you're a poet. You know if I had a gun right now and T.S. Eliot walked into the room, I'd shoot him. Straight through the head.'

Ken's poem ends with: 'I dream of breaking down the door to your room and finding you in bed with T.S. Eliot, the gun asleep under your pillow. That's your problem. You're all talk.' A frisson of stunned horror that someone I'd had bugger all to do with had pegged me so unflatteringly well. Yet (secretly) feeling somehow lauded that, even recognising my utterly wank wee stand-up moment, he must have been either scathingly amused or simply amused. Me being me, I opted for the latter.

On the other hand, when he said, 'No one doubts your angst, Rebecca,' I was dead stoked. I presumed angst meant charming. I was smiling all day, replaying the line in my head until I looked up angst in the dictionary: 'Feelings of dread, anxiety or anguish.' Of course I told him this story several times, as it consistently got at least a small snicker from him.

Lovers? I remember an audience member: 'It's obvious the two of you are lovers . . .' But a strange intimacy grows, spending hours together writing and laughing, gut-buster primary-school giggles.

Along with the writing and rehearsing, we would tell stories to each other; play to the other when in a group of people. Ken: 'What about the time you . . .' Setting me up to launch into a story. Me: 'People just think you say important, brilliant things because you speak slowly in a monotone.' There would be gasps at my cruelty, Ken mock-sagely nodding his head as if considering . . .

That intimacy included a defensiveness of him that mitigated any chance of saying anything I thought would really hurt him. Certainly it must have been picked up on, as no one ever said even a moderately negative thing about him to me. Some of my then boyfriends—rather, associates—were inclined to a bit of jealousy when I'd turn down a party for rehearsal time.

The intimacy was more of an avuncular nature when he directed me. In rehearsal, there was a hierarchy. My same-aged uncle called the shots. Though he still wasn't a precious director—if he didn't agree with my suggestion, it didn't automatically get tossed out or changed.

Some of the lines I'd written for Pam were not well thought-out. The 'fat bit' had Pam saying, '[My mother's] still a fat dwarf.

My sister's still fat. But she's not a dwarf, just plain old fat. Mousy hair, too. She reads a lot, though. Fat people always read a lot.' Unfortunately my mama was only five feet tall and I did used to jokingly call her my favourite dwarf. My sister always perceived herself as fat. I'm amazed they never gave me a moment's grief. It was my father who told me how hurt my sister had been. I was so 'semi-narcissistic' that it simply hadn't crossed my mind it's a mortifying thing to hear in front of people who don't know you. What a bitch I could be, and how gracious others.

I made a few other cock-ups. I had a cold with a runny nose, and during one performance I turned my back and played the fool so I could wipe the snot from my face. Next night, I took some over-the-counter stuff. I got through that one-hour show in, say, 30 minutes. Gobsmacked at the disaster, I realised one of the ingredients was ephedrine. I stuck to nose-rubbing after that horror.

The night before one *Pam* show at Victoria University, my partner had stolen a vacuum cleaner and a container from a parked car. On the front page of the *Dominion* the next day, police claimed fear for the children who had done this, as the box (which we had both held over our heads to look into) contained arsenic powder, since the owner was a photocopier cleaner. I got home from my job as a wig-wearing bartender and barely had the energy to open the flat door. I took diet pills that would normally have had me off my head. They brought me close to normal levels, and the play went well, with no one suspecting I might have arsenic poisoning. Well, what is one to do when gifted a vac? Be ethically ruthless and ban the person from your life? I considered getting a B+ for my 'Morals and Ethics' philosophy paper proved I was above average in that area. No further exertion needed.

Dunedin for *Polythene Pam* was fun. Ken, his then partner Jill and I in a motel; driving round the Octagon twice, presuming we couldn't park there for the lack of parked cars; interviews with the *Otago Daily Times* and student radio. We gave away about eight tickets in the radio session, so were in disbelief at the audience of four: one Jenny Bornholdt, a poet friend of Ken's; another a reviewer; one a walk-in; and Ken himself. This was a huge theatre at the University of Otago, and a huge stage to try to throw myself around to cover the whole space. Ken opined that I could call it quits; not do it. But that hit a nerve with my (our?) belief that doing your best at full throttle was the beauty of the art. I went for it in full-on, almost aggressive determination. There was a great review in the paper and we both thought I'd never done so vibrantly well. We doubled our audience for the second and last shows. I threw off any disappointment or guilt, recognising we couldn't have done more, what with the interviews we organised and the 12am to 4am paste-up Ken and I did.

A few years later I became a *Truth* cover-girl while performing in Auckland, with Simon Bennett directing. It was a full front page of me (cigarette in hand) bending next to Conor, my Irish terrier—the banner headline screaming 'Op Shock Horror Story'. Inside was the full gory account of how, post-replacement, I'd boiled my hipbone and then while it was cooling on the kitchen bench, Conor had snatched it and run away . . .

Previous to *Polythene Pam* it was pointed out to me (as undeniable fact) that I'd need to get my leg lengthened if I ever wanted to be an actress. I'd had a limp since a motorbike (pillion) crash when I was sixteen. I had about six unsuccessful surgeries on my broken hip. But it was holding at that stage (for a while). I've ended up having 24 surgeries, including six hip replacements and a three-month stint in isolation from a 'hospital-induced super bug'. I'm now 15 cm shorter, at last measuring, and walking is a buffoon's mime act with my built-up boots. This year I broke my wrist losing my balance. But I'm sure that remark, which I've remembered for all these years, made me exultant at the idea of writing so that I bloody well could hit the stage, if only for a few plays.

Nothing in my life since those times on stage has come close to the emotional but so, so alive passionate entities that would engulf me. I would feel like throwing up before going on, then a 360-degree upheaval of feeling insanely alive. I didn't feel the pain on stage. I remembered to purposely limp when my pain clinic doctor came to BATS to see *Polythene Pam*—fearing he'd doubt my word. He wasn't to know I got what I refer to as 'paybacks' later in the evening, when the stage-high calmed down. But the paybacks weren't even a consideration, not after the sublime focus of the performance and feeling the mesmerising need to do it again and again.

Simon Bennett:

In 1985 I was 20, and I fell in love. Three years into an LLB/BA at Victoria University of Wellington, my casual enrolment in Phil Mann and David Carnegie's 'Drama 2' course smashed my life plans, expectations and inhibitions to smithereens.

If memory serves me right, enrolment in drama studies was competitive. There was certainly a sense of achievement to have got in. Fellow students in my year included Gary Henderson and Jonathon Hendry, both of whom would go on to make their names as a playwright and actor/director respectively. Drama 2 was paired with Drama 3—a third-year theatre production course, which culminated in each student presenting a 20-minute stage production. Casts for these were usually made up of second-year students. This was where I found a taste for acting. I played Rosencrantz (or was it Guildenstern?) in an excerpt from the Stoppard play, directed by Jennifer Major, as well as the Orator in Ionesco's *The Chairs*, directed by Colleen Foss. In *The Chairs*, Jonathon Hendry and Maria Buchanan had all the dialogue. I made a pretentious entrance at the end of the play, sweeping in to make a formal speech, only for it to become apparent the Orator is mute, and can only speak in gibberish. The Drama 3 students had to work as technicians for each other's productions, and I'm pretty sure that Ken Duncum was Colleen's technician on *The Chairs*.

The highlight of the 1985 season of Drama 3 productions was an excerpt from *Equus* by Peter Shaffer, directed by Ken Duncum. I don't remember a lot about the performance, but an image of a red horse's head projected onto the back wall and the use of the Triffids's song 'Red Pony' will stay with me always. Ken had crafted a stunningly memorable piece of theatre.

Ken was a bit different from the rest of us. We were barely adults, and Ken lived in a house in Miramar, in a grown-up relationship. He had also had real jobs. I was particularly impressed when I learnt that Ken had his own VCR (a luxury in those days), and had a huge collection of music videos on VHS, which he had recorded from *Radio with Pictures* and *Ready to Roll*, and diligently catalogued. Ken's passion for, and knowledge of, popular music was to feature in all his writing, and is something he and I share to this day.

Colleen Foss decided to enter her production of *The Chairs* in the Shell Community Drama Festival competition, which was a big deal for all of us. As well as me, Colleen, Jonty and Maria, the expedition was joined by crewmembers Ken, Jenny Major and Sarah Pomeroy. We called ourselves the Bit Players (I've no idea why), drove up to the semifinals in Hawera, made the obligatory stop at the Elvis Presley museum, and won the competition. This meant we had qualified for the finals in Whangarei. This may as well have been another country to us impoverished students, so funds had to be raised to get us there.

I'm not sure who put it all together, but I remember making the poster for a fundraising performance at BATS Theatre. In 1985, BATS was a run-down venue for hire. The theatre was rich with history, having been the Savage Club, a dance hall, Unity Theatre in the 60s and 70s, and the home of the Bane and Austin Touring Society (BATS) in the late 70s and early 80s. I had first acted there in 1975, when it was Unity, in Goldoni's *The Venetian Twins*, directed by my father. I appeared in the first scene playing the violin, then slept under the stairs in the props room for the rest of the performance. I shared that space with glasses of cask wine and cheese hedgehogs, which were distributed to the audience at interval. My memories of BATS are forever associated with the smell of cheap cask wine and stage-makeup sticks.

The Chairs wasn't deemed long enough to sustain an evening's programme, so we joined forces with a solo play Ken had been writing with Rebecca Rodden: *Polythene Pam*. We'd seen the play in an early form when Rebecca had performed it for us at drama studies. Ken and Rebecca had both done Drama 2, and found it advantageous to write together. I think that Ken gave Rebecca motivation, structure and discipline, whereas Rebecca brought a truly original worldview to proceedings. She had a wonderful gift for spiky anarchic humour and surreal juxtapositions. Her hair, clothes and piercings put her firmly in the punk camp—but this was a way of life for Rebecca, not a young person's affectation. I found Rebecca scarily intense but also fascinating, with a wicked sense of humour.

Polythene Pam sat comfortably next to the absurdism of *The*

Chairs. Pam's abdication speech as ruler of the universe, constantly interrupted by memories and the wayward behaviour of her two life-sized mannequins, was poetic, bold and theatrical. It was open to audience interpretation: was Pam suffering from some type of paranoid illness, or did she only exist as a theatrical construct? Pam had a direct relationship with the audience, and at times her monologue was confronting, making the audience uneasy; at others the audience were moved to laughter and even tears. The play was hard to pin down. I certainly can't imagine anyone other than Rebecca performing *Polythene Pam.* Her charisma and personality fuelled Pam and allowed the audience insight into a very particular world. I was blown away by the writing and by Rebecca's performance, to the point that I felt compelled to remount the work in Auckland in 1994.

It was interesting watching Ken and Rebecca working together. Rebecca adopted the role of the reluctant pupil and Ken was the teacher/parent; coaxing and cajoling, sometimes bullying compliance out of Rebecca.

We raised the money for the trip to Whangarei. *The Chairs* didn't win. Despite the disappointment, we all had a great sense of achievement to be performing at Forum North, and it felt as if we were embarking on something exciting and important.

For me, theatre was in colour; the rest of life became monochrome.

Gary Henderson:

Polythene Pam was the first of Ken and Rebecca's plays I saw. I seem to remember it being performed at Victoria University, somewhere in the Student Union building, I think. It was a solo piece for Rebecca. I'd never met her before, and her punkish appearance along with the striking poetic imagery of the script made it absolutely compelling. I have always remembered 'applause as big and white as icebergs'—even now I can see and hear Rebecca saying it—and the gentleness and serenity of the final speech. To this day I've retained the image, not entirely accurately, I have to admit, of soft rain falling on the skeleton of a bird.

There's also much I'd forgotten about the play, but reading it again brought it back in an instant. I'd forgotten how dark and bleak it really was, the sense of loss and futility in the story about the boy down the well, and the deep sadness, the finality, of that last speech: 'Two weeks after I became ruler of the world . . .'

Ken wrote poetry before he wrote plays. I have a handmade anthology he produced, 'Smalls.' It's a manila folder with typed, photocopied pages, some hand-drawn, with one of those folding metal clasps, a bit rusted now.

I recall Ken formatting scripts as if they were poems; each sentence on a new line, spaces where he thought the actor should pause.

It's easy to see *Polythene Pam* as a transition from poetry to play. There's no story. Instead, it's a series of images, reflections, evocative anecdotes—set up, digressed from, then returned to—which build to a view of life. It's a bleak view, but the beauty of the writing somehow transcends that.

Polythene Pam

by Ken Duncum and Rebecca Rodden

Originally produced 8 September 1985 at BATS, then

10–20 December, 1986

Polythene Pam	Rebecca Rodden
Director	Ken Duncum

Polythene Pam

Polythene Pam strides onstage carrying a large, bulging, black plastic bag. Pam is dressed 'hospital chic', with both wrists bandaged and a pink arm sling around her neck—purely as adornment.

Polythene Pam:

Two weeks . . .

Two weeks after I became ruler of the world . . .

But you think that's funny. I suppose it is really. Me, a ruler. I probably wouldn't be able to 'measure' up. Totally unable to put my best 'foot' forward. I know what you're thinking— 'megalomaniac', 'Messiah complex'—but as a matter of fact I didn't always want to be ruler of the world. When I was little I wanted to be a vet. Veterinarian's always a safe bet. That's what all little girls who know they're not going to be airline hostesses pretend they want to be. It's acceptable to have ambitions about making sick puppies all better. Then, of course, I was completely unaware of the staggering mortality rate amongst sick puppies. When I told my father about becoming a vet he said that sick puppies died and it was a good job too. He didn't like puppies. Either that or he didn't like me. Maybe he'd always wanted a boy. Maybe he'd always wanted a girl. I felt lousy about having a gender at all. Then there was the way my mother kept swelling up. I seemed to be the only one who found it alarming how she was ballooning out in all directions. Her story was that she'd eaten too many green apples, but I knew. She was full of babies. Crammed in there like tadpoles. The way she was going I knew it was only a matter of time before the pressure inside got too much and she'd take off. Streaking round the room like a let-go balloon spraying out babies everywhere.

Pam demonstrates with the bag, tearing it open so that the head of a life-sized dummy hangs out.

There she blows. Call the doctor. Call the midwife. Look at that head—those features. This is the big moment. Snap on the gloves—and out you come. Stop. You call this birth? Look at those bright lights, those harsh sounds. Birth—take two. Muted lights. Relaxing music. Sliding out as slippery as a mud-puppy into a bowl of tepid water. Afterbirth left attached like a built-in swingball set. And there it is—floating in its own dark world. Staining all the water red. What giant thoughts in that little papier mâché head. What a perfect expression of peace. Now . . . GIVE IT AN ELECTRIC SHOCK TO MAKE SURE IT'S BREATHING! A good healthy cry. It must be . . . it is! A boy! Let's circumcise him! Short back and sides? Ah, life's great game of tag—one slip and you're it. Listen to that voice. What a set of lungs. But wait—what's this?

Pam finds the second 'baby'.

Surely not. But it is. A double blessed event. Hold space in the Births column—details coming up.

This one does not come so easily.

Uh oh, looks like a breech birth. There's only one thing to do. A suburban-section. Now don't be defeatist, this doesn't mean there's anything wrong with your baby. Think of all the famous epileptics born by this method.

She wrenches the second dummy out.

Whoops. Well you weren't planning to have any more anyway, were you?

Now . . . electric shock . . . circumcision . . .

She can't find anything to circumcise—looks on the floor; inside the bag.

A daughter! A son! A matching set! Both greeting life with
one concerted howl. You hold him. I don't know how. Just go
ahead—like that. He's crying. He wants his mother. There, there,
little man. He's stopped. And she's started. You don't have to do
everything your brother does, you know. There, there. There, there.
THERE!

Pam throws them down.

I'm sick of it. Sick! Stuck in here. I can't go out. I can't take you
out. People don't want to see babies like you. Stop crying! Stop
crying and crying and crying.

She picks them up again.

If you'd only shut up. Shut up! Shut up!

The Baby Crisis Centre. I can't stand it anymore, I've got to call the
Baby Crisis Centre—'They squawk, we talk'.

She dials.

Baby Crisis? Baby Crisis? . . . What? . . . I can't hear you—the
babies are crying. Shut up! Shut up, shut up, shut up!

*Pam bludgeons them with the phone and then lets them drop to the
floor. Listens for a moment to the phone, then guiltily hangs up.*

Kids, eh? Never listen to a word you say. Cloth ears!

*She cuffs one of the dummies across the head, then stands looking at its
collapsed form, reminded of something.*

I remember this item on the news once. It was one of those
ongoing stories that pace alongside you for a few days, passing you
updates like segments of orange in a marathon. It was a story about
a little Italian boy who fell into a well. A disused well. A dry Italian
well. He was six years old. His parents had told him not to play by
the well because of the danger but, boys being boys, and six-year-
old boys, and Italian boys—he fell in. He fell into the earth, into
the funnel with the dead spring at the bottom, and he slid down
as far as he could go (which was quite far) and then he stuck there.
After that things started to snowball. Someone heard the little

stuck boy crying, or his brother ran off home blaming himself
because his mother had said, 'And don't let your brother near that
old well.' Anyway, soon they all arrive. The parents—concerned
father and distraught mother wringing their hands at the edge of
the well, calling out the boy's name into the darkness and waiting to
hear the faint wail that both comforts and horrifies them. The news
spreads. Out comes everybody from the town, the local fire brigade,
able-bodied men and women of all talents and descriptions.
Arguments begin on the best ways to extricate boys from wells, and
the debate rages around the lip, quoting precedents and weighing
the relative demerits of suffocation, starvation, exposure and shock,
while the purely practical try to push the crowd back to avoid
smothering the boy with a fall of loose shingle. Night approaches at
roughly the same time as the realisation that no one is small enough
to get down as far as the boy.

Mind you, with all that pasta they eat I'm not surprised. I don't
like fat people. I always worry that there's a kind of guilt by
association. When I'm eating with fat people I always make a point
of leaving food on my plate and complaining about how full I feel.
Whether that's to punish them for being fat in my presence or to
let everyone know that food bores me, I'm not sure. I was a ten-
stone eleven-year-old. Not cute and chubby but more like a child
wrestler. And I hate her too. Even at eleven I was learning to use
words like 'rounded' and 'womanly' to get around Milkybar Kid
fits and tablespoons of condensed milk. It wasn't that soft puppy-
fat stuff but more of a solid mass. Statuesque? Hard to be that
when you're still dwarf size. 'Shut up or Pam'll sit on you.' I didn't
even bother to look jolly. I'm not a jolly person. Jolliness is not
in me. My mother isn't jolly either and she's still a fat dwarf. My
sister's still fat. But she's not a dwarf, just plain old fat. Mousy hair
too. She reads a lot, though. Fat people always read a lot. Homer
was fat. As well as blind. Fat and blind: you either go into hiding
or write masterpieces. When I finally give in . . . that's how I see
it—just a matter of time until I give in and gorge, eat till I vomit.
Well, I do that now. Eat and vomit and put Jane Fonda on. But
everyone has that routine—EVF: eat, vomit, Fonda. I'll hide. I'll
wear black; black clothes are slimming. During the day I'll look

slim; at night I'll be invisible. I'll go on cake-shop crawls before heading home to throw out all the biscuit and cake recipes. Fat people do that too. They don't stock up on Toffee Pops—they buy them at the dairy and eat them as they walk. Then they throw the last two away to prove they're not a glutton.

Diet pills are sort of effective. You can lose three pounds in two days, but you also get twitchy hands and a nervous laugh. Sometimes I get afraid to talk after a few days on the old diet pills, because I know my voice is going to come out with that twittery nervous sound. I don't like meeting people's eyes either, so I just sit there—a silent, twitchy Pam. Not that that stops me from going back every month for another supply of twitch tablets. I get a real sense of challenge in the waiting room. Can I get more Duromine out of the good doctor? It's about the only time—okay, not the only time—but one of the times when I feel in control. I sit down in front of the doctor and my voice comes out precise and no-nonsense. I quietly explain that I feel, with all the pressure and life-hassles I'm having at the moment, I don't want to be worrying about my weight. I suppose he knows it's a game, but I always feel rather smug about it.

Actually, that's bullshit. I never feel smug about it because I'm always hoping the doctor will tell me there's no way on earth he's going to prescribe diet pills to me. Tell me that I'm being ridiculous as well as unrealistic and not to bother him again with requests for stupid addictive tablets. Of course I'll go back if he's going to bloody prescribe them. Who wouldn't? But I feel like screaming at him—'You unethical shithead, how can you prescribe diet pills to an eight-and-a-half-stone, five-foot-five-and-a-half-inch jellyfish? . . . You fuck-brained maniac, you must know they make me twitch and I can't sleep and I get nervous and how the fuck would you like it if I gave you things that make you unnaturally bright and make you think you've got incredible willpower, and who said there was anything wrong with being overweight anyway?'

Yeah, that's what I should say to him. Maybe he'd give me some Seconal as well.

Anyway, where was I? I was in the middle of something. Two weeks?

Pam stands up stiffly.

Two weeks after I became ruler of the world . . . No.

Oh, that's right, all the fat Italians around the well. And the little
boy. He's been down there a while now. Overnight a contingent of
emergency services from the nearest city arrives, and after a brief
skirmish they completely rout the local fire brigade. They switch
on their yellow sodium lights and the whole place looks unreal,
like a scene on a distant planet. Morning, and the newspapers flap
in, the radio and the television. By the next evening, on the other
side of the world I know all about the boy in the well. There's
a cross-section diagram on a million screens showing the well
squiggling away into the earth—the crowd of uniforms on the
surface—the attempt to tunnel in underneath the boy (which is
not going well)—and the artist's impression of the boy himself,
tiny and curled like a sulking foetus.

And so it goes for a few days—extra little bits of by-the-way
information fed out across the world to you at home, at work,
driving between the two. An international rescue team is brought
in from Switzerland. The rescue tunnel hits rock. During the
fourth night the boy slips down a further six feet. Until finally
it seems he slips so far that even the media can't reach him and
we hear no more. Not even the announcement of his death. The
diagram never gets updated to put a little cross over the top of the
sulky foetus. As far as you know they're all still there, trying in the
tired way people try when they know they're no longer news.

I'm like that boy. Slipping further and further down despite all
the organisation on the surface. Every day, every night, just letting
myself go, give in, beyond the help that trained so hard just to save
me.

All my problems started because I was the oldest. I always had to
look after the others. I had too much responsibility too young. I
never learnt to really enjoy life. But really it was because I was the
youngest. I was always the baby of the family; nobody ever took
me seriously. Nobody seemed to expect or even want me to grow

up—and so in the end I never did. Personally, though, I think it was because I came middle of the family. Not one thing or the other, not the oldest and not the baby. I was just one more kid, one in a crowd—nobody even seemed to notice me. It was so hard, it was too easy, it was so mediocre it makes me want to scream. To scream. To throw up. I disgust myself. It's always been like that. Mouth, mouth, mouth. I talk my way in, I talk my way round and I talk my way out again. I could convince anyone, and the first sucker to fall for it is always me. Mendacity. Lies. That's all there is to me. Tissue of lies, litany of lies. Stories, fibs, distortions. Nothing in the least little bit true. To suffer, to hurt, to be happy is to be real. And I'm none. Nothing. Cipher. Absolute zero. So I lie myself into suffering—to hurt to be human. Do you understand? I can't be hurt. I can't be reached. I'm like the core of the moon—not even properly dead. I'm the negative of a person, as clean of features as the most horrific, the most hidden away of all the burns victims. Finally what's so ghastly is not what's there but what's missing.

Pity me.

She laughs.

Applause. Applause. Gimme an H. Gimme an A. Gimme an N. Gimme a D. Give me your hands. Cos you're wonderful.

I love it. I love applause. I fantasise about it. Leaning into a blizzard of the sound of hands. Applause as big and white as icebergs cracking off and sliding down to me. Nothing else can measure up. All that approval, all that pity, warm and runny and pouring all over me. I just want to forget everything and swim length after length in it forever. But it disappears, of course, it all gurgles away before you've had enough, and you're left licking round the plughole like some sort of crazed junkie. And you never know where to get more. What tricks to play. How to get a lifetime supply.

I used to dream about being blind. Blind or dying or with some major affliction. I was probably the most beautiful woman to ever be struck blind. I was this silent, too beautiful for words angel who broke hearts by just being so beautifully, beautifully tragic. People could see how strong I was. I wouldn't crumble, never shed a tear. I just had this look of quiet strength on my face.

Nothing much else happened. I was just blind or dying and strong. I laughed a lot, which would constantly amaze people and bring tears to their eyes because how can such a beautiful woman laugh and be strong when she's blind or dying? I was astoundingly beautiful: a picture, a dream. I didn't look like me at all but I knew it was. I was tiny as well, tiny as you can imagine without being ridiculous. Raven cascading hair falling in ripples down my back, eyes that glowed, noble, radiant face. Kind of a dying Nefertiti.

It made life simple. Simple because suddenly I didn't have to do anything. Just being alive was a cause—a major cause. What could be simpler than cutting out all your options to get a sense of achievement? And I knew, I just knew bone deep, that all apathy would vanish once I had a real, live, legitimate pain that I could wear every day and that nobody could ever doubt. Whatever I decided to do would ooze pain and suffering. But no one could call it self-pity. See? Who would get away with calling a blind person sorry for herself? Blind, you don't catch some bus or train in the morning. You don't pick up a career. Never have to find anything fulfilling. That's me, the beautiful blind one in the corner. Just drifting blindly.

Not very tasteful, is it? I've never heard of anyone else getting off on that sort of thing. Maybe people do and I just don't read the right magazines to find out about them. You know, magazines for people who fantasise about being incredibly handicapped. Perhaps I could set up a support group. When I say 'Perhaps I could set up a support group', obviously I have no intention of that whatsoever and it's just an attempt to make light of the fact that I enjoy making up these long, involved stories about being crippled. I don't like to admit it, you know. I mean, I know enough to be ashamed. I wouldn't like to stand up and recite it at a Braille meeting or anything.

Pam unwraps one wrist bandage slowly and suggestively, finally revealing a watch.

Schizophrenia is not what it used to be. It's bigger. Stronger.

Gradually it's taken over all the other mental diseases like a corporation buying them all out. Schizophrenia. You remember when it meant split-personality? Three faces of Eve. Sixteen sides to Sybil. That sort of thing. Now it covers everything. Going bed to bed in great big strides like Paul Bunyan crushing heads underfoot. From the Greek, 'to split the mind'. To shatter it.

'During acute schizophrenic episodes, people often report that the world appears different to them; noises seem louder, colours more intense. Their own bodies may no longer appear the same, hands may seem too large or too small, legs overly extended, eyes dislocated in the face. Some patients fail to recognise themselves in a mirror, or they see their reflection as a triple image. Most of us are able to selectively focus our attention. From the mass of incoming sensory information we attend to those stimuli relevant to the task at hand and ignore the rest. However, the schizophrenic appears unable to screen out irrelevant stimuli or to distinguish relevant inputs. Sometimes he or she may express emotions that are inappropriate to the situation or thought being expressed. For example, the patient may smile while speaking of tragic events.'

Those are the bones.

This is the flesh/I hit the surface
& slide under
my feet through a hoop of light
& then no effort
no lift from the blind bottom
to rise
requires effort
I will try
in a minute
in a minute
I will remember where to go

The skin is unimportant.
The head can't be overlooked.
The hole is where the heart was.

What you doing down there, Mum? Up you get, Dad. Family photo time.

Pam arranges the dummies for a 'photo', smiles, poses, puts their hands together. The hands fall apart. She tries again. Same result. She punches Mother off the seat.

A family is a horrifying thing—like a dog hit by a car but not dead yet. I read about this girl, she dreamed there was a burglar in the house. She chased him from room to room with her father's rifle—all the time asleep. Killed five of her family in their beds. Jeez, an honest mistake. Son. I thought you and I should have a little talk. How are you getting on with that book I gave you? Read it all? The bit about the chickens and how when the rooster gets on top of one it's not necessarily being mean to it? Good.

Son, what I wanted to talk to you about was . . . that there'll probably come a time when you get older that you'll have a girlfriend. And probably you and your girlfriend will go out to parties. And probably at these parties there'll be a certain amount of . . . gatecrashing. And many times these gatecrashers will no doubt be repelled, especially if it's a sport-oriented kind of party. And no doubt these disgruntled gatecrashers will go away and return three-quarters of an hour later, armed to the teeth with baseball bats, pieces of wood with nails in, steel pokers and such like. And perhaps you and your girlfriend will decide to go home and will walk out to your car. Or my car, as the case may be. And there they'll attack you. Spilling out of a van across the street and coming for you. And you'll find both of you running. Immediately. Instinctively. Flying back towards the house, knowing from just one look, beyond a doubt, that to stop is to be killed. And it could happen in the final analysis, within reach of the house, the party, your friends, that your girlfriend could trip in the driveway and fall. Skinning her hands. And you could reach the door, not knowing she isn't with you, and turn around and see the poker come down. Across the back of her head.

Then, son, what are you going to do? Go back or forwards? When that happens to you, what are you going to do? What? Tell me—would you rather have your head chopped off with an axe or be

eaten by a crocodile? Which one? Which? The axe? The crocodile?
The poker? Conscience? Peace of mind—lacerations—manhood—
death? The axe is the action. The crocodile is the consequence. Do
the action or take the consequence. The axe or the consequence?
The action or the crocodile? What's it going to be from you, son?
You. What? WHAT?

It's alright son, no bones broken. It's all part of growing up and
being New Zealand. Just a true story, son, and the truth can't
hurt you, can it? Always best to tell the truth as you read it in the
paper, as you see it on TV and then forget it. If you can. If you
were born with that little piece of a human being, that tiny drop-in
component that perfects the beast, that pulls it back on the station
when it looks like wandering off. The precious ability to disregard.
To see, hear, feel, know and understand the calamity, to suck
slowly on someone else's misery, to smoke it down and then just
flick it out the window so it drops behind you.

All my life I've tried to be like that—to consume and consume and
keep consuming so as not to look like the mourner at the wedding,
the vegetarian at the cannibal feast—but I just can't do it. It
comes back, it all comes back; trapped in wells, raped, murdered,
incest, loneliness, voices everywhere crying. And everyone just
puts on that embarrassed, slightly mortified look that people get if
someone vomits on the bus. 'Do you always have to bring that up?'
When I want to scream 'How do you keep it down?' Every story,
every human horror stuck to my fingers when I tried to throw it
away. I close my eyes and they're all still there. Sparkling. The kind
of pain people mean when they talk about seeing stars. So I see
the funny side. Well, we're meant to, aren't we? The good Kiwi.
No wheels on the car. Missing a vital part of your personality.
You've got to laugh. Well, I do. My laugh—the vast in-joke of the
obsessed. It's real wrist-splitting stuff, folks.

Two weeks after I became ruler of the world I began to notice
some changes. Men began to wear fewer clothes and women
to exhibit that mercury smoothness in their dressing that had
eluded them previously. In addition the weather changed in such
a way as to make a warm shower at about 3:30 in the afternoon

most days entirely acceptable. This rain particularly nourished waterlilies and behaved on the open spaces of water as if the carp had become small and were surfacing in excited competition. These showers inevitably cleared at 4:15, when opportunities were afforded to watch the birds feeding on the lawns, making the most of the damp ground. At this time the light was of such a colour and quality as to be warm even in the thin sheeting of precipitate water which quickly adapted itself to its surroundings. Old and twisted trees, pines oaks and mangroves held honour, while younger willows and elms showed both symmetry and flexibility. These things satisfied me that processes were underway, though I had taken no steps myself. It occurred to me that my acceptance of the role of ruler had altered the balance and set these changes in motion. I decided to do nothing as long as the pattern was smooth, preferring to oversee rather than to intrude my will. This remained the same for fifteen years. Wherever I went the patterns of men and women, of birds, of trees and the lightness of the afternoon shower served to remind me of the world's unity. Then I found the waterlogged body of a thrush in a fountain. I was tempted to do nothing, and for some time this was my predominant emotion. This morning things were taken out of my hands. Beneath the trees amongst the pine humus I found several bone-like slivers and then unmistakeably the small angular skull of a bird. It is for these reasons, fellow citizens of the world, that I must offer, and you must accept, my resignation.

She exits.

The End

Truelove

Stiletto   Theatre   Presents

TRUELOVE.

& Polythene Pam

A COMEDY

By Ken Duncum & Rebecca Rodden

BATS Theatre 1 Kent Tce.   Dec 10th~20th 8pm
Bookings State Opera House   (no perf. Sun 14th)

assistance from . Flash Instant Printing

Ken:

We needed a play.

To put *Polythene Pam* on where people would see it—to have a proper season like the real plays did—we needed to make an evening of it, which meant there were 50 minutes of something missing. Rebecca and I went back into writing mode. The plan was to write about relationships, romance and love—as far as we understood those concepts at the time.

Rebecca wrote. I wrote. We looked at what each other had written. It became evident it was not going to be a fusion this time—it was going to be a two-headed cow. Rebecca wasn't good at inventing names for characters, so she had just put down keyboard symbols. Her initial scene of outrageous self-centeredness took place between '–' and '*', and gleefully destroyed any idea of giving oneself in a relationship. I said we had to have some way of talking about these characters. So '*', the voracious female character who admits no rules and must have all the attention all the time, was transliterated into Asteris. Likewise '–', the stolid passive-aggressive man-in-waiting, became Dash. Later, when they needed a son, I christened him Hyphen. My scene was between the deliberately mundanely named Liz and Brian. Whereas in Rebecca's scene Asteris dominated the conversation, on my side the blustering Brian Jimmy-Porter-ed it all over the place, barely letting Liz get a word in. Worlds clearly had to collide. But first—what worlds were they?

There was something of the cartoonish already about Asteris—so Brian and Liz became roughly 'our world', leaving the other side able to be different in any way we liked—monsters, elephant boys, parrot phones . . . And from the beginning I envisaged that it was about sides—one couple stage left, the other on the right, with our attention flicking back and forth like a tennis match.

We pushed and squeezed and developed the two relationships— the difficult moments we find the couples in—then got Brian to cross over after finding a hole in space and time. Worlds collide. A knock-down death match of the two love-titans ensues. Brian ends up getting the ungettable girl, but of course wants the one he can't get. Asteris fixes on him as an ideal, the man who can always beat her in an unfair fight. Dash follows along, devoting a life to low horizons. Liz seems perfectly reasonable, but in the end prefers a shell to live ammunition. A vision of alienation and the impassable gap between human beings surfaces—not unlike Polythene Pam's sense of herself in the world . . .

I had been thinking about what might connect the two plays that would make up the evening's entertainment—and found it in the idea that *Truelove* was taking place in the mind of Polythene Pam. A divided mind where her inventions refused to 'play nice', and one in particular would openly rebel in the search for a deeper truth about love. The title—*Truelove*—was intended to reverberate with all its saccharine, ironic and genuinely yearned-for meanings.

So Polythene Pam also became a part of the staging of *Truelove*. She was there, on a lifeguard's perch, overseeing and interceding in the action. The characters all wore soul-dolls in the likeness of Pam. I realised we needed to create a beginning to the play which theatrically set this up; something growing out of the swampy murk, a bubbling of primordial idea into images, words, characters, dialogue . . . Thinking about William Burrough's cut-up technique, I cannibalised the already existing script for truncated phrases which I coaxed into a groping-towards-coherent-thought, rhythmic mish-mash to be distributed between undifferentiated voices. I didn't (just) want talky theatre: the intent was to make space for the visceral and the ritual. And a bit of magic. It began to be clear that this was our true step into theatre—this play had characters, relationships, concepts of style and design. It was complex and, yes, challenging to put on stage. What director was going to be able to realise such a thing? Oh, I guess that would be me, with the necessary help of a lot of people who would bring their creativity also. Somehow *Truelove*—once an add-on to *Polythene Pam*—had now become very important.

We actually tried to do the show at the New Depot theatre behind Courtenay Place. They were the fresh kid on the block when a new wave of New Zealand plays were being done—Greg McGee's *Out in the Cold*, James Beaumont's *Wild Cabbage* and *Blood for Tuppence* . . . It's worth remembering that's where we wanted to be at the time. We applied for a season—the New Depot collective turned us down. I was told, possibly mischievously, that someone who had just come out of the same theatre courses as Rebecca and I had closed down discussion of our application by saying the Depot was supposed to be for professional productions. Great—you need a comment like that every five years or so to keep you motivated. So we turned our attention to BATS Theatre as the black box in which our dreams would come true. It's interesting to speculate on what might not have subsequently happened at and to BATS if we'd got that gig at the Depot . . .

Who was going to pay to rent BATS? I've got a little notebook from the time, in which I tried to keep a kind of diary of the process. It says in there that we estimated the budget at $3500 and I put up $1000 of that. Why or how I had a thousand dollars I'm not sure—I must have scratched it together from my wages. I was working a rotating shift as a trainee postal clerk at the Post Office headquarters building on Waterloo Quay. I had wanted to be a postie like James K. Baxter, Ian Wedde, Bill Lake and a bunch of other arty and actor types. It was a cool Wellington thing to do. But they didn't need any posties at the time I enquired—instead I was directed towards being a postal clerk, always indoors on the giant sorting-room floor, supervisors walking around shouting 'Face the case!' No poets there. No intellectuals. No one who'd ever been to a theatre, let alone tried to write for one.

BATS was booked for December. Or at least I thought it was. From the notebook:

22 September: It turns out our pencil booking at BATS was never recorded, and the guy who took it verbally is overseas

until next year. Someone else has pencil booked our time. This could be a major disaster if she doesn't back off.

After a tense week or two, she did.

Casting was the first concern. The tight-knit group of people who'd taken *The Chairs* to the Shell Community Festival of Drama final in Whangarei had been the first readers, responders and actors for *Truelove*. Looking back through that notebook reminds me just how much, how often and how widely I sought feedback on the play. Phil Mann, David Geary and Ron Mikalsen (later Michael Peck) all read various drafts. David appears to have given me notes several times while we were standing around at parties. Ron suggested swingeing edits which (would have) reduced the play to half its length, and Phil wasn't sure the play had the personality evident in *Polythene Pam*. Besides those early commentators, the core of people loyal to the cause consisted of Simon Bennett, Jonathon Hendry, Maria Buchanan, Colleen Foss, Sarah Pomeroy and Jennifer Major. Throughout the long development process of readings and workshops Jennifer read Asteris, Jonathon read Brian, Simon read Dash and Maria read Liz. They developed and bonded with the roles. But I determined to throw it open to audition. I wanted to be professional in the sense of making sure I got the best people available—if this was a career I wanted to start it off on the right foot.

Simon was good for Dash—he stayed. As did Maria with Liz. Brian was a problem. No one who read the script liked him—they thought he was an irredeemable asshole. I wanted—no, needed—him to be a redeemable arsehole. I saw Tim Balme in a Victoria University Drama Society production called *Bloodsports*, written and directed by Michael Wilson. It was a matinee, I remember, in the Memorial Theatre on campus. The play was about a rugby tour to Transylvania. Tim played an Igor-type character (maybe called Igor) and had his wrist tied to his ankle to give him the appropriate walk. He came on about ten minutes into the show and provoked a sudden shuffling of paper in the audience as everyone opened their programmes to see who this actor was. Tim was not the only one who had a hunch at that moment. I thought he might be the one to make people see the irritating Brian in another light. I managed to get him to an audition—BATS Theatre was free that day, so we met there—and he was terrific. Charming, funny, able to deliver the venom with finesse. One of Tim's fellow drama students was Carol Smith, and I mentioned I was thinking of asking her to audition. Tim volunteered that she lived round the corner in Roxburgh Street, and if she was home she could audition right now. With no minutes notice, Carol read Asteris and was also great. The role, originated in the writing by Rebecca, was Rebecca's voice—monstrously and amusingly self-centered—and to find someone who could bring it off with similar sparkle was not easy. Carol had the warmth, the humour, the angst, if necessary. Michael Galvin completed the cast with his rendition of the petulant adolescent monster Hyphen, pigmented green and walking on paint cans disguised as elephant feet. To tell Jennifer and Jonathon that I'd chosen someone else for the roles they'd helped to develop was hard—this was a first professional show for all of us and now they wouldn't be in it. I held on to the idea that this was an artistic crossroads—was I serious about this theatre thing or not?—and maybe the echo of that comment from the New Depot collective helped to steel me as I pulled the trigger.

We started rehearsing two months before the season—up at 93 Kelburn Parade, the old faithful theatre space—most evenings of the week, alternating nights for *Truelove* and *Polythene Pam*.

> October 19: First proper rehearsal. Everyone was late. Tim phoned from the Railway Station to say that he'd just hitched from Tauranga and was on his way. Then Rebecca came in stoned off her face. It was obvious within two minutes. As soon as everyone picked it up she started playing to them. She was incoherent a lot of the time. I dragged her downstairs and gave her the verbal ice-water treatment. She said she'd be able to pull herself together. I was so mad I could hardly speak . . .

In Rebecca's defense, it was the first and last time that ever happened. Next day when we met to rehearse *Polythene Pam*, I was remorseless in guilt-tripping her. I've never given anyone the evils the way I did her. I'm sure she remembers it to this day.

October 25: You can't get a squeaky toy hammer in Wellington at the moment for love nor money.

November 3: Simon said to me he was hating rehearsals, doubted his ability to act the role and wanted to get out if I could replace him. I said no way and that I didn't want to hear a word about getting out ever again.

So, in fits and starts—one step up, two steps back—we moved forward. I remember rehearsing on Guy Fawkes and lighting a firework outside 93 Kelburn Parade because Simon in particular didn't want to miss the festivities. It was a useful reminder—then and now—that most of the cast were barely out of their teens. Swiftly we were into December and into BATS for the run-up to opening—and the play was not rehearsed. I was struggling to pull it together, to give each section the attention it needed, to get from the actors what I needed. Two months we'd been working and yet I was running out of time.

I resigned from my job. I was just reaching the end of 18 months' training as a postal clerk; I'd spent three weeks at Post Office school and graduated with 100% (still got the certificate), I was being groomed for the overseas branch, where only the cream of postal sorters worked—but working revolving shifts would not fit with rehearsal. Damn those arty posties and their early afternoon finish—I was doing night shifts every third week. So I quit. It was another crunch moment—was I a sorter or a playwright? Stan the Man—the Post Office stalwart who'd employed me—would have been totally within his rights to be pissed off. The Post Office had invested in my training and I was about to become useful. Instead, when I explained I had to rehearse this play I wrote, Stan suggested he get me a job in private boxes on the 6 to 10am shift. I'd be finished work mid-morning, and free to write in the afternoons and rehearse in the evenings. If the overseas branch was the most highly esteemed and elite wing of the post office sorting world, private boxes was by comparison Siberia. It was underground and staffed by people who couldn't or wouldn't cut it elsewhere—if you washed out of Post Office school, that's where you ended up. I took the job and was there for years. I saw the sun come up six days a week on my way to work, if I wasn't already underground. Stan the Man still remembered James K. Baxter and the poem he wrote about the soap powder lock-out when posties refused to carry free samples—I guess he figured if he could, he'd support the arts.

As it was, I didn't even turn up for my early shift at private boxes on the day we opened. I was in a state of collapse. We'd had a fraught dress rehearsal the night before—the details would've been in the notebook, but from late-November I'd had no time to write in it so I'll just hazard a guess that nothing felt right, most things went wrong, technically it was a nightmare, we were all exhausted and I, as director, had to fix a rictus of a smile and pretend to the actors that it was all going to be alright. That covers most dress rehearsals I've been associated with. It ran late and, as mentioned earlier, I then dozed fitfully through a post-midnight dress of *Polythene Pam*. I found my way home without driving into the sea, fell into bed and did not rise three hours later when the alarm went. By the time I did drag myself out of bed to meet my fate, it was after knock-off time at private boxes and I was bitterly repenting my decision to repudiate a career as a high-flying postal sorter in favour of the theatre. Unbelievably, egregiously, I had never—*never*—rehearsed the beginning of *Truelove*. The actors did not know how the show started because somehow I'd left it till last and we had run out of time. How was this possible? Opening night was hours away. I had never felt such pressure. I checked the mail. My mother and father had sent me an opening night card, from 'your two biggest fans'. I cried.

Then I went to BATS and tried to fix everything that was wrong. The actors came in early and we blocked the beginning of the play—it was a lot of new moves to remember and they had to do things in unison without being able to see each other. There was a sense of controlled panic. Sarah, as stage manager, had to come in and stop us, saying there were people outside who wanted to come in. She basically pushed the actors off the stage, and next minute I was looking at actual audience members. Bloody hell . . .

One thing: we had great design, a design that a lot of people had poured their hearts and souls into. A lot of it was Simon Bennett's work. Simon has a really strong visual sense. He took all the publicity photos, mostly of Rebecca—and came up with the idea of projecting transparencies of some close-ups of her face onto massive banners, then painting the blobs of black and white to create giant images of her. He also engineered the process by which these were stretched between lengths of four-by-two and hoisted on pulley systems so they loomed over the stage. There were three—one each side of the stage and one at the back. The timber was heavy—if a cord had snapped or a hook come out it could have literally brained an actor. But they looked great. Each image of Rebecca/Polythene Pam's face had a different expression—the masks of comedy and tragedy—and the most threateningly intent one, centre-stage, had holes cut out in the pupils of the eyes, with two spotlights mounted behind which would catch Brian in a paralysing blue glare at the climax of the play. To complete the idea of this being the inside of Pam's head, we had a curtain across the front of stage showing the hugest image of all—a serene Rebecca with eyes shut.

Rebecca had her hair cropped and bleached with a black stripe down the middle. We had the idea of reversing this between plays—that she could turn it into black with a white stripe during the interval—but I can't now remember whether we went with that or not. When the curtain rose, there were the banners dominating the stage. There was a bed with a custom-dyed duvet cover of blue shading into black, and a chair on the other side. Upstage in the middle there was our version of a lifeguard's perch, from which Pam oversaw everything. It was actually a tennis umpire's seat from the university tennis courts, which somewhat surprisingly they'd let us borrow. Hanging on the side of the seat was the inner-tube which Pam would throw at Brian and which would then become his portal to another world. On the back wall of the stage were two large fake video displays which could light up the symbols for play, pause, stop and fast forward. My partner Jill's brother was an electrician who'd helped me wire up this display so the various symbols could be lit up from backstage. Supposedly it was being operated by Pam via a remote control. This remote was actually the big clunky one we used for our TV at home. I impressed myself by carefully removing the guts of it and replacing them with a simple circuit I got from Dick Smith Electronics which meant whenever you pressed any button a red light on the end of the remote went on. It could well be that no

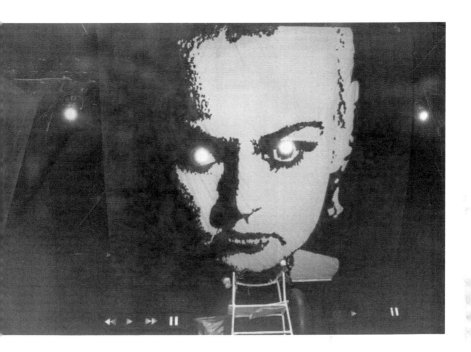

one noticed and our domestic sacrifice during these weeks of having to walk to the TV to adjust it was in vain. You have to understand that this was at the time when VHS recorders were exciting new technology and the whole idea of being able to pause, rewind or fast forward things was an arresting visual concept. This is when the theatre invented all those now-tired tropes of freezing or going-backwards-at-high-speed. Before video they would have made no sense whatsoever.

Just as an aside, all the set—banners, everything—had to be taken down and removed every night after *Truelove* in order to create a bare stage for *Polythene Pam*, then be put back up before the next night's performance.

My partner Jill customised dolls into images of Polythene Pam for use as the soul-dolls each character wore. They came out looking a bit macabre; bald except for bristly black mohawks, black knitted jerseys and wrap-around miniskirts over laddered black tights. Their eyes remained bright blue under thick black lashes. Jill then created a tribe of smaller versions which Simon's sister Rachel sold off a tray during interval. I didn't expect her to, but Rachel did in fact sell some—for me it was more about keeping the feeling of the show going during the changeover between plays, to give everything a sense of event.

There was a reason Rachel was available every night to sell dolls—she didn't come in specially for that. In her more crucial role, she spent most of the evening lying under the bed on stage. She would be positioned there—invisible to the audience—before the curtain went up and spend about 40 minutes keeping perfectly still and silent. Then, on her cue and while the audience (some of them only ten feet away) were distracted by action on the other side of the stage, Rachel would slither into the bed already occupied by the characters of Dash and Asteris. When the lights came up on them, Asteris would peek under the covers and moan, 'Oh God, I've had another monster.' She and Dash would then vacate the bed, leaving a large, moving lump of something that wasn't there a minute ago. Dash then stripped off the duvet, revealing a large, wet-looking green stain on the sheet, under which something definitely alive was writhing in a grotesque way. Carefully bundling up the sheets, Dash pulled the figure off the bed and dragged it—still struggling—offstage.

The idea behind it was simple. Magic. How did they do that? Where did that thing come from? What is it? First lesson: It's amazing what you can do right in front of people if you misdirect their attention for a moment. Second lesson: The best theatrical thrills come from taking the trouble, doing things that are hard or time-consuming or the opposite of labour-saving. Have an unseen performer hide on stage for most of a play just so you can have one special effect? Hell, yes.

Every time Simon was over by the bed, he would kick his sister to make sure she was awake. She always was. Take a bow, Rachel.

Simon also designed our posters—three completely different designs; one gave *Truelove* prominence, a second prioritised *Polythene Pam* and the third featured equal billing for both. All of them were striking. I watched and helped Simon create them on the big high-quality photocopiers at Teachers' College, where his mother worked. In those pre-computer days he literally cut, copied and pasted until he got the image he wanted. There were also fliers which I think were hand-delivered to letterboxes; there was a window display in Courtenay Place; print ads in magazines; a press release; an illustrated begging letter to potential sponsors—the multiplicity of designs and design-material was huge and the publicity campaign as wide-ranging as we could make it. I'm pretty sure we did the postering as well—making the rounds of the city and environs with a bucket of paste, and all too often finding our efforts plastered over within hours by some alternative Wellington band or big touring show at the State Opera House. Incidentally, with BATS just a venue, the booking system was through the State Opera House box office. If you wanted a ticket to our show you called them.

I hope I'm giving a sense of the level of activity, commitment and determination of all involved—because that's what I want to do. It was everything to us in that moment. Perhaps, with tentacles of the project spilling in every direction, it's no surprise that I'd left the opening of the show unrehearsed.

Besides Hyphen's monster-pyjamas costume (made by Kri Leitner) and the parrot-phone which we flew in and out using more cords and hooks, the other significant design elements were the masks the actors wore for the opening sequence. These were made by Dolores Hoy and consisted of a dark stocking pulled over the head with a flat black-and-white painted image of Polythene Pam's face on one side. The trick was, as Dolores and I discovered by playing around with them, that they were especially freaky if you put the image on the back of the actor's head. The four actors started *Truelove* lying on the floor. Simply by sitting up—the masks on the back of their heads facing the audience—and putting their hands down beside them, it created a weirdly voodoo backwards picture which was accentuated when they stood and moved about. It gave a powerful sense of the uncanny and inhuman, which underpinned the primal thing I was going for in the opening—inchoate thought separating into words and then characters.

My friend Gary Henderson was up in the lighting box as designer and operator. I think we designed the lighting together, actually. I've got a very clear memory of just the two of us rigging and tech-ing late night at BATS, I guess a couple of days before opening. We got in there and discovered there was no extension cord to reach the lighting board in the box. I think they were all locked away in a cupboard we didn't have a key to. It was late—there was nowhere we could just pick up an extension cord—but if we didn't get this done overnight it would be disastrous. We racked our brains for probably half an hour, coming up with all sorts of workarounds that didn't work. Finally I was struck with a realisation. I told Gary he was going to laugh . . . I climbed up to the box, picked up the very basic lighting board, which was of course completely portable, brought it down to the stage, plugged it in, and Gary did the plotting and cues while sitting in the front row. I'd met Gary the previous year in the theatre department at Victoria University, and I'd cast him as Jesus in Edward Bond's *Black Mass*, which I'd directed for an Amnesty International day. We then did *Black Mass* as one of the *Apocalypso* one-act plays at the student union smoking lounge, along with *Polythene Pam* and an early David Geary play called *Kiss Me Baby, I'm Dying*. Gary, of course, is a bit of a dab hand at this playwriting lark himself . . .

So, I know I left you hanging with the curtain about to go up on opening night, and I'm starting to feel that I've lured you all this way for not a lot. I don't have any definite memories of that show, or indeed any of the others in the season. Perhaps that's what the years do, or that's how it always is—you recall things, people, conversations, crises around and about the actual performance but not what happened on stage itself (unless the set fell down). The curtain did go up that night, *Truelove* was premiered to an actual paying public and the occasional reviewer, banners were lowered and dolls touted at half-time, Polythene Pam stalked the stage for her hour, and then it was over. After, I'm sure, appropriate applause.

I can remember afterwards swimming in a sense of relief. Survivor ecstasy. No one got killed. It was a sensation I would feel repeatedly over the years—but perhaps most keenly that first time. I'm not a big drinker, but after watching a first performance of any of my plays, boy, do I need a drink.

Laurie Atkinson's review in the *Evening Post* observed both plays were 'written and directed with a burgeoning theatrical talent which displays youthful vigour and imagination as well as passages of youthful self-indulgence'. Looking back from this distance, I don't think I could put it better myself. David Geary—under his nom-de-critic Kurt Davidson—wrote a three-page article for *Illusions*, a magazine set up by our film classmates of the previous year. Bon mots about *Truelove* included 'Structurally the play is all over the place like a pig in a fit, but what a wild hog!' and 'It is by now obvious this is not for the squeamish or low bewilderment thresholders, but the shops are almost closed now and it has been witty so the punters hang in there'. It was one thing to be given notes at a party but Rebecca and I took a dim view of fellow playwrights reviewing us in print—especially when it happened again on the next play. By the time *JISM* rolled around, the show included a character called David Kurtson—a mortuary assistant and the butt of various jokes. Coincidence?

I do remember doing the wrong thing one night during the run. As director I was giving notes nightly and was frustrated, feeling *Truelove* could lift further, that the performances were somehow variable and porous. My post-show comments this particular night fell like dull blows on an overloaded mule and I capped them off by suggesting to the actors they all go round the front and see what Rebecca was doing in *Polythene Pam* (implication: if you want to see a really committed performance). Eyes were downcast. Carol cried. Maria was furious and pursued me out of the dressing room, across the stage and bailed me up in the foyer where we had one of those hissed arguments you have in public while people are standing around waiting to go back in for the second play and trying to ignore the thesps having a really intense moment right beside them. Upshot—I felt shit. I apologised to Carol, we all went out for a drink and I made a private resolution to lighten up a bit. And maybe not direct my own work . . .

We were all very buzzy and happy on the last night. It was a few days before Christmas and we went out post-show to Emmanuel's, an open-late Greek restaurant and gathering place for the night-people. Looking at everyone chattering animatedly around the long table, I felt proud—of myself, of Rebecca, of each person who'd contributed their time and energy, their imaginations and abilities. I didn't go in for team sports much as a kid but I understood what it was about. Here was my team—assembled for maybe the last time, flying high on endorphins that made us feel kind of crazy in love with each other. And why not?

Should that be the full stop? Should I leave us there? *Freeze-frame on laughing group in long-defunct Wellington restaurant.*

I'm tempted to, but like the end of my favorite movie (*American Graffiti*) my mind also inevitably slips to a round of 'Where are they now?'

Sarah works for Creative New Zealand; Jennifer has lived in the UK for over 25 years; Jonathon became head of acting at Toi Whakaari: New Zealand Drama School and is currently artistic director of Fortune Theatre in Dunedin; Maria was absorbed into her life of work and family; Jill gave birth to my daughter and son; Colleen is a drama teacher; Simon went on to Toi Whakaari, then to revolutionise BATS Theatre, then on to a successful career as a director and producer for stage and screen; Carol also graduated from Toi and has had a long acting career; Tim and Michael went through Toi the year after Simon and went on to successful acting and writing careers; Gary regularly looks like the best playwright in the country and is definitely the best teacher of playwriting; Rebecca has had six hip transplants, a roughly equal number of dogs, and she lives round the corner from me; Rachel was killed before her adult life could even get started—and none of us have ever forgotten that.

Rebecca:

I dug that (in the main) we allocated characters. My Asteris and Dash were clichés most of the time, and contained my reflections on a relationship I'd been in from ages 14 to 18. Asteris was stroppy and would throw out accusatory lines which left no room for defence, such as the old familiar 'I just need space! Space to grow! Space to be me!' Dash would lower his sad-arse face in pain or despair, perhaps, mumbling of just wanting to love her, to be near her. In my real life relationship, my boyfriend wanted to buy a house with a granny flat I could live in and pay no rent, and he would give me money every week to get to university. I was 17 and, like Asteris, I'd thought a relationship would just grow in excitement and passion. Similar to Dash, my man was prepared to never touch me if he could only have me near him, to know that I wasn't seeing anyone else. I perceived Dash as so rolled in guilt that he assumed all Asteris's issues or tantrums stemmed from a lack in him, with the consequence of heightening Asteris's fury at him.

As the referee on top of the tennis ladder making presumptuous decisions about which world could shut up for a bit, I had a remote control that I pointed from one side to the other when I was bored or perhaps curious. I never said a word, dressed in extremely unbecoming towelling board shorts, a T-shirt and sunglasses, and holding a lifeguard-like tyre. It was fascinating so closely watching and listening to actors, seeing scenes grow and fit the performers; Asteris and Dash deepening into feverish self-righteousness and despair; Michael Galvin playing Hyphen, drawing out more laughter from audiences; and Liz strengthening her pragmatic approach into a determined guide for love and life.

I remember one of the huge black and white sheet paintings of me/Pam was hanging in the window of the ANZ. Somehow I'd managed to be blind to its arrogance. To my horror, I had a fag while talking to a friend right next to it. I did notice people in passing buses on Courtenay Place seemed to be staring. I was mortified when I finally saw it. 'No! No! This one time I truly wasn't doing an exhibitionistic set-up!'

Oh, well. Almost as freaky was the time a group of bootboys and skinheads I knew came to watch the plays and, uncaringly confident and casual, cruised onto the stage to offer a cask of wine as a 'Not bad, mate' tribute. Eight or ten guys like that are overwhelmingly unpredictable. Would they miniature riot if I told them, 'Inappropriate time to leave, lads'? I took the obsequious coward approach, squealing in girly delight, followed by a piss-your-pants round of sycophancy and body-blocking towards the exit. I wasn't ashamed of my associates, I hasten to add, but trying on new personalities doesn't cut out awareness that they looked damn intimidating in their boots and braces. I'd already experienced the horror of Ken coming to pick me up for rehearsal and having one of them greet him at the door by throwing his arm forcefully round Ken's neck with the endearing invitation, 'Come and have a drink with us, cunt.'

Or the time Ken saw my best friend and flatmate slip one of the soul dolls inside his jacket and was forced to tell him, 'That's a prop, mate, you need to give it to me.' I stood paralysed with shame over my friend—probably less than he felt, handing it over and going home to repeat and reiterate, 'I really wasn't thinking of it as stealing. I thought there would be new ones every night.' Of course Jill's handcrafted beauties, with tiny knitted jumpers and heads of hair tweezed out one by one, including the smaller ones we sold during the interval, must have taken so much hard work and time. My dear deaf Uncle Fred bussed from Palmerston North to watch a play he couldn't hear and buy himself a doll. A proud but slightly dubious parent bought two.

It was stunning that dollars didn't come into the over-the-top manner in which people turned themselves inside out to give and give for no public recognition. Stage managers, front of house, set design, lighting—shit, a trillion essential jobs and done by folk who had a theatre bug and substantially giant hearts and energy.

Another unpaid visitor was Creature, my tiny Oriental Shorthair cat, who would come running and jump through a window to the dressing room cum green room. I lived directly behind BATS at the bottom of Roxburgh Street. Creature would visit, presumably enjoying the human high we exuded after the show, as we climbed over each other's excited verbals to throw in another on-stage highlight of the night. It flipped me out to have Creech come and join our heightened state.

Simon Bennett:

I remember Ken's announcement that he and Rebecca had written a new play—this time, for more than one actor. Ken would direct, Rebecca would act (Polythene Pam would be a character in this new play), and the rest of the roles would be cast by audition. I vaguely remember auditioning for Ken in the BATS auditorium. Jonty also auditioned. It was strange to be auditioning, as we had all been working together as a tight-knit group for the last 18 months or so. I was surprised to be offered the role of Dash, as by then I saw myself much more as a director than an actor.

I have no memory of *Truelove* rehearsals—I probably blanked the experience out. I do remember auditioning for drama school while the season was just opening at BATS. There was no place for a trainee director, so I had to audition as an actor. I was accepted into a cohort of 10, which included Jonathon Hendry. The following year would see Carol Smith, Tim Balme and Michael Galvin in the intake.

My memories of *Truelove* are more of design and stage management than they are story. I suppose that's often the case when you're actually in a play. Over the season, it became increasingly clear to me that I was too self-conscious to ever be a good actor. I remember being painfully aware of my arms and hands while on stage and was embarrassed by the scene where Dash and Asteris had to kiss. My Fair Isle jersey, spun and knitted by my mother, was part of Dash's costume and I sweltered every night. My sister Rachel had to hide under the bed every performance until I dragged her off stage, wrapped in bedding as some sort of surreal menstrual event. Michael Galvin had a one-scene cameo role as an elephant-footed green creature. The star of the show, as far as I could tell, was Tim, who went on to become a hugely successful leading actor. Tim's Brian was funny, charming and charismatic; likeable, despite being a completely self-centred shit.

Tim and Michael would go on to play the Everly Brothers in three productions of Ken's play *Blue Sky Boys,* and Tim would play James K. Baxter in Ken's *Horseplay* at Auckland Theatre Company.

While *Truelove* helped to dispel any ambitions I may have had as an actor, I was fully immersed in the production experience. I took publicity photos and designed the set—including the three images of Polythene Pam's face that seemed to loom over the audience.

The set design was made possible thanks to my mother Jane, who worked at the Wellington Teachers' College resource centre. They had state-of-the-art photocopiers which would produce solid black copies as well as reduce and enlarge images. I worked with Ken on the three posters we ended up designing for the show, cutting and pasting and blowing up images on the photocopier. This was before the advent of desktop publishing. The text on our posters was either hand-drawn or made with Letraset—each letter was a rub-down transfer. This gave the posters a certain punk, homemade quality.

Ken's partner Jill made Pam dolls, which were sold at interval like ice creams. I still have and treasure my doll.

Truelove sat well as part of a double-bill with *Polythene Pam* and was very much part of the same oeuvre. In fact, in musical terms, *Truelove/Polythene Pam* was the precocious early double-album.

When I was accepted for drama school, I asked movement tutor Rona Bailey what she had thought of *Truelove*. She was circumspect. 'I thought you gave a very . . . intelligent performance,' she said.

Gary Henderson:

When *Polythene Pam* was performed at BATS Theatre in a double bill with *Truelove*, I was lighting operator and saw every performance. *Polythene Pam* was pretty much lights up at the start, lights down at the end. Its companion piece, *Truelove*, was new and adventurous. The two plays were given a coherence by having Pam—Rebecca—also appearing in *Truelove* as a kind of guardian angel/demon, perched silently above the action, controlling it with a TV remote (signifying her 'ruler of the world' persona, maybe). Above and behind her was a gigantic image of her face, with holes in the eyeballs through which harsh spotlights blazed down on Brian in the last moments of the play.

The surreal vision shared by Ken and Rebecca and written into their script was given solid form. The simple trick of an inner tube becoming a portal into another world where time passed at a different speed; the bizarre and brief appearance of Michael Galvin as Hyphen, the green-faced elephant boy clumping on with big paint-can feet; the amazing theatrical sleight of hand that enabled a squirming slimy green monster to materialise in a bed, as though Ken and Rebecca had thought of the most impossible thing to do on stage, then done it.

And under and over all this was the writing: poetic and cruel and funny and incredibly insightful. I recall the imagery in Brian's last speech being quoted in a review. I also recall mishearing a line from that speech—'I wish I had memories'—as 'I wish I had mammaries'. I made the mistake of telling the actor, Tim Balme, and every night I could hear him carefully pronouncing 'memories'. But once some things are in your head, there's no budging them.

Truelove

by Ken Duncum and Rebecca Rodden

Originally performed at BATS Theatre,

10–20 December 1986

Brian	Tim Balme
Liz	Maria Buchanan
Asteris	Carol Smith
Dash	Simon Bennett
Pam	Rebecca Rodden
Hyphen	Michael Galvin
Monster	Rachel Bennett

Director	Ken Duncum
Set Design and Graphics	Simon Bennett
Operator	Gary Henderson
Stage Manager	Sarah Pomeroy
Publicity	Jennifer Major
Front of House	Colleen Foss
	Jonathon Hendry

Truelove

Huge images of Polythene Pam look down on all sides. Pam herself is perched high on a lifeguard's seat, an inflated rubber inner tube beside her. She uses a remote control to play, pause or rewind.

Actors rise from the darkness wearing Polythene Pam masks.

Brian: It's like being locked.

Liz: In a cage.

Brian/Dash: It's like being locked.

Liz/Asteris: In a cage.

All: It's like being locked in a cage.

Brian/Dash/Asteris: It's like being locked.

Liz: Some kind of.

Brian/Dash/Asteris: In a cage.

Liz: Vengeful monkey.

Brian/Asteris: It's like being locked.

Dash: We happen.

Liz: It's like being locked in a cage with some kind of vengeful monkey.

Brian: In a cage.

Dash: We happen to be members.

Asteris: Tomorrow it burns.

Dash: We happen to be members of the human race.

Brian: Like that bastard should burn.

Liz: I asked him if he still loved me.

Asteris: Arctic breezes.

Dash: Don't you want me to be happy?

Liz: I asked him.

All: Don't look at me!

Actors pull off their masks one by one—

Asteris: I don't know which I'd rather believe—that you're stupid or that you're vicious.

Brian: You're a bit pink around the eyes.

Liz: That's obscene.

Asteris: Let's fuck.

All: Seminal recognition.

Asteris: I'm sorry I can't make it more clever or dazzling than that.

Dash: What do we do when we stop it?

Liz: Well I'm sorry, but I'm your mother

Asteris: I thought you said jealousy wasn't in your repertoire.

Brian: Within certain parameters.

Dash: I scent blood.

Liz: Put on your rubber gloves.

Asteris: Dead because he didn't take the time to listen.

Brian: That close, that wrapped up.

Liz: And then the room disappears.

Dash:	Room . . .
Asteris:	. . . to breathe.

They all take a breath.

They separate into couples. Each character wears a Polythene Pam doll.

Lights up on Liz and Brian.

Brian:	What are you doing?
Liz:	Writing a letter.
Brian:	Ah.

He watches her.

And another letter. And another. A whole word!

Pause.

Brian:	Who are you writing to?
Liz:	To all my ex-lovers. I'm going to have it photocopied.
Brian:	Dear All-and-Sundry, in case you've been wondering I'm still just as uninterested in sex as I ever was. Love and tight-lipped kisses, Liz.

Liz looks at him.

Brian:	Well you started it.
Liz:	Then you just stop it.
Brian:	Right.

Pause.

What do we do when we stop it?

Liz:	What?
Brian:	What do we replace 'it' with, Liz?
Liz:	Real life?
Brian:	Real life?

He slaps his forehead.

Oh, what a silly-billy I've been. Of course.

(*with venom*) Real life!

Pause.

What has Liz been writing? Perhaps we should turn her off and see.

Slowly and intimately he strokes his hand down over her eyes, his other hand taking the letter from her. He moves away to read it.

Liz: Give me that.

Brian: I turned you off, Liz.

Liz: For God's sake don't be so—

Brian: I TURNED YOU OFF!

He begins to read.

Now . . . 'Dear Carol'—no surprises there. No moment of seminal recognition.

'How are you?'—well you didn't have to go to the trouble of writing away just to find that out, Liz. I could have told you that most probably she's still the bitch that she ever was. 'Things are not very good here. He just seems to get worse.' He—Now there you should have written 'Brian' so she knows who . . . in case she doesn't . . . 'He just seems to get worse.'

'Everything I say is wrong'—that's an interesting one. Everything . . . I say . . . now there are you referring to a random pattern of vocalisations emanating from yourself? Are you suggesting that I, brackets, Brian, am arbitrarily responding to the sound of your voice by assigning it a negative value? Or does it just mean that you've tried everything and nothing works?

Why don't you look me up in your book of handy hints?

How to remove stains, how to shine brass doorknobs, how to produce your own orgasm, how to keep your man satisfied. Do you really think that you can just put on your rubber gloves and pull the unhappiness out of me like giblets out of a chicken? Without actually having to touch me? Without having to look at me? Look at me. Don't you see what you're saying here?

Liz: It's a letter, Brian.

Brian: You don't see, do you?

Liz: See what? Is this the Marxist or the Freudian analysis? You just go ahead and twist it around any way you like.

Brian: Well let's leave sex out of it for the moment, shall we? Now where was I? Ah, yes . . .

'It's like being locked in a cage with some kind of vengeful monkey. Most of the time it's just all this mad chattering, but I know there's no way I can avoid getting bitten every now and then. Yesterday he hit me. That sounds dramatic, I suppose, but it wasn't really. I mean I'm not creeping down to the shops hiding my black eye or anything. Anyway, you know how feeble he is from that time you got him to push your car. It was the viciousness, though, that really upset me. Of course, then he just collapsed on the floor and howled like a baby for half an hour. I know you'll think I'm stupid but I held on to him and told him everything would be alright. Over and over again. After a while he went to sleep and I just stayed looking at him. He looked so completely wrung-out and unhappy. Every now and then he'd make some hurt little noise in his sleep like the sound of a . . . wet cork on a bottle?'

He looks over inquiringly at Liz. She shrugs, half-smiling.

'It's strange, isn't it, but I can love him like that. And now today he's just as pent up as ever, crashing around the house trying to hurt me. I know it'll sound as if I'm always complaining, Carol, and I know you've already told me what you think I should do, but please write, tell me how everything is, and as for you Brian . . . stop reading my fucking letters.'

Pause.

I'm speechless.

Liz: Good.

Brian: Why did you leave me, Liz?

Liz lets out a 'not again' sigh.

Why did you leave me?

Liz: I'm still here, aren't I?

Brian: Why did you do it?

Liz: I never left you, Brian.

Brian: Why?

Liz: God knows why. I know I should have.

Brian: Why did you leave me?

Liz: Give it a rest, for Christ's sake. Stop fantasising yourself into the role of the victim all the time. I'm the one who has to put up with you—not the other way round.

Brian: Tell me!

Liz: Because you can't stay that close, that wrapped-up in each other forever. It's just not . . .

Brian: Practical?

Liz: Possible. It's not possible. There's the small matter of the rest of the world out there, for instance. We happen to be members of the human race.

Brian:	Not me. I'm from another planet.
Liz:	Really? Well, when in Rome, do as the Romans do.
Brian:	I see you from my orbiting spaceship. I come down and I climb out and I say 'Greetings, Earthwoman. I am from the galaxy Truelove. Take me to your Blender.'

Liz turns away in disgust.

Pam uses her remote control to pause them, and start the other characters.

Lights up on the other half of the stage. Dash lies on the bed pretending to read the paper.

Asteris:	(*melodramatic*) I . . . hate myself.
	Look at me—dressed to the hilt . . .
Dash:	Very nice.
Asteris:	This is the first and last time I wear it. Tomorrow it burns, just like that bastard should burn.
Dash:	Right.
Asteris:	I told him this could be it. The big one. Over the edge stuff. Obviously that wouldn't bother him.
Dash:	No heart, no compassion.
Asteris:	That's what I said. But oh no, he had to meet someone at the pub. Of course that comes first. That comes before his ex-lover who could be having her first proper nervous breakdown.
Dash:	Bastard.
Asteris:	I could have killed myself. For all he knew. I thought of it—believe me, I thought of it. Suicide.
Dash:	That would have shown him. He'd have been bloody sorry then.
Asteris:	Pills. That's how I was going to do it. Quietly. Simply.

You would have come home and found me lying on the bed, eyes open, staring at the ceiling.

Dash considers.

Dash: I would have phoned him up, got him round here and said, 'Now look what you've done.'

Asteris: Imagine how you would have felt. The woman you love—

Dash: Like.

Asteris: —dead because he didn't take the time to listen to a cry for help. Doesn't it frighten you—that I could have done that? Just reached into the bathroom cabinet, taken out a bottle of pills . . .

Dash drops the paper.

Dash: Of course it frightens me. Which would you have used—the aspirins or the herbal laxatives?

Asteris: I suppose it's very cool to be cynical. Unfortunately for me I'm not like you. I feel everything. Everything.

Pause.

How could he do this to me? One year, only one year later and he's found someone else. I asked him if he still loved me. I was crying and I said 'My God, do you still love me?'

Dash: What did he say?

Asteris: He just said, 'Of course,' and asked me if I loved the guy I was living with. That's you.

Dash: Oh.

Asteris: You see? He has no conception of the pain I'm in. He always looks at things instead of feelings. Instead of feeling my pain he brings up things like living with people.

I wonder if she makes him laugh the way I do? She

doesn't sound that bright from what he's said. It's just the idea of him screwing her. Yick. How could he?

Dash: Well, I suppose he just—

Asteris: And that post-screwing cuddliness . . . I hate the idea of that the most. I hope she's tall. I hope she's really tall because you know he always used to make that mistake of not starting far enough down the bed, so that in all the excitement he'd end up with his head wedged up against the wall like the Hunchback of Notre Dame.

She imitates him.

So he was going, 'Was it good for you?' And I'd say, 'Don't move. Just don't move.' Like that, so it sounded like I was reaching some high plateau of inner peace. And he'd be stuck there, saying, 'I'm not moving.' He was so cute. I just hope she's so tall that she gets her head banged against the wall every time they try and do it.

Dash: You know, listening to you, you'd never guess it was you that dumped him. Because he liked you too much. Because he thought he loved you.

Asteris: That's not the point. The point is that he doesn't love me now.

Dash: Not if you define love as coming running any time you call.

Asteris: It wasn't just any time. I was having a nervous breakdown.

Dash: Then why not call me?

Asteris: Because you would have come running. I'm having a nervous breakdown and I called him because I thought maybe he wouldn't come this time. I'm having a nervous breakdown because he's got someone else. It's frightening, isn't it? One more person in the world tonight doesn't love me. Just when I thought I was making progress.

Pause.

Tell me you love me.

Dash: I wouldn't give you the satisfaction.

Asteris: Let's keep sex out of it for the moment, shall we?

Dash: It has been a year, you know, a whole year since you told him to piss off.

Asteris: Love is meant to be forever.

Pam pauses, restarts the other side.

Brian sniffs once or twice, as if he might be about to cry, but instead he vigorously blows his nose on the letter. He holds it out to Liz. She doesn't take it. He lets it fall.

Liz: If that's the way you want it, Brian.

Brian rounds on her.

Brian: THAT IS NOT THE WAY I WANT IT!

Liz stands facing him.

Liz: What are you going to do—hit me again? Will that make you feel in control?

Brian: I'd love to, but what's the point of beating you into insensibility when you're there already?

Liz: Me, me, me—always me. When are you going to take a good hard look at yourself, Brian?

             You used to give so much. What happened to that?

Brian: I can't believe I'm hearing this. You—the local black hole. I don't know which I'd rather believe—that you're stupid or that you're vicious.

Liz: You bastard. Any hurtful thing and you just can't wait to say it. After . . . after . . .

Brian: After all you've done for me?

Liz: FUCK YOU!

*Liz tries to rush past Brian and out. Brian stands
directly in front of her. Pam signals and Liz tries to side-
step him. Brian moves to block her again. Pam signals
and Liz breaks past Brian on the other side but he grabs
her hand and pulls her back, holding her there.*

Brian: Wait.

Liz: (*stage-whisper, trying to pull away*) But Brian . . .

Brian: No, wait.

Liz: This bit comes later on.

Brian: I'm sorry.

Liz is still trying to get away.

Brian: I don't even know what it is I want.

I just . . . want.

Liz: Oh, come on, Brian—you've got what you wanted.
You wanted me to react, you wanted to upset me . . .

Brian: I don't want to lose you.

I'm sorry.

Liz is unimpressed.

What would you like? A confession?

He drops down on one knee, still holding her hand.

Forgive me, for I have sinned. I have acted like
a complete and total arsehole. I have been loud,
obnoxious, uncaring—

Liz pulls her hand away.

I'M SORRY. Why won't you believe that?

Liz: Because you're not going to do anything about it.

Pause.

Brian: You expect me to take that seriously? Coming from a woman who eats as fast as you do?

Gobble gobble gobble. I mean, I don't even have enough time to say, 'Slow down.' I just go, 'Uh—' and it's all gone. Eating fish and chips with you, your hand is just a blur.

I can change if I have to. I think.

And you grind your teeth in your sleep. It sounds like icebergs splitting up or something. I love it. I can feel that arctic breeze in my hair. Hear the penguins.

It's just you whistling through your nose.

I can't promise to promise. I can promise to try. I promise to try.

He salutes.

Scout's honour.

He puts out his hand.

Shake?

After a moment's hesitation, Liz puts out her hand. They perform a complicated handshake ritual. They hold each other.

Liz: I'll see you later.

Brian: What?

Liz: I've got to go. I'm late already.

Brian: I'll come with you.

Liz: You don't go. Only me.

Brian: I want to be with you.

Liz: It's in the script, Brian.

Brian: Well what kind of a stupid fucking reason is that?

Liz:	Oh, don't be so naïve.
Brian:	I don't believe it. We actually start getting close . . .
	Doesn't any of that mean anything to you?
Liz:	Yes. Yes, it does.
	It means that you did it again, didn't you? For a minute there you really had me believing you could be different. Just for a minute.
	Well that's it, Brian. That's it.
	She goes to rush out.
	FUCK YOU!
	She rushes out.
	Brian is enraged. He looks around for something to vent his anger on. There's nothing. Pam tries to pause Brian but his frustrated energy can't be contained. Pam snaps the light down on Brian's side and brings the light up on the other side of the stage. Brian's tantrum can still be heard.
Asteris:	What's that?
Dash:	I don't hear anything.
Asteris:	Listen.
	Aggravated, Pam snaps the light up on Brian's side to see what he's doing. Brian has bumped up against her lifeguard's stand and is blindly kicking at the base of it. Losing her temper, Pam clobbers him with the inner tube, knocking him flat but dropping the tube in the process.
Asteris:	It's the phone. He's ringing up to see if I've killed myself.
	The phone—a brightly painted plastic parrot—appears from above. Asteris hesitates before answering it.

Let his imagination work a bit.

She saws her wrist with a finger, mimes swallowing pills and hanging herself.

Brian gets to his feet as Asteris picks the phone up.

Asteris:　Hello. Oh. Hi.

No, just sitting here thinking. By myself.

She looks at Dash.

Oh, I don't know. Out somewhere.

Brian notices the inner tube, picks it up and looks through it.

Brian:　Bloody hell.

Asteris:　No, I'm fine.

She laughs in an unhinged fashion.

Why should you worry about me?

Brian:　Bloody hell.

Asteris:　Do you? Still?

(to Dash, hand over phone) Told you.

He says he's missed laughing.

Liz enters.

Liz:　I'm leaving, Brian.

Brian:　Liz, Liz, look at this. I've discovered a hole through into another universe.

Liz:　Oh, for God's sake, Brian.

Brian:　No, look, look, it's true.

Liz is unwillingly induced to look through the inner tube.

Asteris:　Me too. I could never forget the way it was with us.

She does the hunchback impression again.

Brian: See? See?

Liz straightens up.

Liz: Well, that's just bloody typical.

Brian: What?

Liz: Typical. As soon as you realise you've gone too far you have to throw in some kind of distraction.

Well this time it's not going to work.

Brian: But this could make us both very rich or something.

Liz: I don't want to talk about it, Brian. I just don't want to talk about it.

Liz exits.

Brian: (*gesturing through the tube*) We could go on a holiday. Think what we'd save . . .

Asteris: Of course.

Brian watches.

No. I'll come round there.

She puts the phone down.

Dash: You're going.

Asteris: Well I couldn't turn him down, could I? He's so worried about me.

Dash: And you're going to stay the night?

Asteris: If I don't stay I won't be there when his girlfriend shows up.

Dash: Right.

Asteris: I thought you said jealousy wasn't in your repertoire?

Dash: I'm not jealous. I'm resentful.

Why should I be jealous of some poor bastard who's

in exactly the same situation as me?

Asteris: You said you wouldn't pressure me.

Dash: I'm not pressuring you. I just want you to tell me what it is you want.

Asteris: This feels like a classic pressure situation to me.

Dash: Tell me what you want.

Asteris: I just need . . . other things.

Dash: Like what?

Asteris: Like . . . some space. I need some space.

Dash: Yes . . .

Asteris: Room to breathe.

Dash: Yes . . .

Asteris: I need time to think.

Dash: Uh-huh . . .

Asteris: Time to decide what I want out of life. I need to get in touch with my own feelings. Find out who I really am. It's so funny how we don't talk any more.

Dash: I can give you all the space and time you want. You know that.

Asteris: I don't want to lose you . . .

Dash: Don't, then.

Asteris: But I have to . . . leave.

(*carrying on quickly*)

I'll still see you all the time. I think it'll strengthen us. We'll be pleased to see each other rather than just automatically being together.

Dash: Bullshit.

Brian: That's right.

Asteris:	You're not even considering that it might be the best thing to do. You don't understand how I feel.
Dash:	I understand. You need space, time, room, other people, excitement that old dreary deadhead doesn't provide.
Asteris:	I knew you'd take it personally. Don't you want me to be happy?
Dash:	That's not fair.
Asteris:	I just asked a simple question.
Dash:	So loaded it's going to blow my head off.

Pause.

Yes, I want you to be happy. Don't worry, I'm not going to be tiresome or dull. You go ahead and do whatever it is you want. I'll still be here when you're finished.

Asteris:	See? You do understand a bit. But you wear me out.

She kisses him quickly and goes to the door.

It's nobody's fault. It's just one of those things. Are you crying?

Dash:	(*crying*) No.
Asteris:	Oh. Good. See you later then.

She exits.

Brian is outraged by this.

Brian:	OH, WHAT!

He climbs through the inner tube.

What the hell do you call that? That was the most pitiful display I've ever witnessed. You as good as had her, and then you threw it away. I mean if I'm going to be watching you instead of TV from now on, I'll want to be seeing an improved performance, more flying of the flag. You'll never get anywhere with her like that.

Dash puts his hands over his eyes.

Dash: Go away.

Brian: It's no use doing all this sulking. You've got to stay on your toes.

Shuffle, shuffle, dance, *jab*.

See? Sarcasm, sarcasm, irony. Battering blows to the body. Home truth, home truth, home truth. Duck. Weave. Clinch.

He holds on to Dash, pinning his arms, they stagger around.

Holding, holding, holding. Get your breath back. Break. More probing analysis. Sting. Sting. Line her up. Get her ready. Then the king hit. Honesty.

Dash: That's obscene.

Brian: War is hell.

Dash: I don't need your advice.

Brian looks around pointedly.

So she's gone off with someone else. She'll be back. I can wait.

Brian: Like a vulture?

Dash: The first thing I learnt was that you don't put her on the spot. She just runs from anything like that.

Brian: Not if you don't let her.

Dash: She can't love. She can't give anything. And the thing that terrifies her most is having to face that in herself.

Brian: Now that really is obscene.

You mean to tell me that she's got a problem—you can see that—but you're not going to help her to change?

Dash:	She can't change.
Brian:	And you think you're good for her?
Dash:	Nice to have met you. Goodbye.
Brian:	Look, I'll show you what I mean. We'll play that over again.
	Stand over here. Pretend you're part of the furniture.
	I'll be you. We all look the same to her.
Dash:	Don't be ridiculous.
Brian:	Wait. That's what you're good at, isn't it?
	Okay. Action replay.
	Nothing happens. Pam is not cooperating.
Brian:	Oh, come on, just a little diversion. It's educational.
	Still nothing. Brian adopts a more stubborn attitude.
Brian:	I'll just wait here then, shall I?
	Grudgingly, Pam relents. Asteris reappears with the telephone.
Asteris:	No. I'll come round there.
	She puts the phone down. Brian is acting uninterested. There is a pause during which Asteris registers the fact that there are two Dashes. Her confusion is resolved when Brian speaks and thereafter she finds it simpler to treat Brian as if he was Dash, and Dash as if he didn't exist.
Brian:	You going somewhere?
Asteris:	Well, I couldn't turn him down, could I? He's so worried about me.
	Pause.
Asteris:	Well, don't wait up.
	Brian lets her get almost to the door.

Brian:	Is that what you're wearing?

Asteris stops.

Asteris:	What's wrong with it?
Brian:	Nothing. I've always found the cargo cult very interesting myself.
Asteris:	Are you saying I'm overdressed?
Brian:	(*shrugs*) New Guinea highlanders would find it very attractive.
Asteris:	That's cruel. That's not like you.
Dash:	It's not me.
Brian:	You mean I'm not lying on my back with my paws in the air, whining?
Asteris:	I'm going.
Brian:	Okay. (*to Dash*) She won't go.
Asteris:	Why are you changing everything? You promised it wouldn't be like this. I've told you. If I could be happy with you, I would.
Brian:	Who asked you to be happy? Who said you had any God-given right to be happy?
Asteris:	Well if I can't be happy, what can I be?
Brian:	Useful.
Asteris:	If you push me, I'll just go. You know that.
Brian:	Then do it. Walk out. For good. Now.

He takes out some chalk and draws a line behind her.

Step over this line.

He draws a line in front of her.

Step over this line.

Asteris:	I just want . . .

Brian:	I don't care what you want.
	He draws a line to the side of her.
	Step over this line.
	Come on.
Asteris:	I . . .
	He draws another line to the other side of her.
Brian:	Step over this line.
	Step over it. Step over it. Step over it.
	Dash moves forward—
Dash:	Alright, that's enough—
Asteris:	You keep out of this.
	Brian draws a tight outline round her feet.
Brian:	Step over that line.
Asteris:	I want somebody better than myself.
	Why do people try to make me responsible for them? Why do they make their happiness depend on what I do, on what I say?
	What I want is to be like them. To fall in love. To lose control. To not be responsible for myself, let alone anyone else. To make someone else take the blame for whether I'm happy or miserable. For love to rain or shine on me like the weather; out of my reach, none of my concern, no decisions to make, just to stand there and get an even tan or get drenched.
	But for that I need someone I can trust. Someone I can trust not to trust me. Someone who doesn't show any of those cracks that I can work at and widen and crumble away until all of a sudden they split wide open and all the sawdust spills out.
	Someone better than me.

Someone else.

Brian: I see.

Dash: 8 . . . 9 . . . 10. Out for the count.

Asteris: Look, we'll just . . .

Assuming she has escaped, Asteris goes to take a step.

Brian: Step over that line.

Asteris: But I've just explained—

Brian: I forget.

Leave me—break my heart.

Stay with me—make me the happiest man in the world.

Asteris: I can't choose. It's not like that. It's just—

Brian: One of those things? No. Not this time.

This time you're going to choose.

This time you're going to have to live by it.

Asteris: Alright, I'll go.

Brian: Risky. That might mean you'd have to explain to yourself what you're so frightened of.

Asteris: I'll stay with you, then.

Brian: Even more risky. Who knows what I might find out about you. Well, never mind. Just close your eyes and step.

Asteris: I can't.

Brian: Step over that line. Move. Step. Move. Step. Move. Move. Move.

Asteris: I can't!

Brian throws the chalk at her.

Brian: MOVE!

Asteris:	I CAN'T!
	Pause.
	Brian walks up to her.
Brian:	(*quietly*) Are you going to stay there for the rest of your life, then?
Asteris:	I don't know.
	Brian reaches out, takes hold of her and pulls her gently out of the square and to him.
Dash:	Let her go. If the display's over, let her go.
Brian:	Actually I don't think I can do that. Now.
	He kisses her.
Dash:	You bastard.
Brian:	You're talking about the man she loves.
Asteris:	Let's just go to bed.
Dash:	Emotional fascist!
	Brian hesitates.
Brian:	(*out*) Well, I'm better off here. Aren't I?
	Brian and Asteris go to bed.
	Dash considers his situation.
Dash:	I'll wait.
	He settles down on the floor.
	Liz enters.
Liz:	I think you should know that I'm taking the bedside clock radio. I'm only . . .
	She notices Brian isn't there.
	Brian? Brian?
	Seemingly by instinct she manages to step over Dash.

(*out*) Everyone wonders why I've stayed with him this long.

Carol, my friend, said she couldn't understand how I could even like him, let alone love him.

I don't like him. He doesn't like me.

You see, Brian's got no time for the emotion of liking someone. He says it's like margarine—a pale imitation of the real thing.

The real thing. Eyes meeting across a crowded room. It's so much a cliché that it's embarrassing. But true. When I first saw him I felt such a jolt . . . it was like being hit. I must have looked stupid, just standing there, staring. Not moving. Not saying anything. And him. His mouth was hanging open and the dip was dropping off his potato chip onto his shoes. Love at first sight.

And then we got talking and I realised we were totally incompatible.

A partnership, working together; that's what I was brought up to think you could expect. To look at my parents, you'd think that liking—simple honest liking—was 90% of it.

What's wrong with that? What's the point otherwise? Love can't just be two people staring into each other's eyes forever. It's got to fit into everyday life.

In the end, it's what you *do,* not what you feel.

And Brian does nothing. Does less and less all the time to test me, to see how much I love him.

What right has he got to test me?

Liz waits.

Pam crosses over to the bed. She takes Brian's doll off him and returns. She takes out a plastic squeaky toy hammer and hits the doll on the head with it. Brian jerks upright in bed. Asteris turns over sleepily.

Asteris: What is it?

Pam hits the doll again. Brian jerks. He finds the doll is missing and searches frantically for it.

What are you doing?

Pam hits the doll. Brian jerks. He moves towards his own side but then comes back, willing himself to stay put.

Brian: No. No. I'm staying. I don't care. I'm staying.

He is pouring everything he has into resisting the pull to the other side. Pam starts to beat the doll with the hammer in a regular headachy rhythm.

Asteris: You're dreaming. You're still asleep. Come back to bed.

Brian turns suddenly towards Asteris.

Brian: Give me yours. Lend it to me. We can share it.

Asteris: *(a little alarmed by his intensity)* What?

Brian: Just a loan. You'll get it back.

Asteris: What do you want?

(retreating) I don't know what you want.

Brian: I'm empty!

Asteris is bailed up, her arms crossed over her doll to protect it.

Give it to me.

Brian makes a grab for her doll. She fights his hands off and hisses/snarls at him. Brian raises his fist but then turns and stumbles through the inner tube back to his own side. Asteris lunges after him—

Asteris:	No!

—but is too late to stop him. She ends up with one of his shoes.

Pam drops the doll.

Dash does a Marcel Marceau-type mime of a wall through which Brian has just passed.

(*scathing*) Knock it off.

Distressed, she crawls back into bed and pulls the covers over her head. Dash takes out a toothbrush and smugly brushes his teeth before getting into bed himself.

Pam accidentally puts Asteris and Dash on fast-forward, but doesn't notice. She takes the inner tube back.

Brian puts his doll back on.

Brian:	Liz! Liz. I had a nightmare. I . . .

I was over there. I got . . .

Liz:	I'm taking the bedside clock radio.

I'm only packing a few things, so I think that's fair.

Brian:	Do you ever get scared, Liz?
Liz:	I think there's an old wind-up one in the cupboard somewhere that you could use.
Brian:	Arctic breezes.
Liz:	What?

He mimes walking into a strong wind emanating from Liz.

Brian:	I'll play Shackleton and you can be the pack ice.
Liz:	That's right, Brian. Nothing is the least little bit serious.

He grabs Liz and starts to waltz.

Brian:	Strangers in the night—exchanging glances.

Strangers in the night—exchanging glances.
Strangers in the night—exchanging glances.
Hmmm.

She's laughing a little bit.

Liz: But not enough.

I won't be around to watch you turn into Mr Hyde again.

Brian: Or to heckle Jekyll.

I don't know what to do, Liz.

She turns to leave.

Liz.

She looks back.

At least admit you let me down?

She goes.

Alright, go on then, leave me. I know you're just going over there to stand in the dark. Leave me? HAH!

Asteris suddenly jerks up in bed, her hands going to her face. After a moment she lifts the sheets and looks underneath.

Asteris: Oh, God.

She shakes Dash.

Wake up. Wake up.

Dash: What? What?

Asteris: I've had another monster.

Dash: It's only two weeks since you had the last one.

Asteris: So I'm not regular. This is a difficult time for me.

Dash: Alright . . . alright . . .

You want me to get rid of it?

Asteris: Please.

They get out of bed. Dash pulls back the duvet. The sheet underneath has a huge green wet-looking stain. There is a full-size figure moving under the sheet. Dash bundles up the sheets around the figure and, dragging it onto the floor, he exits with it.

Dash: I hope the rubbish truck hasn't been yet.

As soon as Dash is out of the room, Asteris reaches under the bed and gets out a shoebox from which she takes Brian's missing sandshoe, now yellowy and aged. She caresses and kisses it, then regards it sadly.

Asteris: Stained with tears.

She puts it back in its box under the bed. Dash reenters with new sheets.

Dash: Boy, I'd hate to have to handle one of those things once it cuts its real teeth.

Asteris: You're lucky. This woman I know up the road has them with wings on. One of them got away once and flew all over the neighbourhood. God, if it had been me I would have just died.

They start making the bed.

Dash: What's on for today?

Asteris: Well I thought I'd have a little breakfast and then take a stab at curing cancer. Oh, and before lunch I must get around to bringing peace and goodwill to all men.

Dash: Sorry I asked.

Asteris: It's just a stupid question—'What's on today?'

The same thing that's always on. Nothing.

Dash: You never know, some cosmic cowboy might fly in and rope you to the bed if you're lucky.

Asteris: I wouldn't expect you to understand.

Dash: Maybe I understand better than you think.

Asteris: Don't try to be mysterious. It just looks ludicrous.

Dash: Someday you're going to have to accept that he's not coming back.

Asteris: Yes, you're very big on accepting things, aren't you? You'd just love that—if I accepted this dump, accepted this life . . .

Dash: Accepted me.

Asteris: My head aches. First thing in the morning and my head aches.

Is there any coffee?

Dash: I just put it on. I'll see if it's ready.

Oh, the boy's lurking around outside in a suspicious manner. Shall I let him in?

Asteris: I suppose so.

Dash goes out. An awkward adolescent with a green head and elephant feet comes in.

Hyphen: Hi, Mum.

Asteris: Did you sleep well? You look run down. You're a bit pink around the eyes. Have you been masturbating again?

Hyphen: You said it was normal.

Asteris: Within certain parameters. What have you got behind your back? Show me.

Hyphen produces a frilly black bra.

Hyphen: It's for you. I want you to wear it. Will you wear it for me, Mum?

Asteris: Well, what a surprise. How thoughtful of you. Where did you get it?

Hyphen: Oh, you know . . .

Asteris: I think this makes a dress, a pair of shoes, some slightly laddered pantyhose and a set of contact lenses that you've given me in the last week, doesn't it?

Hyphen smiles weakly.

Have you got a dead girl in your room?

Hyphen: (*whining*) That's not fair. None of my friends' mothers ask them things like that.

Asteris: Well, I am sorry but I'm your mother and if you've got the mouldering corpse of some female under your bed then I want to know about it.

Hyphen: You're always putting me down.

Asteris: I am not putting you down. You just have to realise that this house belongs to your father and myself and as long as you're in it you have to observe certain courtesies.

Oh, for God's sake, don't sulk. Just don't let your father find out, that's all. Well go on, go on, don't you have something to do?

Hyphen starts to go.

Aren't you going to give your mother a kiss?

She leans towards him but at the last minute turns her head so that he kisses her on the cheek. She waves him away. On the way out he almost runs into Dash, who is returning with the coffee.

Dash: Look out, son.

Hyphen glowers at him intimidatingly and exits.

I'm sure I wasn't like that at his age.

	How about we just rest up today? In fact . . . why don't I come back to bed now and . . .
Asteris:	I'll say one thing for you—you've got a strong stomach if you can dump one of those things in the bin and be thinking about sex five minutes later.
Dash:	Incorrigible.
	He starts to kiss her. She responds. Suddenly Brian leaps in, dragged by his shoe which he holds in one hand.
Brian:	Howdy, neighbours!
	Asteris throws Dash off.
Asteris:	It's him!
Brian:	(*out, regarding the shoe*) They mate for life, you know.
Asteris:	You haven't aged.
	You bastard, you're still the same and I've aged . . . years.
Brian:	You don't look any . . .
Asteris:	Don't look at me!
	She throws the bedclothes over her head.
Brian:	Peekaboo.
Dash:	Look, don't you ever knock or anything?
	I mean just because the planets are in conjunction or whatever doesn't give you the right to come barging through our bedroom wall.
Brian:	(*himself and Asteris*) Don't you mean 'our' bedroom wall?
Dash:	That was twenty years ago.
	Asteris pokes her head out briefly.
Asteris:	Eighteen!
Dash:	Alright. She's been waiting for this for years. It's the

second coming. Hallelujah! Go ahead. Don't mind me. Let's see this grand passion I've heard so much about. Let's see the miracle. Let's see you do what thousands before you couldn't. What I can't. Let's see you make her happy.

Brian: Actually, I've just come for my shoe.

Asteris drops the sheets.

Asteris: At least you haven't changed.

Brian: I didn't have time, so I came casual.

He starts to sniff round the room with his shoe.

Asteris: I've been waiting for you.

Brian: Uh-huh. Runs in the family, does it?

Asteris: I've changed. I know I can give myself now. To you. I love you.

Dash: What?

Asteris: (*to Dash*) I'm sorry.

Dash: Sorry?

Asteris: (*to Brian*) I love you.

Brian jumps onto the bed.

Brian: Great. Let's fuck.

Asteris: I wish I could make it more dazzling or clever than that.

The shoe starts to twitch. Brian finds the other shoe under the bed and starts putting them on.

Asteris: But that's it. I love you.

Brian: So you said.

Asteris: I like saying it. I've never said it before. And it annoys you. I—

Brian: DON'T . . . say it again.

Pause.

So I'm the one, am I? Perfect in every detail.

Asteris: You're not perfect. I'm not perfect. I've learnt to forgive myself for that. I learnt that everything can't be exactly as you want it. You do your best . . .

Brian: And then you settle for what you can get.

Asteris: Don't you think that's hard enough—just getting what you can get? It doesn't have to be a defeat.

Brian: Just one of those things.

Okay then. Let's set up shop together. Sell each other short for the rest of our lives. Think of all the happy hours we could spend—nursing each other's limitations like a couple of amputees.

Asteris: What do you want? Because whatever it is—you can't have it. It's impossible.

Brian: What if it is? What's the alternative? To settle for less and tell yourself it's an heroic victory?

Not me. Not that.

Asteris: I just want to be with you. Is that a crime?

Brian: Loitering with intent.

Liz enters, and discovers Brian has disappeared again.

Liz: Brian?

Brian: Liz.

Liz: Brian?

Brian: Ahoy there.

Brian seizes the inner tube from Pam and places it over Liz's head.

The queen of my dreams.

Liz: Brian.

Brian:	Liz! You look just like a trophy. Five feet across the antlers, she was. I could see the whites of her eyes rolling as she charged towards me. It was me or her . . .
Liz:	I'm leaving now.
Asteris:	Who is this?
Brian:	Don't.
Liz:	It's too late for that.
Asteris:	Well you can just get your face out of my wall.
Dash:	Our wall. It is our wall.
Brian:	Just don't, alright?
Dash:	I live here too.
Asteris:	What does she mean to you?
Liz:	I won't lose myself in you.
Asteris:	I don't care about her. Just tell her to go.
Brian:	I was ready to lose myself in you.
Liz:	And that's what's so . . .
Brian:	Frightening.
Asteris:	You've got me now.
Dash:	All this time. All the years . . .
Brian:	Don't leave me.
Dash:	We've got a son. Of sorts.
Asteris:	I understand you.
Brian:	I want you.
Dash/Asteris/Brian: I love you.
	Pause.
Liz:	And I love you. But it's not enough.
	She pulls her head back through the inner tube.

Brian:	Wait. Just let me talk to you.
	He goes to follow Liz but Asteris throws herself at him, grabbing his legs.
Asteris:	No, you can't. I'll be 90 by the time you get back.
Brian:	Just let me talk—
	Liz goes to leave. Brian is struggling.
Asteris:	Help me.
Dash:	Like fuck.
Brian:	NO!

He kicks Asteris in the face. She lets go.

Outraged, Pam blows her lifeguard whistle. The lights snap out everywhere but on Brian, who is caught in the glare of spotlights from the eyes of a huge Polythene Pam image.

Pam climbs down and stands in front of Brian, blowing her whistle and gesturing angrily.

Brian jerks the whistle out of her mouth and throws it away.

They stare at each other.

Pam turns on her heel and stalks to the back.

I've done it now, haven't I? Oh yes. I've been a naughty toy and now I have to go back in the box.

You know, it's times like these I wish I had memories. So I could explain it all. Say it was something that happened to me, some traumatic thing from childhood or something.

Whatever story it was, it would have a second in it. Just one second. And in this second I would know everything.

And what I would know is that I'm alone. And

because I'm alone I start to want someone else. And
that's the start of it all. You see? You do see, don't you?

Pam starts to move forward.

No!

Alright—a story, a memory. You ever had one of
those days when you vowed to improve yourself?
Build up your mind and your body. Become a better
person.

Let's say I'm young. Let's say I'm a kid, throwing my
spear made out of a broom handle across the lawn as
it gets dark. Right, I say, I'm going for a run round
the block. Get in training.

My sister wants to come too. Let's say.

Halfway round there's a man standing on a corner.
Worried looking man. Have you seen a little girl?
This high? She's my daughter. She's lost. Would you
help look for her? Why don't you look over there
and your sister can look back in the schoolgrounds
and I'll go down here?

I might remember asking in the shops but no one's
seen the little girl. It might get dark. So completely
dark. I'm on my way home when the car pulls up
beside me. My father and my brother. Get in. Are
you looking for the little girl too? Silence. Your sister's
been assaulted.

Pause.

Don't stop.

Stay with me because we're almost there, almost right
up to that second. Remember?

When my father thought it was safe to go home
without encountering anything too intense, we did.

My brother waited until we were home, all together,

before he said . . . before he jumped at me.

How could you be so stupid? How could you let him separate you?

I waited.

I waited for my mother to come straight back with, 'Don't be ridiculous, it wasn't his fault, it was nobody's fault.'

I waited.

A second passed.

No, it didn't. It never passed. It still hasn't passed.

My mother said something. Weak. Late. Too late.

I knew then that was what they thought. All of them.

Why didn't he do his job properly?

He salutes with the cub-scout salute.

A cub-scout always does his best to do his duty to God, and to the queen and to his country. He is always courteous and kind and helps others at all times.

He drops into the cub-scout crouch.

A-ke-la-we-will-do-our-best!

He lets out a wolf howl.

He slowly stands up.

You think I want you to feel sorry for me?

Feel sorry for all of us. For my imaginary mother. For my fictitious father. For my brother. For my sister. All of us standing on different stars. All cut off, unable to reach a single other person.

And I say, 'Good.' I'm glad it happened. Because now I know where I am.

You see, I used to be troubled by these hallucinations. All the time I was trudging through the frozen waste, I thought I was home by the fire. But then came that second, like a crevasse—a little set of footprints leading up to it, nothing coming out the other side.

So here I am.

Alone.

With all the rest of you.

Still in that second. The ragged cleft in the ice.

Still waiting.

And, strangely enough, hoping.

Because impossibly, irrationally, romantically, I believe that someone is going to come past and see me.

See me.

And this time they won't stop halfway because they get scared. This time I won't be left shouting, 'I'm here, I'll catch you, *jump.*'

I won't give up hope.

I WON'T GIVE UP HOPE!

So now I sit back down and I wait for the right one. And for her I keep the faith.

Pam comes up behind him. She drapes an arm over his shoulder and rests her head against his.

With her that faith will make sense.

She's coming.

I can feel her.

Pam tears the head off his doll and, holding it out at arm's length, crushes it. She lets it fall.

Brian's knees buckle. He is neutral, expressionless, silent. Pam climbs up into her chair again and starts both sides.

Liz is standing ready to go. Asteris is crouched, crying, with Dash standing behind her.

Liz: Goodbye, Brian.

Pause.

Brian: It's like being locked . . .

Dash puts his hands on Asteris's shoulders.

Dash: That's right, you have a good cry.

Brian: It's like being locked . . .

Liz: Brian?

She goes towards him.

Dash: In a while I'll make us a nice cup of coffee.

Liz pulls Brian's head back and looks into his eyes.

Brian: It's like being locked . . .

She cradles him in her arms.

Liz: It's going to be alright now.

Brian: It's like . . .

Liz: It'll be alright, Brian. It'll all be alright.

It'll all be alright.

The lights fade. Pam is left sitting with her head in her hands.

Blackout.

The End

Flybaby

Ken:

Now we knew how this get a play-on-at-BATS thing worked, the question was what to do next? There was no doubt we would do something—and in fact we did it quite quickly, as these things go. *Truelove/Polythene Pam* closed late December 1986—in May of 87 I was calling for auditions for a July season at BATS of our next project.

It was three one-act plays, advertised as *Stiletto Theatre: Three more stabs in the dark*. One of the plays was *Flybaby*—written by Rebecca and me. The others were *David's Books* by Gary Henderson and *The New Step* by Leonard Cohen.

Rebecca and I wrote the first draft of *Flybaby* by actually sitting together and passing the paper back and forth, scribbling a few lines that lobbed the ball back over the net. There was a lot of 'Hah—get out of that one.' I've got that original draft and it's titled 'Serpent', which was just the first word I thought of and put down to accentuate to Rebecca that this was just brainstorming, to free us up. The intention as always was to write a good play with a good part for Rebecca.

Also, this was going to be a comedy, a bit of a breather from the intensity of the previous year. For that reason I possibly decided early on that I wouldn't direct; it was a good light project to find out what having someone else direct our work might be like.

Having her usual trouble with names, Rebecca provisionally called her character Lassie—not after the dog but because her Scots family used that to mean 'girl'. Quite late in the day I changed it to Nadine, which I thought better suited the spikiness of the character.

Carrying on the punctuation theme of *Truelove,* I named the male character Phil Stop.

Nadine was modelled on Rebecca, of course—but a Rebecca going through a nightmare worstcase scenario of being expected to care for and be responsible for another human being; a reversal of a natural flow of things. When I think about it, babies were also the subject of discussion in my house at the time—my daughter Katherine would be born the following year. So, again, it was some kind of fusion of both our lives and concerns.

My memory of the writing is that it was relatively painless, and the idea from the outset was that we were going to put *Flybaby* on as part of an evening of short plays, thereby making it viable as a BATS show, i.e. meaning likely to repay the rent. Ron Mikalsen agreed to direct. Ron had been in the 1984 theatre course where Rebecca and I had first met (I remember him playing the emperor and Rebecca the blind beggar in Brecht's *The Emperor and the Dead Dog*). He had read my writing and given me feedback since then, was now working at Radio New Zealand in the drama department and had (or would soon) direct Rebecca in a small-scale production of *Salve Regina*, a truly astonishing and mostly forgotten New Zealand-written play by Edward Bowman (it was originally a BBC TV play featuring Glenda Jackson—check it out, all the way from Palmerston North to the apocalypse . . .)

Things went fine with Ron (I'm going on the assumption that if they didn't, I would remember)—the only thing was that he wouldn't do the end of *Flybaby* as written. His reason was the fact that it required three more actors—one of particularly short stature—and some special effects just to provide a couple of minutes of excitement at the end. My point of view was, 'But what excitement! What a couple of minutes that will be!' I was trying to up our game on last time in terms of audience surprise and theatre magic. 'Go to the trouble, go to the trouble—no one will expect it and they'll be amazed.' Ron just shook his head. So we had to think again . . . and we came up with something quieter and more achievable. But I'm adamant that the original end is the end of *Flybaby*. That's why the other conclusion is presented here as the alternate—and the wrestling Angel/Demons ending takes its rightful place.

Michael Galvin played Phil—not only as a reward for turning up every night in *Truelove* to be painted green for a few brief and weird moments on stage as Hyphen, the elephant boy, but also because he was a great actor on the rise. He was smart, he could do comedy and he was a good match for Rebecca; she'd have to work for the spotlight. Michael was a year behind us in those theatre courses and had played the boy in my 25-minute excerpt of *Equus*, presented at the end of my time in the theatre department. In that play, Michael had stripped down to his grunds and totally went there in terms of sexual anxiety and blinding horses. He was electrifying. That little play in 93 Kelburn Parade was also a (maybe *the*) turning point in my life. Five minutes into it I looked around at the audience of fifty-some souls and was struck with the realisation that if I happened to find a pin and drop it, everybody there would actually hear it. They were that intent on the performance. The performance that I had chosen, edited and sculptured. I was talking to them and they were listening. Really listening. Give me more of this, I thought . . .

Colleen Foss was by now working as a postie—those posties again!—and thought one of her workmates might be good for the role of the policeman. So Mick Rose came in and auditioned, and another great actor joins the roster of 'We saw him first'. Was there something in the southerly back then? I don't know what it was, but it blew a lot of incredibly talented people through the door of BATS. Mick had, I think, done some earlier amateur acting but had given it up. *Flybaby* got him back on the road to a long career of giving up acting many more times.

Jeremy Donovan completed the cast as the sinister Vatican emissary. Jeremy was another fugitive from the theatre department. I'd met him at the same time as Michael, since the two of them—along with Bruce Thompson—made up a tight-knit triumvirate of precociously talented theatre guys impatient to show the world what they could do.

Flybaby gave rise to two quintessential BATS moments in the same performance. On one particular night, when Michael as Phil read out the royal congratulatory telegram, it magically coincided with the Buffaloes, upstairs, lustily singing *God Save the Queen*. Later, as Phil squinted through the venetian blinds saying he couldn't live his life hiding from the police, sirens wailed all round the building as engines raced off from the fire station next door. The audience loved it.

A more excruciating moment was when the actor playing the old man in *David's Books* dried during a performance. I was watching it from the side. He lost his line. Silence. His fellow actor tried to prompt him with an improvised leading line—nope, no takers. He tried again—the old man just grunted. Silence: a Grand Canyon of silence opening and opening a mile wide and still growing . . . while he just sat there, the focus of all eyes and ears, doing . . . nothing. I jumped up and ran out. Out of the theatre, all the way down the corridor and out onto the street. I was out there on Kent Terrace gibbering with the tension and the torture of it. It was the worst dry I ever saw. An actor's most fevered nightmare would still not be as bad. Don't ask me how they got out of it. By the time I could bring myself to creep back up the corridor, things were miraculously in motion again.

The play I directed for this season was *The New Step* by Leonard Cohen. I had found what appeared to be his first and last play in a blackened book of Cohen's poetry which, by the look and smell of it, had gone through a house fire. It was mordant and funny, full of acute observations of those of us—as he had written elsewhere— 'who are oppressed by the figures of beauty'. It also featured a massively obese woman, played by Caroline Lowry in a fat suit. Carol Smith played her victim, and Anne Chamberlain was the figure of beauty. A brief bluff boyfriend role was played by two more theatre department refugees—the ever-urbane Donald Holder and, on the last night, Stephen Wainwright (currently head of Creative New Zealand). It's worth mentioning that Leonard Cohen was not at that time the universally loved grandfather figure he is now; instead he was thought of as a kind of groaningly depressive has-been. Time has correctly altered the balance—but let history record that Ann Hunt's *Evening Post* review of the show ended with, 'One wishes Mr Cohen had written more plays and perhaps fewer of his somewhat dreary songs.'

One night during the run, two guys doing a photography course at the Polytech came in and shot a photo-essay of preparations for the show. Consequently I've got a handful of photos of scenes such as the crowded dressing-room, me on stage standing in for Michael so we could tighten the cue for him to be hit by a bale of nappies, some great images of the performances, and, perhaps my favourite, a cold and wet BATS exterior showing Roy's Burger Bar—in the distance, Carol hurrying towards the theatre because she was late even though she just lived round the corner.

Another memory from that season is of Rebecca and I doing a radio interview. I can't remember what station it was for, but this was a new thing for us and we were both nervous—Rebecca showing it and me trying not to. I assured her it would go fine. The first thing the interviewer said—looking at the *Evening Post* review in front of him—was, 'Your play is described as black and Satanic—what's that about?' I stared at him. I looked at Rebecca, who stared back. My brain whirled, seeking a way out. There wasn't one. I had to tell this guy on-air—and his thousands of loyal listeners—that he couldn't read for shit. 'I think you'll find,' I ventured, 'That it says "satiric". "The humour is black and satiric."' I wasn't even sure he knew what that meant . . .

Elsewhere in reviews, Ralph McAllister in the *Dominion* proclaimed '*Flybaby* is an anarchic, witty and skilful piece of new writing by playwrights Ken Duncum and Rebecca Rodden, names that should be noted.' Yes, indeed. He also panned the other two plays, saying *The New Step* was 'sloppily directed', and finished with 'The evening belongs to *Flybaby,* so either arrive late or be prepared to grit your teeth till about 9pm.'

David Geary once again assumed a superior tone in *Illusions* to observe, 'This year the kid gloves appear to be back on as *Stiletto Theatre* draw a paper knife to fashion a tight, straight farcette.' He thought it had a weak resolution—which he wouldn't have said if it had the angel and demons wrestling! Two pages of similar comments later he ends with, 'The quandary facing *Stiletto Theatre* would seem to be what direction next. *Flybaby* has been an affirmation of comic talents after the mixed response to *Truelove/Polythene Pam*, but at the expense of an edge. Rumour has it a new work is in the offing. Plunge it to the hilt and twist would be my inclination.' 'Don't worry, David,' I would have thought when I read that, buried somewhere in the writing of that rumoured new work, 'Already on it . . .'

After the season closed Colleen organised a picnic at Makara. I've got a couple of photos of us on the rocks, looking—particularly Rebecca—out of our natural habitat; bedraggled moreporks blinking in the sun. By the time we did our next play, a lot would have changed . . . I'd write two more shows with Rebecca, but she wouldn't be in either of them, and would rarely act again.

Rebecca:

O the cruelty of that watching, analysing man—with a matchless assessment of people's foibles or failures, and a black sense of humour.

To start writing *Flybaby*, Ken announced to me we would *both* write a 25-page version of what angle we thought the play could take. I rolled up, overtly impressed that I'd actually followed through with the deal. After we calmed down from our hilarity at the piece of crap I'd flipped out, Ken explained that it was a shortcut to get me to write the shit out of my head before starting. 'Oh yeah, yeah, but show me yours now,' I responded. The bastard looked genuinely surprised at my chagrin as he stated, 'Oh, I didn't do it.'

Outmanoeuvred and outwitted. As far as I'm aware he still has my pathetic attempt at humour and comic wit filed away. What if he gets ugly and Facebooks it or loads it onto a creative writing site? Who really knows the perversions of an apparently empathetic soul?

Gary Henderson:

There are a couple of things that made *Flybaby* a landmark for me, not least of which was the revelatory debut of Mick Rose as the Policeman in two brief scenes, which he completely stole and hasn't given back to this day. (Mick would later portray Father Maximilian Kolbe in Ken's *The Temptations of St Max*.)

Flybaby was performed alongside two other short plays—*The New Step* by Leonard Cohen, and *David's Books*, a fifteen minute play by me, written as part of a theatre course I was taking at Victoria

University, and directed by Colleen Foss. Its inclusion marked the first time someone else had staged one of my plays. A small personal milestone.

Flybaby was about two aimless no-hopers played by Michael Galvin and Rebecca, who had somehow given birth to the Messiah. By making the expectations of them that much more extreme, it relentlessly dismantled our rosy stereotype of new parents. Ken would offer a more measured and complex examination of parenthood in his later plays *Cherish* and *Picture Perfect*, but in the meantime, *Flybaby* was uremittingly, hilariously brutal.

A counterpoint to Mick Rose's cop was Jeremy Donovan's cadaverous Vatman, a special envoy from the Vatican popping by to test if the baby really was the Messiah, which he did by tossing it backwards over his head to see if it would fly. It didn't.

But it did. At one point the baby was stashed in a cupboard, and in a remarkable moment, one of the pair opened the door a crack and the baby flew out. It was a moment of theatrical magic, achieved really simply. The cupboard had a false back, of course, and someone just flung the baby through from behind. However, the three plays were performed on the same set, so the cupboard featured in all of them. Between each play, it was opened wide and its contents replaced to suit the next play. The real purpose of this though, was to cement in the audience's mind the apparently solid back wall, which was removed once the door was closed. Subverting the audience's expectations from behind: I still think of it as a genius move.

I was intrigued by the two shiftless characters, and wanted to write something like that myself. I even asked Ken if I could continue their story. In the end I didn't, but my attempt morphed into *Tigerplay*, which I wrote for the first Young and Hungry season. *Tigerplay*'s Russ and Alison were spawned from *Flybaby*'s Phil and Nadine.

Flybaby

by Ken Duncum and Rebecca Rodden

Originally performed at BATS Theatre, 9–25 July 1987

Nadine	Rebecca Rodden
Phil	Michael Galvin
Policeman	Mick Rose
Vatman	Jeremy Donovan
Director	Ron Mikalsen

Flybaby

An inner-city flat. A 'WELCOME HOME MESSIAH' banner has been hung up.

Crowd noise. Enter Nadine, with baby. Pause. Enter Phil, who slams the door.

Phil: Bloody hell, I thought they were going to tear me apart.

He gets his breath back.

Quite good media coverage, I thought. We'll be headlining the 6:30 news again tonight, no doubt about it.

'And today police were unable to restrain excited wellwishers from tearing the father of the baby into little strips and taking him home as souvenirs.' You could have at least talked to that reporter. He seemed like a nice guy.

Nadine: (*mimics*) 'Seemed like a nice guy.' They all do to you.

What a stupid question—'Was she conceived in love?'

Phil: Well saying 'no' was hardly diplomatic.

Nadine: I'm well past being diplomatic.

Phil moves to look out the window.

Phil: Some of those old ladies can really move fast when they want to.

123

Nadine: What am I supposed to do with this?

Phil: (*still looking out the window*) With what?

Nadine: With the baby.

Phil: I don't know. Feed her? Put her to bed? Something like that.

                Nadine puts the baby in a cupboard and closes the door. She sits down and picks up something to read.

                Did you see my sign?

Nadine: Yeah.

                Phil looks round the room.

Phil: Where's the baby?

Nadine: What?

Phil: The baby. Where is it?

Nadine: In the cupboard.

                Phil goes over to the cupboard, opens it, looks in, then closes the door again.

Phil: Are you just going to leave her there?

Nadine: Got any suggestions?

Phil: Well, what did they tell you to do at the hospital?

Nadine: Nothing. They were too busy taking photos and running around squawking, 'It's the Messiah, it's the Messiah.'

Phil: But what about changing nappies and all that?

Nadine: I don't know. I don't care.

Phil: Well, I do. That's my slot car set in there. I don't want it getting rusty. Or worse.

                Imagine that—final lap of the Indy 500—Phil Stop in his customised black Corvette Stingray exploding into the last corner, burning rubber, and then . . .

He makes sounds of skidding, crashing and exploding into flame.

. . . baby crap on the track.

He takes the baby out of the cupboard.

Phil: Hell-oo. Hell-oo.

Nadine: Don't you dare.

Phil: What?

Nadine: Don't you dare talk to that baby.

Phil props the baby up on the couch.

Phil: Why don't you read some of your telegrams?

He picks up a bunch of telegrams and holds them out. She doesn't take them.

Come on, just the one from the queen. I'll read it to you.

He opens it and reads.

'The realm is overwhelmed. Stop. Salutations to all. Stop. Er.'

Er?

Nadine: E.R., dickhead.

Phil: I knew that. Look, here's one from . . .

Nadine: How long are you going to keep this up?

Phil: What do you expect me to do?

Nadine: Nothing. Anything. What are you even doing here?

Phil: Well, I couldn't just walk out on you, could I? Not after I'd been on television.

Nadine: I suppose there have to be some drawbacks to being an overnight media celebrity.

Phil: I think I can cope with the fame.

Nadine: Well, I can't. Not a single other woman in my
            antenatal class has had to put up with what I have.
            Not one of them has had to go through anything like
            what happened to me in that delivery room. There
            I am—squatting away, minding my own business,
            when all of a sudden someone busts in yelling 'She's
            having the Messiah, she's having the Messiah. It's just
            been on TV.'

            Charming, I thought.

            Then it started to come and the doctor was telling
            me to push, and every time I did a crowd of people
            behind me shouted 'Hallelujah'.

            'Push—Hallelujah! PUSH—HALLELUJAH!'

            I think half the bloody hospital was in there by the
            time it finally dropped out. They were all dancing
            around and singing, and when I asked what the baby
            was, they all said 'It's the Messiah.' And I started
            screaming, 'But what is it? What is it? WHAT IS IT?'

            And finally one nurse stopped dancing around and
            said, 'Oh. Well, it's a girl as well.' As well. I was so
            excited I vomited.

Phil: Did you miss me?

Nadine: Yeah, I missed you, but I got it all over one of the
            doctors.

Phil: I mean, did you want me there?

Nadine: We agreed, didn't we?

Phil: Yeah. We agreed.

            He picks the baby up.

            A-bouncy-bouncy . . .

            He looks at Nadine and stops.

Phil: Is it supposed to be this colour?

Nadine:	Is it blue?
Phil:	No.
Nadine:	Then it's alright.

Phil puts the baby down again.

Phil:	I ended up at the hospital anyway.
	It was just like New Year's Eve.
Nadine:	Just thought you'd come and soak up the atmosphere, did you?
Phil:	They came and picked me up.
Nadine:	Who?
Phil:	Reporters. I don't know how they found out my name or anything. It was only about an hour after God came on TV. They said that my place was up at the hospital.
Nadine:	Did they give you lots of cigarettes and tell you to pace up and down the corridor?
Phil:	No, they just took pictures of me getting the news. Of course I'd already got it, but we re-enacted the scene. I was doing this really good surprised look. I was clutching my forehead and going like this.

He demonstrates.

That was the one that got front page of the *Dominion*. '"STRIKE ME PINK, IT'S THE MESSIAH!" SAYS DELIGHTED DAD'.

Actually I didn't say 'Strike me pink', I said 'Jesus Christ'—but they thought that might be a bit confusing.

Nadine continues to leaf through a magazine.

They say you grieve for a while.

Nadine:	What?

Phil: You grieve. When your baby isn't normal. You grieving?

Nadine: Actually, I have a pain.

Phil: Probably because you're not bonding. You've got to bond with your baby, you know. It's hormonal.

He picks up the baby and offers it to her.

Here, have a go.

Nadine reaches out a hand and pats it.

Nadine: Bond. Bond, bond. Alright?

Phil: Who's going to look after her if you don't?

Nadine: She can look after herself. She's the Messiah, isn't she? That lets us both off the hook.

Phil: Well, hadn't you better feed her at least?

Nadine: You do it.

Phil: Me?

Nadine: I haven't got any milk.

Phil: Are you sure?

Nadine: Of course I'm sure.

Phil: Bummer. I thought it was automatic.

Nadine: I've had enough of this. I'm going out.

Phil: Where?

Nadine: Anywhere. Some place normal.

She opens the door and the roar of the crowd erupts. Flowers, dummies and rattles come flying in. After a moment, Nadine shuts the door.

Phil: The police said we should wait here.

Nadine: What for? For her to grow up?

Phil: They said either that or another royal wedding to take some of the attention off us.

Nadine: Great.

She sits down and starts to cry.

Phil: Ah. Post-natal depression.

Pause.

Most people would be overjoyed. It's you and the Virgin Mary—an exclusive club.

Nadine: I thought it would be an ordinary baby. Not this.

Phil: She's ordinary. Look. Two eyes. A nose. Arms and legs down there somewhere. She doesn't cry much though, does she?

He rattles the baby.

Nadine: I didn't even want a baby. Now everyone's treating me like I'm just an incubator.

Phil: I don't think of you as an incubator. You'll always be more to me than that.

Nadine: Well if they think she belongs to the whole world, then they can take care of her. It's nothing to do with me.

Phil: Don't be ridiculous. She's your baby. She looks just like you. Alright, she doesn't look anything like you. But she will. It's me that's got nothing to do with it.

Nadine: What do you mean?

Phil: You know. God . . . and you . . .

He makes vague hand motions.

Nadine: You what?

Phil: I'm not jealous, if that's what you think. I've told you, I believe in an open relationship.

Nadine: Oh yes, I see. Who needs a blood test to establish paternity when you can plead divine intervention?

Phil: Well, I can't be the father of the Messiah, can I?

Nadine: Why not? I'm the mother.

Phil: Because I've got convictions.

Nadine: Religious ones?

Phil: No. Drug ones. I'm not fit.

Nadine: The newspapers called you 'dad'.

Phil: Media hype.

Nadine: Don't you think I'd know if you weren't the father?

Phil: Maybe you weren't paying enough attention. Maybe you didn't recognise what was going on. They say the Virgin Mary was impregnated through her ear.

Nadine: Come again?

Phil: You could have been asleep. Or semi-conscious.

Nadine: So this is how you're going to wriggle out, is it?

Phil: I still stand by everything I said when you first told me you were pregnant.

Nadine: What? 'Who's the father?'

Phil: After that.

Nadine: That you couldn't promise anything and we should just take things day by day?

Phil: No. After that.

Nadine: That you might be able to help out with the money?

Phil: Yeah. That.

Nadine: I never doubted you for an instant.

Phil: You said it as well. No ties. We both agreed. Are you going to go back on that now?

Nadine: You still don't get it, do you?

She walks to the door.

Phil: What are you doing?

Nadine throws open the door and shouts.

Nadine: He's leaving us. He's abandoning me and the kid . . .

The roar of the crowd cuts in. Phil runs over and drags Nadine away. Before he can shut the door he is hit by a box of nappies.

Phil: What are you trying to do? Get me killed?

Nadine: See? It's not me who's going to force you into anything. It's them. Unless we can think of a way out we're going to be stuck here and stuck together.

Phil: I'm psychologically unfit. That must be worth something. I'm far too highly strung to be a proper father figure. I'm a child beater. Yeah, I feel it coming on . . .

He makes aggressive moves towards the baby . . .

Don't mess with me, baby.

. . . and ends up poking her gently and going 'coochy-coo', etc.

Nadine: (*taking a breath*) We've got to put her up for adoption.

Phil: Okay.

He continues to play with the baby.

Nadine: Okay?

Phil: Sounds fine to me.

Nadine: Well at least recognise the enormity of the situation. I'm suggesting upstaging Lindy Chamberlain and all you can say is that it sounds fine to you.

Phil: What would you like me to say? That, just because everyone wants us to, we should stay together and be the greatest little set of parents ever? Despite the fact that we can't even run our own lives properly?

Nadine: Don't lump me in with you. I can run my life perfectly well.

Phil: If you could, we wouldn't be in this situation now.

(*to the baby*) Hah, she's got no answer to that.

Nadine: Give me that.

Phil: Why?

Nadine gets up.

Nadine: Give it to me.

Phil: No.

(*to the baby*) We didn't like all that about Lindy Chamberlain, did we?

Nadine faces him.

Nadine: Give me my baby.

Slowly Phil hands the baby over. Nadine looks at it.

Just a bundle with a face. No big deal.

Go on, then. Save the world or something. Perhaps you'd be more comfortable if we tacked you up on the wall?

Phil takes out a joint from a hiding place.

Phil: So okay, this wasn't what we expected. But if we just stay cool, don't get excited, then everything will probably work itself out.

Nadine: You mean if we go with the flow, mellow out and keep it together?

Phil: Well, what's the point in getting worked up?

He offers her the joint—she doesn't take it.

I mean, look on the bright side. We're famous.

Overnight. I don't know about you but I think it's about time I started getting some attention.

There is a knock at the door and a Policeman enters.

Policeman: Afternoon. Sorry about not waiting for you to say 'Come in'. It's my training.

Phil moves incredibly deliberately, as if in slow motion, taking the joint out of his mouth, concealing it in his hand, exhaling almost imperceptibly.

Delighted dad, is it? Congratulations.

He shakes hands with Phil, who gets burnt.

And delighted mum, I presume. So this is the baby, then? Well, would you look at that. I've got a daughter, you know. Big head. Unnaturally big. Ears like an elephant.

Nadine: Indian or African?

Policeman: Well, actually coffee, if you've got any.

Phil: (*quickly*) No. No, we haven't. Sorry.

Policeman: Quite right. Bad for you anyway, eh?

Nadine: Anything else we can do for you?

Policeman: Oh. I just came to tell you we've cleared the street. We didn't want the crowd disturbing her.

Nadine: Oh, that's lovely. Isn't that lovely, Phil?

Policeman: Have you noticed anything funny about her yet?

Nadine: No.

Policeman: Of course I didn't mean 'funny', as such. I meant . . .

Nadine: Peculiar.

Policeman: Different. Indicative of powers beyond our ken.

Nadine: Phil found her in the cupboard a few minutes ago. Didn't you, Phil?

Phil:	Eh?
Policeman:	What, just found her in the cupboard?
Nadine:	One minute she was here, the next she was in the cupboard.
Policeman:	Amazing.
Phil:	(*changing the subject*) So, how are things outside?
Policeman:	Fine. We've secured most of the rooftops.
Phil:	What for?
Policeman:	Snipers.
Nadine:	Snipers?
Policeman:	Police jargon for people who kill you from a long distance. No cause for concern, though. Out there it's what I would describe as a carnival atmosphere. We've all been having a few laughs and getting on like a house on fire.

Now, anything you need in here? |
Nadine:	A sniper?
Policeman:	That's right, a sense of humour's what you need. I can see why you were visited with the holy occurrence.
Nadine:	That's a relief—just visiting, is it?
Policeman:	It couldn't have happened to a nicer couple.
Nadine:	Couple of what?
Phil:	Well, we don't want to keep you from the party. Don't worry about us, we'll be fine.
Policeman:	I get you. Ready for a feed, is she? It's okay, I did a couple of papers in sociology last year so you don't have to worry about embarrassing me. As a matter of fact, I find breastfeeding very soothing. But my wife won't sit still for long enough.

(*laughs*) My wife won't . . .

He clears his throat and stands up.

Sorry about that. It's the job. It brutalises you. You wouldn't believe some of the things I've seen. And of course, outside the station it's even worse.

(*on his way to the door*) If there's anything you want . . .

Nadine:	I love you. Take me away from all this.
Policeman:	That's right. Keep it up. Ha ha ha.

He goes.

Phil:	Did you see that? I almost got snapped. In my own home.
Nadine:	They're only here to help us.
Phil:	I can't live my life surrounded by police. This isn't how I imagined it would go. I thought that once she was born, once you'd seen her, you'd get all those feelings you're supposed to get and you'd want to take care of her so I could piss off somewhere and not have to worry.
Nadine:	That's funny, I thought the same thing about you.
Phil:	I mean, you're going to do something, aren't you? Even if you have her adopted, you'll make sure it's to a proper family, won't you? She might get spoiled. All this attention she's getting. She needs proper training, like the royal family. She'll have to learn control, composure, diplomacy, how to sit still for hours on end . . .
Nadine:	Don't worry.
Phil:	But who's going to teach her? We don't know anything about those things.
Nadine:	What are you getting so excited about?
Phil:	I don't know. It's a responsibility attack or something.

Look, she's been home 15 minutes and we haven't even changed a nappy. Neither you nor the fridge has got any milk and we need police protection to put the bottles out.

Nadine: Calm down.

Phil: I tried that and I almost got arrested. It's all this not-crying. It's getting on my nerves. At some stage someone's going to have to tell her about sex, you know.

Nadine: What?

Phil: All those things: right, wrong, grey areas . . .

Oh God, my nose has started to bleed.

Nadine: Sit down. Sit down. Now, baby, your father's got something he wants to say to you.

Alright. Tell her the facts of life.

Phil: Me? It's supposed to be the mother. You go to one of those film evenings . . .

Nadine: You don't want her to think you're scared, do you? Just tell her about mummies and daddies.

Phil: Never mind the bloody mummies and daddies—it's the consenting adults you've got to watch.

Nadine: And now tell her not to get pregnant or she won't be allowed the car.

Phil: Why doesn't she cry?

Nadine: She's waiting to see what I'm going to do. But pinch her if it'll make you feel better.

Phil: Sometimes, you know, I wish I wasn't quite so useless.

Nadine: What do you mean?

Phil: I could have done something back when you were first pregnant, couldn't I? I could be doing something now.

Nadine:	Like what?

Phil: I don't know, get married or something.

Nadine: Get a grip. I don't mind admitting you live here, but the thought of introducing you to people as my husband . . .

Phil: I've had other offers, you know.

Nadine: Who?

Phil: Well, I saw this ad in the paper once. But I didn't answer it. See? I couldn't even get myself properly organised to run away.

Nadine: I don't mind. No. I mean, I'm glad. I'm glad someone's here.

Phil: Of course that doesn't mean you can take anything for granted. It's just that I haven't got that many friends at the moment. I got this funny haircut at primary school and things just seemed to escalate from there.

There is a knock at the door. The Policeman reenters.

Policeman: Did you say come in? Probably not.

Everything alright your end? The reason I've popped back is that we've got this gentleman . . .

The Vatman enters.

Vatman: Thank you, officer, I'll take it from here.

Nadine: Who are you?

Vatman: Vatican Special Envoy in charge of Messiahs, false and otherwise. I trust my coming here isn't an intrusion. But we at the Vatican believe there's no time like the present. Unless it's the past.

He utters a short bark of laughter.

I'll just get down a few details.

Nadine: What is this?

Vatman: Now you're the mother. Correct?

Nadine: Yes.

Vatman: Right. The father?

Phil: Yo.

Vatman: You're not trying to claim parthenogenesis, then?

Phil: No, I'm just on the ordinary benefit.

Vatman: Parthenogenesis means virgin birth.

                Phil and Nadine look at each other.

Phil/Nadine: No.

Vatman: (*to Nadine*) Have you experienced visions, healings, voices, teleplasm or other unusual sensations?

Nadine: That's a bit personal, isn't it?

Vatman: Just answer the questions, please, and we'll be through much more quickly. Otherworldly experiences?

Nadine: No.

Vatman: Any signs, portents, intimations of impending doom?

Nadine: Plenty of those.

Vatman: Yes?

Nadine: The doctors said I'd soon cheer up, though.

Vatman: This is the baby?

                He approaches cautiously.

Vatman: It appears to be asleep.

Nadine: Probably tired out from all that flying.

Policeman: Flying?

                (*punches Phil on the arm*) You son of a gun.

Vatman:	May we have a demonstration? A little turn round the room perhaps?
Nadine:	I told you—she's asleep. She's worn out.
Vatman:	Wake her up.
Policeman:	Just a little flit, that's all.
Nadine:	I don't think so, officer.
Vatman:	You're lying.
Nadine:	That's right, I made it up. She can't fly at all.
Vatman:	No?
Nadine:	Not a bit. She can't even walk.
Vatman:	You're protecting her. What are you trying to hide?
Nadine:	Nothing.
Vatman:	I don't believe you.
Nadine:	Believe what you like.
Vatman:	I will. Now wake her up, please.
Nadine:	No.
Vatman:	Then I will.

He steps towards the baby.

Phil:	Have you got a warrant to wake this baby up?
Vatman:	Restrain this man, officer.
Phil:	Hey, no problem.

The Vatman picks up the baby.

Vatman:	Now, I wonder . . . can she or can she not fly?
Nadine:	You know she can't.
Vatman:	On the contrary. I try not to pre-judge.
	OUT, BEELZEBUB!

He throws the baby high in the air.

Phil: Hey!

Phil goes for the catch, fumbles it, and Nadine gets it on the rebound.

Nadine: You bastard! Nobody throws my baby round the room but me.

Vatman: Congratulations. Your baby is not possessed by a demon.

Phil: We already knew that, wanker.

Policeman: That was a bit on the nose, wasn't it, sir?

Vatman: Not at all. The old methods are still the best. An evil spirit will always save itself.

Policeman: You don't believe in that stuff, do you?

Vatman: I haven't got much choice in my line of work.

          (*to Nadine*) Now what exactly are you claiming about your child?

Nadine: Nothing. *We* are not claiming anything. Now piss off.

Vatman: (*to Phil*) Is this correct?

Phil: You heard her.

Vatman: Sign here then, please.

He produces a form.

          It's just a simple waiver stating that you don't claim your daughter to be the one true prophet.

Phil: Do you want it in blood?

Vatman: What do you think this is? The Dark Ages?

Phil signs it.

          Now spit on it.

Phil: What?

He spits on the form.

Vatman: Now if you could just provide me with an icon. Toy, article of clothing, half-chewed rusk . . .

Phil: I thought you said she wasn't the Messiah?

Vatman: I can't be too careful. It'd be worth my job if I missed the big one.

Phil gives him a bootee.

Right. The Pope will issue a statement in a few days saying that it's not the end of the world and everyone should keep sending the money.

He starts to pack up.

Policeman: If it was a demon, wouldn't it know that someone would always try and catch it?

Vatman: That would require trust. (*to Nadine and Phil*) Have a nice day.

He exits.

Policeman: Not the Messiah, eh? Bit of a shocker. But look at it this way—at least she's got a nice set of ears.

He exits.

Pause.

Phil: A few days, he said. The Pope will say it was all a mistake, maybe the crowds will go home, things'll settle down a bit.

I suppose I'll be off then. If I ever get packed.

You going to have her adopted?

Nadine: Whatever.

Phil: Yeah. Whatever.

They sit down. A Demon emerges from the couch and tries to kill the baby with a squiggly bladed knife. The cupboard door bangs open and an Angel comes out.

Angel: Go ahead. Make my day.

They wrestle. The demon is the baddie, the angel the 'Gorgeous George' variety of wrestler. The fight displays all the usual Hollywood drama and vicissitudes of big-time wrestling, with underhand tactics, etc.

Phil and Nadine are completely oblivious, perhaps carrying on a desultory conversation.

The demon is caught in a painful hold but manages to stretch out its hand towards the couch.

Demon: Tag.

Another hand comes out of the couch and a dwarf demon enters the fray, leaping on the angel's back.

Phil: I wish we had a television.

Eventually the demons are subdued and driven back into the couch. The angel goes to salute the baby, but wrinkles its nose in disgust. The angel gets back into the cupboard.

The lights start to fade.

Phil: Can you smell something?

They both look at the baby.

Blackout.

The End

Alternate End:

Policeman: Not the Messiah, eh? Bit of a shocker. But look at it
this way—at least she's got a nice set of ears.

He exits.

*Nadine notices something strange. She unwinds then
shakes out the baby's blanket—no baby. They look at
each other . . .*

*The sound of crying from inside the cupboard. Phil
opens the cupboard—the baby comes flying out and into
Nadine's arms. She rewraps the baby and soothes her.*

*Phil reaches into the cupboard and takes out a slot-
car, relieved to see it is okay. He turns it over. A stream
of urine pours out. He gingerly puts it back in the
cupboard and shuts the door.*

He joins Nadine and the baby on the couch.

Pause.

Phil: A few days, he said. The Pope will say it was all a
mistake, maybe the crowds will go home, things'll
settle down a bit.

I suppose I'll be off then. If I ever get packed.

You going to have her adopted?

Nadine: Whatever.

Phil: Yeah. Whatever.

Lights slowly fade.

The End

JISM

Ken:

The idea was originally for Rebecca and Carol Smith. During the season of *Flybaby/David's Books/The New Step*, Carol and Rebecca were getting on really well—and made a great double-act backstage. One night when I came into town for the show, I parked the car and was walking to BATS when I thought as a joke I'd tell Rebecca and Carol we'd do a play with them as conjoined twins. I'd had to park particularly far away that night, and all the way along Kent Terrace I thought about it. By the time I arrived at BATS it wasn't a joke any more. I was serious.

Lily White, Rose Red, spleen versus ideal, sex and love, the bodily and the spiritual, concepts of womanhood . . . all naturally arose from that original joky idea. Other aspects drifted in and were caught in the gravity, fell into orbit as if they'd always been there, giving rise to characters: advertising exploitation (Clara and her perfume, JISM), the alienation of fanaticism (Gerald), the loneliness of madness (Clark). The challenges and symmetries of a play featuring conjoined twins were absorbing—we knew from early on, for instance, that one sister would have an affair with the other's boyfriend literally behind her back—but how? It was clear that once Lily and Rose had done everything they could together they must be separated and then do everything they could individually—but what were their disparate trajectories and towards what?

Between that initial idea and the season of *JISM* at BATS, almost two years passed. And a lot had changed in the interim. Jill and I had our first child, Katherine, in 1988. Round that same time I attended the Playmarket Playwrights' Conference, where an early draft of my first solo-written play, *Blue Sky Boys*, was presented. I started to work for a local production company, Gibson Group, writing sketches on spec for their puppet political satire, *Public Eye*. When they offered me a weekly wage for a further series I left my job in private boxes and set sail on the uncertain sea of a freelance writing career, which I would navigate precariously for the next 15 years. No more 10am finish, the-day's-your-own; I was a breadwinner now, a family man. I was writing and getting paid for it. I was somehow on the pathway the careers advisor at school had assured me didn't exist.

Meanwhile Carol successfully auditioned for, and was accepted into, drama school. During her two-year course she wasn't allowed to do outside productions, so she wouldn't be a *JISM*-sister after all.

Neither would Rebecca. Nine years on from her motorbike accident, her hip had deteriorated to the point where she had to have a replacement. I remember meeting her in the street one lunchtime looking very sorry for herself. She'd just come from the dentist, who—in the lead-up to the big operation—had pulled all her wisdom teeth to ward against post-hip-replacement infection. I took her round to Carol's and she cheered up a bit. We passed a pleasant afternoon before the pain medication started to wear off. Following the hip replacement Rebecca was on crutches a long time, and after that usually needed a stick for balance. Somewhere along the line it became apparent that she was never going to cope with being physically attached to another actor on stage. The writing may have been on the wall—but I had to read it to her nevertheless. That was hard. As Rebecca says in an interview about the play, 'I'd kill to act—I'd only maim to write.' The deal we'd always had—if she wrote it, she could be in it—crumbled away with her hipbone. Rebecca did play the Fool (ha!) in Simon Bennett's Summer Shakespeare production of *King Lear* at Victoria University early in 1988, but a bit of physical impairment works well for the Fool, and there were only a couple of acting roles after that. Simon remembers Rebecca's Fool as 'magnificent, with a plastic exoskeleton on one leg and a battered pair of Mickey Mouse ears as her cockscomb'.

The revolving door of the drama school might have spirited

Carol away, but it had also dropped Simon back on the street after a two-year stint as an acting student. (As he says, probably the most reluctant actor to ever graduate from Toi Whakaari!) He emerged with some grand plans. One was to transform BATS Theatre along with Simon Elson—and the other was to direct *JISM* at the duly transformed BATS.

While old BATS resounded to the snarl of power tools wielded by a rag-tag band of theatre soldiers the two Simons had pressed into service, I don't remember lifting a hammer or paintbrush. That's not really where my talents lie anyway. Instead Rebecca and I were grappling with the responsibility of ensuring the bright new BATS didn't launch with a dud play. Writing and rewriting—and a bit of reading and workshopping—went on in the background as the new theatre took shape. A major reason Simon Bennett was taking the reins at BATS was to ensure *JISM* got a production—he'd been part of its development from early on—but also to ensure that plays like *JISM* (New Zealand-written, young-ish, ambitious and a bit edgy) could be staged. A new wave of playwrights was emerging— or trying to emerge—and BATS-as-we-know-it-today was set up to provide them (and of course the new actors, designers and directors coming through) with an outlet. Yes, there were a lot of theatres in Wellington, but they had their own audiences and agendas and, though they might cheer from the sidelines, they weren't usually prepared to take a punt on the new and untried, or the proud possessors of a 'cult' audience (a term bandied about in regard to Rebecca's and my work at the time). For a while there—a long while, actually—BATS was as close as New Zealand got to having a 'writers' theatre'. It still provides that service—though mysteriously plays have got shorter, ambitions lower and authorship more diluted (but let's leave that for another day). If you were a writer, BATS was a theatre you could get yourself and your work into. Getting out again could later prove to be more of a problem: once you'd developed your craft and career at BATS and were looking for the next step up, there was no natural direction to go in. A few years after *JISM* I was picturing my career as stranded in the Taj Mahal (once public toilets; now the Welsh Dragon bar)—by which I mean stuck on the no-man's-land traffic island with been-there-done-that

BATS on one side of the road and the unreachable Downstage on the other.

However, I digress. I hear the buzzsaws singing as Simon and Simon cut the radical new centre entrance to the BATS auditorium, so I'd better get on with my story . . .

Casting. Having lost both Carol and Rebecca, we now had to find actors to play the roles written with those two in mind. Emma Robinson and Kerry Fox were tight friends who had gone through drama school a year ahead of Simon. They were cast on their individual abilities—but the fact they had an already-existing rapport was also useful. Emma persuasively played the serene, loved-by-everyone Lily and excelled at taking that to a disconcerting level of stillness and alienation. Kerry played Rose as a whirlpool of emotion and appetite, a character with no off-button whose every response radiated through her skin. Stephen Lovatt and Michael McGrath were cast as the flatmates. I'd first met Stephen when he acted in my Radio New Zealand radio play *One Day at the Ayers Rock Hilton*, about a kangaroo considering a career as a motivational speaker. Stephen's acting had an intensity which made the steadily growing arc of Gerald's fanaticism mesmerising. I'd also recently worked with Michael when he played the part of Phil Everly in *Blue Sky Boys* at the Playmarket Playwrights' Conference. Michael played Clark with a beautifully gentle manner that made audiences adore him. Emma Kinane came from Simon's year at drama school. She played a lovely, slightly goofy doctor; an exuberantly angry activist; but most challenging of all, Manson the giant axolotl. To watch her every night, in her spectacular though cumbersome costume, surge up the tight spiral staircase in pursuit of Clark was truly an awesome sight. Emma also sang hauntingly the second song I had ever written (my first song—the *JISM* rap—concludes precisely one minute previously in the show). John Leigh played Philippe Mignon and a couple of smaller, both fatal roles—the dog-owner who meets a grisly end, and Mr Grant, who chokes on a caramel and ends up donating his heart and lungs. Some time previously I had been directing a section of *Waiting for Godot* for the Victoria University English department—I had one half of the music-hall tramp duo in the shape of Alan Brough. While looking for an Estragon, Alan suggested his flatmate, who he said was the funniest guy he'd ever met. I rolled my eyes—yeah, right—and cast someone else. John Leigh turned out to be the flatmate, and within five minutes of meeting him I was cursing my stupidity. I didn't make that mistake twice.

This was a big cast—we still needed more actors! Tina Regtien was a drama school graduate also from the same year as Emma and Kerry. She delightfully and comically caught Clara's bizarre mix of sophisticated menace and out-and-out childishness, and contrasted that brilliantly with her portrayal of 'mustn't grumble', organ-donating Mrs Grant. The final onstage actor was Leigh Ransfield, a lithe, clever and physical actor who'd trained in Australia. He played the largely straight-man role of boyfriend David with verve, and the highly excitable animal-activist Erwin with evident enjoyment. Only seen on video was a final actor—Andrew Laing playing chat-show host Tad Maniacal. Andrew was yet another drama school graduate from Simon's year—and a close friend of Simon's. Andrew smoothly trowelled on all the flashy smarm and looks-to-camera required for a show entitled *Innuendo*.

We rehearsed in empty office space upstairs in Wakefield Street (the old Market Gardeners buildings). Emma Kinane took some rehearsal photos and they all seem very sunny. I've only got a few rehearsal memories. One is of all of us trooping round from BATS to the rehearsal space on the first day and having a co-op meeting in which Simon laid out expectations. In her notes, Emma talks about the Mike Alfreds method of rehearsal that Simon took the actors through—and she wonders what Rebecca and I made of it. Speaking for myself, I loved it. All the homework—the lists and the actioning—made everything clear, detailed and checkable. Best of all, it operated on the assumption that everything was in the script of the play—any question could be and would be answered by burrowing into it. The Alfreds method enshrines the writer as the source of the play and encourages actors, directors and designers to pay the kind of concentration and attention to the script that authors fervently hope for but don't always get as they labour over every word, line and stage direction.

Having said that, one of my other memories of rehearsal is of coming in at lunchtime and Kerry, Emma and Leigh excitedly showing me the Lily/David lovemaking scene. They'd added a bit where Leigh reached out and shut Emma's eyes with his fingers. Great, huh—cause he works as a mortician? I carefully observed that David was meant to be a legitimate romantic choice for Lily—that was important for the dramatic stakes—and this one small action turned him into a necrophiliac who could only have sex with a woman if he was fantasising she was dead. They looked crestfallen—Do you think? Oh, yes . . . no doubt about it. Sometimes being the writer can make you feel like you're spoiling all the fun.

I also remember, once we were in BATS for the final rehearsals, Rebecca bursting out in raucous laughter as Simon took the actors through the newly rewritten last scene of the play. They all stopped and looked over, wondering what was so funny about what they were doing. I was forced to admit that Rebecca was pissing herself because I had just whispered to her that this scene was the best thing I had ever written. Philistine.

The *JISM* rap was set to music by Christiaan Ercolano and used some early days sampling from Prince and Frankie Goes to Hollywood. It made a great start to the play with everyone singing and dancing, and then (starting as we meant to go on) wrong-footing the audience by revealing itself to be a prospective (and rejected) advert. I remember Simon and Emma Kinane telling me that my lyrics for the 'Stick Together' song didn't scan. Musically illiterate, I had somehow imagined that if I could hear the melody in them, so could everyone else. I was forced *way* out of my comfort zone to mumblingly sing it for them. Luckily that was all Emma needed.

The video inserts of *Innuendo* were shot by Marty Walsh in a small studio just off the Basin Reserve and owned by director of photography Waka Attewell. In return for donating his time and expertise, Marty wanted to shoot a video of *Polythene Pam*—so Rebecca had to gear back up to perform that for the camera. I never saw the video—except through the monitor on the night—and don't know if it's still out there somewhere . . .

I'm on the *Innuendo* videos as the intro voice and as a crew member wrestling with the crazed Tad Maniacal at the end. I'd first invented Tad for a university revue—but he really came into his own in *JISM* (so to speak). As mentioned earlier, this was all on VHS video, the height of technology at the time, and using it on stage was cutting-edge and daring. Opening night: disaster! Nothing but white noise on the TV screen. The actors waited in darkness and the operator was at a loss. As it turned out, the video had not been rewound after the previous night's dress rehearsal. Simon realised this. I looked back to see him climb from his seat and scramble across the (full) top rows to get to the lighting box. We then got to watch the entire two *Innuendo* scenes backward at high speed as Simon rewound the tape until he reached the start and normal transmission could resume.

Andrew Foster—whom I'd first met up a ladder at BATS three years before—designed the set. It was a groundbreaking design, showing what was possible in BATS; a multi-purpose structure of levels full of exposed scaffolding pipes and grungy darkness, featuring a metal spiral staircase to a fetid bathroom, all overhung with the white-on-black *JISM* logo. The effect of this was amplified by an intricate sound design (requiring its own operator) that ranged from stagnant dripping to foreboding deep-bass rumbles, to Christiaan's purpose-written music, and by innovative lighting around and under the stage. Judiciously add some dry ice, and the assault on the senses was immersive in a way BATS had never been host to before. When Manson emerged out of the shadows—a six-foot Mexican walking fish in that spectacular costume by Natasha Christie—accompanied by horror-movie chords and his own Psycho-type theme, the audience was torn between disbelief and delight. Yes, *Baby with the Bathwater* was technically the first show in the revamped theatre (directed by Guy Boyce, who would later take his turn at running BATS) but it was the soft launch, enabling Simon to snatch the rehearsal time he needed for what would really be the flagship show, the one that had to impress. And it succeeded. Sound, lights, set, costume, acting and writing—everything about *JISM* did what we intended it to do—rule a big black line that said 'This is the new BATS'. That was then; this is now. Everything, that is, but the vat of boiling JISM which I thought was ridiculously small and underwhelming. But let's not quibble . . .

Publicity, too. We ran a teaser campaign of cheap newsprint posters—'*JISM*: it's coming'—to raise profile in advance. Our main poster was the opposite of cheap—a beautiful purple and gold image of Emma and Kerry at their most glam and elegant, joined at the face. We grabbed whatever media we could. The *Dominion* and *Evening Post* reviews blew all the wind into our sails we could want. Both were uniformly excellent; not a negative word. Headlines proclaimed 'Awesome in production and performance' and '*JISM*: roses all the way'; elsewhere 'a remarkable presentation', 'an extraordinarily exhilarating show' and a 'a true theatrical event'.

'Too long,' said David Geary in *Illusions* (not mentioning the fact that there seemed to be a character named after him). 'Lacking dramatic tension—circling in eddies of plot . . . bizarreness trying to be reality,' said Ron Mikalsen in the *Listener*. Hang on, wasn't that one written by the director of our last play? *Come on, guys.*

I should mention here that David is a good friend of mine and always sends me an email on my birthday, which we happen to share. Ron moved to Australia years ago, but I would love to have a drink with him any time. It's just that, back then, Rebecca and I sincerely wished that our friends would *stop reviewing us*.

That aside, everything went swimmingly. I'm pretty sure—with the newspaper reviews and word of mouth—that we packed out. That didn't mean anybody made any money, of course. But we were the toast—if not of the town, then at least the top of Courtenay Place. Peter Hawes's *Aunt Daisy!* musical was across the road at Downstage, but he kept telling people they should see our show instead. Either we weren't 'cult' anymore or the cult had gotten substantially bigger.

I got particular pleasure from inveigling a couple of my ex-workmates from private boxes to come to the show. Nami and Venus had never been to the theatre—any theatre—before, and it blew their heads off. I loved the way they talked about the characters like they were real people. 'Wow,' they said, 'is every play like this?'

Another workmate—this time from Gibson Group—highlighted a miscalculation I'd made. Knowing *JISM* was our first truly full-length play, so therefore would have two acts and an interval, and that people thus far had only seen one-act work from us—I worried that they might mistakenly go home at half-time. The solution, I decided, was to create such a cliffhanger at the end of act 1 that they would have to come back to see what happened. Accordingly we concluded the first act with Lily and Rose being surgically separated—in a gruesome and ritualistic scene—before both going into cardiac arrest and flatlining. We go out on doctors frantically trying to revive them . . . brilliant! I was working at Gibson Group with Arthur Baysting (whom I'd first seen from a distance in 1978 entertaining the main stage crowd at Nambassa with his character Neville Purvis at your service) and brought him along to a performance of *JISM*. The twins were separated, the lights came up and we shuffled out into the foyer. 'Great,' said Arthur, 'but a bit bleak.' And he pulled on his coat and prepared to head out into the night . . . There were reports of others making the same mistake— depressed playgoers who didn't have a writer there to stop them before they reached the door. Note to self: make sure the cliffhanger hangs and doesn't just go over the cliff.

One last point that has to be addressed, I guess: my name— which appears as Ken Duncan on everything connected to this show. 'Because it is my name!' as John Proctor cries in *The Crucible*. But his name was only slightly silly—mine was a major laugh-out- loud handicap when put beside the title *JISM*. Seriously: if you were me, would you put your head in that lion's maw? Let's just pause here to consider that I changed my name rather than the title of the play—which must say something about my dedication to my art. The title was perfect—it was there from the start and the play couldn't be called anything else. Despite intending it to be (professionally) permanent, I changed the spelling back after *JISM*. I just didn't seem to have Bob Dylan's knack for being someone different than whom I was christened as. Listen, when I was born 'cum' did not have the meaning it has today—so maybe it will duly fall out of usage and in 500 years my name will have the same classic ring as Shakespeare.

Yeah, right . . .

In our world *JISM* was a pretty important experience—a milestone for Rebecca and me, for the actors in it, the design team making their bones on it, for Simon as a fledgling director—and for BATS Theatre itself and all who have sailed in her. From that point on BATS was an acknowledged feature of the Wellington theatre

scene—nay, of the New Zealand theatre scene. It developed its own audience, only some of whom you'd see at other theatres. Best of all, there was a feeling that if you didn't keep your eye on it, if you didn't know what was going on at BATS, you ran the risk of missing something new and exciting. That's where the great actors, writers and directors were coming through—and you could see them there before the rest of the world knew. 'Yeah,' you could be boasting years later, 'I saw her at BATS. Front row, close enough to touch...'

Driving to a *JISM* rehearsal one day I saw Kerry Fox on the street and picked her up. She'd gone home at lunchtime to answer a special phone call (there were no mobiles then). Consequently I was the first person she told that she'd just been cast as Janet Frame in Jane Campion's *An Angel at My Table*. That project changed her life, and soon she was in the UK. Emmas Robinson and Kinane and Tina Regtien are all still actors—and writers as well. A few years back Emma Kinane did the MA scriptwriting course which I teach.

Stephen Lovatt has had a successful acting career both here and in Australia, Michael McGrath has lived in the UK for many years, and John Leigh went on to be the much-loved Lionel on *Shortland Street*, and has been in numerous projects since then (including playing Ronald Hugh Morrieson in my play *Horseplay* at Auckland Theatre Company).

Simon went from strength to strength as a theatre director—then as a TV director and producer, and more recently a feature film director. Andrew Foster, in addition to his many talents, is now a member of the Circa Council—if you needed proof that the world has indeed changed.

Rebecca and I didn't write together for a while after this—life took us in different directions. But as it turned out, we had at least one more play in us...

Leigh Ransfield didn't make it through the AIDS epidemic of the 90s. He was a kind of mischievous personality. We were different people with different approaches to theatre, and he used to enjoy winding me up. I can still hear Leigh a row behind me at a performance of *The Cherry Orchard* loudly saying, 'I hate fucking Chekhov,' knowing it would make me turn round—and laughing when I did.

Rebecca:

The phrases 'cult following' and 'cult icons' obviously transfixed me with ego-hungry absorption—for a while.

When *JISM* came out I went to every opening night of other plays at Circa, Downstage and the theatre off Taranaki Street; which has a different name now. Fortunately for my (as I believe) universally experienced assumption of being special, I assessed the likelihood of popularity, recognition and duration of accolades. I'd given the 'starry wondergirl' response a guesstimation of a week's duration. So I settled for the buzzy, brazen indulgence of having a fine time for that week. Drinking champagne at openings, smiling politely or indulgently at the actors I'd only seen on TV coming to shake my hand and eulogise my talent. Delicious as it was, I intuited that these people certainly hadn't recognised me; I'd been pointed out to them. And I further intuited that they would fail to recognise me in a week's time. I was right, but this caused no grief.

The real treats-to-tears for me has been people who've seen the plays and 25 years later choose to make me feel that one short part of my gimpish life has been a kind of success. It doesn't entail financial or social recognition, but to be told someone still has a poster from 'back in the day' is both weird and flattering. Two years ago, after one of seven operations, my district nurse was swabbing the part of my hip that had failed to entirely close. She called herself a fan, then suggested I consider amputation, as there are plenty of film parts for amputees. 'It would be a "hindquarter" amp [takes the buttock on that side, as well as leg] and you'd be sure to be wanted for scenes.' I tried to raise a modicum of requisite interest, and failed.

I never got to drama school, like many of the actors who'd first acted in our plays, but I think that was due to my funky, punky dyed hair; maybe my limp; and more likely to a reference I sent in from a highly regarded theatre academic who suggested I secure a reference from someone else, as he felt the need to explain that I could be a liability to a company due to my mental instability. You had to have two references from people involved in theatre. I only had one. But my supreme arrogance assured me any such wee slur on my brain's normality would be totally eclipsed when they saw and heard me.

I applied two years in a row and never even got to interview stage. I internalised a total belief that the plays I'd written with Ken and had acted in would nullify a teeny-weeny negative. Watching people I had adored—Carol Smith, Tim Balme, Simon Bennett and Mick Rose—interview, audition and get accepted was a double-edged sword. I truly was effervescent on their behalf, knowing they would have craved it as much as I had, but the duet of emotions included a weep-inducing desolation that I was never going to get the learning that any would-be actor sorely needs and yearns for.

It's easy enough to console myself now, knowing that the chronic pain would have dulled me. And I wouldn't hire a person who takes three scene-stealing minutes gimping across the stage. Theatre is about suspending your belief for a time and indulging, luxuriating in the story, drama and acting; not about thinking, 'Ugh, that person really is physically fucked up.' Too much reality can spoil a good idea.

For *JISM* I prostituted myself a little. We badly needed a studio and film work done—for free. A film dude I knew said he would provide equipment and expertise if he could do an abbreviated filming of *Polythene Pam*. Who held the cards? The dude took me to a makeup artist and I was stunned when I looked in the mirror— this woman was, goddamnit, beautiful. I was substantially freaked out that I would never ever look like this again. A day's shoot playing Pam as a stunner rather than half-humorous, half-unhinged, was certainly a different take on the matter. I never did see that video but if I did I'd probably be either tragically traumatised or angry at this ageing business. But hey, we got the gear. No money down and it was quite novel at the time.

Simon Bennett:

JISM was a huge deal for me. It marked my first professional production after finishing drama school, it was my first production at BATS—which Simon Elson and I had taken over and refurbished— and it was a success for all of us, getting excellent reviews and audiences. I felt that with this show I had arrived as a director.

Ken and I had been discussing the play while he and Rebecca

were writing it through 1988. We tried to shop it around, but could not find it a home. This convinced me at the time that Wellington theatre was a closed shop, and that if *JISM* was going to have a professional home, I would have to make it happen myself. Having a play like *JISM* ready to go (as well as Ken's play *Blue Sky Boys* bubbling under), was instrumental in spurring Simon and me to take over the BATS lease and establish the venue as Wellington's fourth professional theatre (after Downstage, Circa and the Depot). We vowed BATS would become an accessible theatre dedicated to new work, new practitioners and new audiences. It succeeded beyond our wildest dreams and, 27 years later, is still going strong.

For a co-op show, *JISM* was ambitious. It had a large, two-storey set, designed by Andrew Foster; a cast of eight; an original electronic score composed by Christiaan Ercolano; a video segment; two songs; lots of blood, dry ice and smoke; and a giant axolotl. I loved the play for its audacity and its refusal to play by the rules of 'safe' theatre. It dealt with madness, the advertising industry, codependency, terrorism, vegetarianism and monkey semen. It was like a punk manifesto made theatre. And I adored it.

We had a wonderful cast: Kerry Fox, Emma Robinson and Tina Regtien had all been in the same year at drama school. John Leigh was a very talented unknown, whose claim to fame prior to *JISM* had been a lovely performance in David Geary's *Gothic but Staunch* at the Depot. I knew Michael McGrath through his partner Peter Gordon—together they worked at a small restaurant on Vivian Street called the Sugar Club, where I washed dishes. I didn't know Leigh Ransfield, but he auditioned with such a high level of preparation and determination to get the role that I had to cast him. Stephen Lovatt was a drama school graduate with a string of leading roles behind him. He was a dynamic and brave actor, perfect for Gerald. Emma Kinane had been in my year at drama school and we were close. The video clip featured my best friend Andrew Laing. As the unctuous, suited talkshow host Tad Maniacal, Andrew was perfect. Sadly on opening night the video malfunctioned. I felt dreadful for him.

I had recently participated in a two-week masterclass run by English director Mike Alfreds, who ran a company in the UK called Shared Experience. He had devised a system of rehearsing a play based on Stanislavsky's teachings, which included: exploring text, character and the world of the play as separate threads through rehearsals and gradually seeing them inform each other and come together; a rigorous text-based exploration informing character work and text work; breaking down lines into impulses or 'actions'; playing actions in a physical improvisation; and then moving on to objectives, then point-of-concentration work. This approach made perfect sense to me, and despite getting bad press from a lot of actors, most of whom weren't on the course, this has been the bedrock of my approach to directing. Starting with *JISM*, the shows where I have had the time and trusting cast to be able to utilise these tools fully have been the most rewarding, surprising, original and successful shows I have directed.

I have happy memories of *JISM* rehearsals in the cramped, shabby and condemned Market Gardeners building round the corner from BATS. Ken and Rebecca came to most, if not all, rehearsals, which I treasured. I don't understand why some directors don't want the writer in the rehearsal room, particularly when it's the first production of a new play. Changes can be quickly suggested or made, points clarified and questions answered. It makes perfect sense to me. I've always seen the director's job as being to communicate the writers' story and ideas to an audience as clearly and as compellingly as possible—rather than an opportunity to make my own statement, using a piece of text as a vehicle.

I have always enjoyed technical theatre—pushing the limits of what can be achieved with design, music, lighting and sound (this is possibly why I have taken easily to screen directing). *JISM* was a prime example of all these elements colliding with a truly original text and wonderful cast at exactly the right time. It was a triumph.

Coupled with the show was a marketing and publicity campaign, at the time unheard of in its scale and scope. As well as our glamorous purple poster, we had newsprint banners made which shouted the headlines 'JISM IS COMING' and 'SAMPLE JISM AT BATS'. Every night our paste-up teams would go out with buckets of wallpaper paste and blitz Wellington. We did live performances of the show's opening *JISM* rap outside Chelsea Records in Manners Mall and (bizarrely) at a women's festival day in the Victoria University quadrangle.

The season sold out quickly, and we tried to get a subsequent life for the production. I remember going to see the Paragon Arts people with Kerry Fox. Paragon were, at that stage, touring Anthony McCarten and Stephen Sinclair's *Ladie's Night* all around the country to a lot of commercial success. I don't think *JISM* was quite their cup of tea. I learnt something then—that my taste is very much in the niche area of storytelling, rather than the mainstream. Success with a niche show in a 100-seat theatre is quite different to large-scale commercial success. Later in life I had to learn how to put my own sensibilities aside to make mainstream dramas such as *Shortland Street* and *Outrageous Fortune*.

I went on from *JISM* to direct as much theatre as possible over the next eight years, jumping between New Zealand works, Shakespeares and Sondheim musicals. I moved to Auckland, where there seemed to be more opportunities to make a living directing. All that time, the fire to keep working, to keep pushing, to keep making, never faded. I feel fortunate that I have been able to stay in touch with Ken's writing ever since *JISM*—directing *Blue Sky Boys* three times, *Horseplay* in Auckland, *Flybaby* and *Polythene Pam* in Auckland, *Flipside* at Circa, and *White Cloud*, Ken's collaboration with Tim Finn, at BATS in 2012. I spent years trying without success to get a film version of Ken's play *Picture Perfect* happening. I suspect technology has now caught up with some of the ideas in the play. Everything I undertake now is shaped by those formative years when I was discovering what I am best at and wrestling with the challenges and fierce joys of Ken Duncum and Rebecca Rodden's peerless writing.

Emma Kinane:

There was a pre-rehearsal workshop two weeks before the actual rehearsals began. The idea was to workshop the play during the day, then Ken and Rebecca would do rewrites at night. As the time went on they started to look pretty rough from lack of sleep and being overworked. Someone had the brilliant idea that the actors should never play their own role during the workshop and instead we took turns playing all the other roles. I think the intention was that the writers wouldn't be influenced or limited in their rewrites by an actor's strengths and weaknesses or by us owning our characters too soon. And for the actors: we wouldn't get stuck in rhythms and choices too early, and also we would see other people's interpretations of our characters, which might surprise us. But looking back, it seems like this was more wonderful for the actors than the writers. For the actors it was two weeks of playfulness, exploration and discovery, knowing we were helping the play develop but with none of the responsibility of building a performance, whereas the constant role-swapping probably wasn't the best idea for the playwrights. If the purpose of the workshop was to test the play, it must have made it harder to see the play clearly through a revolving cast of actors having a fabulous time prancing around in roles they weren't given.

JISM both suffered and benefited from the fact that the Mike Alfreds technique was theatre's current craze. Actually it was less of a technique and more a collection of oldies-but-goodies cherry-picked from Stanislavsky and friends and repackaged to look shiny and new. Most of the cast and the director were recent New Zealand drama school grads and we were soaked in it. We 'actioned' the fuck out of our scripts. We 'beat-ed' our scenes; we compared our objectives and super-objectives; we made our lists of what we said about ourselves, what other characters said about us. (Were they lying? Who knew? At the time, every word was gospel.) We played the action, not the line. We 'dropped in' our lines, which meant other actors quietly read out our lines just before we said them so we could bypass memory and be totally in the moment. We ran scenes with a 'point of concentration' that might have nothing to do with anything in the scene. There was no blocking; you went where you felt was right in the moment. It must have been hell to light. I sound like I'm mocking us, and I am, but only because it's easy to mock your own youthful intensity. In truth, those techniques are all good stuff and they all come back to the text, which must have been good news for the playwrights, right? But thinking back to those rehearsals I wonder if it was absolutely terrifying for Rebecca and Ken to see us approach the text like it was the word of God and at the same time analyse it all through this well-intentioned wankery. Or perhaps they left the room and laughed long and loud at our po-faced cult rituals.

JISM was a joy to perform. I played three roles, I think. The doctor was forgettable (there are no small parts, only small actors—my bad), but for years I was able to claim in my bio that my first professional role was as a six-foot axolotl. The best and most challenging aspect of playing Manson was a journey up a tight spiral staircase in the amazing costume, which included a huge foam-lined head. Limited vision, keeping low and wide (my abs and arms must have been so fit) and curling myself round the stairs was potentially disastrous every night. But the third character was the most fun; being part of the Animal Liberation Army and going mad on stage every night. I got to rip open John's cheek with my teeth. The challenging part of that was actually the first half of the scene; attempting normal dialogue with a mouth full of blood capsules ready to spit onto his face. Poor man. (Bet he loved it.)

Gary Henderson:

JISM was Ken and Rebecca's first full-length play; their break-out work, even. Directed by Simon Bennett, with a cast of people who would become very well known, it was to me both the first and second plays staged at the then new BATS.

Chronologically, it was the second. The first was American writer Christopher Durang's *Baby with the Bathwater*: a strange, edgy, six-year-old play directed by Guy Boyce. However, in the spirit (dare I say the urgent need) that drove the creation of the new BATS, *JISM* was always going to be the flagship production. Brand new, written, directed and acted by a loose collective of restless young Wellington theatre folk, this was what the new BATS was meant to be about.

Part of Simon Bennett and Simon Elson's vision for BATS was that one show would end on Saturday night and the next would open on Wednesday. *JISM* was a big play with a big design, and the four-day turnaround was a challenge.

Oddly, I have very few recollections of sitting in the theatre watching it. I wasn't associated with its production, and I think I saw it just once. I did turn up to see it one night and mingled with the strangely animated pre-show crowd in the foyer, only to have someone say to me, 'It's amazing, isn't it?' It was an early show that night. This was the interval. I slunk home.

What I do remember was the bold, anarchic sense of people who were truly playing with theatre, running with ideas as far as they could. My idea of theatre wasn't particularly conventional, but the vision of Ken, Rebecca, Simon and designer Andrew Foster was something else entirely.

1. We have a commitment to getting the play <u>Jism</u> by Ken Duncan and Rebecca Rodden <u>on</u> and will toil beyond the call of duty to do so. This entails the ordinary theatre obligations such as turning up to all rehearsals on time, unless excused by prior arrangement with the company, or vanquished by flood, fire or earthquake

2. In agreeing to work as a cooperative, we agree to forgo all hope of equity wages and will do our utmost to promote the show so that we can get something out of it at the end of the run.

3. We agree to abide by the contract between the cooperative and Nomis Productions.

4. We agree not to piss off and do anything elso once we're in rehearsal, no matter how lucrative the contract.

5. We agree to grit our teeth and submit to consensus where conflict occurs and not to undertake public smear campaigns.

6. We agree to the following co-op share system:

7. If the unmentionable occurs, and we run at a loss, the extent of our personal liability is limited by our co-op share, i.e. if 14 full shares exist and the show goes down by $140, a full share holder is liable by $10 and a half share holder is liable for $5.

8. We agree to allow Simon Bennett to act as an agent on our behalf in dealing with administrative matters.

9. We agree to hold regular production meetings where everyone can abuse everyone else.

10. We are committed to this show until June 3rd.

11. At the end of the season, we won't evaporate but will help strike set and do all that menial sort of stuff, after curtain closing night.

12. We will maintain a sober state while rehearsing and performing.

13. The actors agree to be in the theatre by the ½ hour call during the run of the show.

14. During the run of the show, Simon Rayner has absolute authority.

JISM

by Ken Duncum and Rebecca Rodden

Originally performed at BATS Theatre, 4 May–3 June 1989

Lily	Emma Robinson
Rose	Kerry Fox
Clark	Michael McGrath
Gerald	Stephen Lovatt
David Kurtson/Erwin	Leigh Ransfield
Clara/Mrs Grant	Tina Regtien
Mignon/Mr Grant/Dogman	John Leigh
Manson/Doctor/Gabrielle	Emma Kinane
Tad Maniacal	Andrew Laing
Director	Simon Bennett
Set and Lighting Design	Andrew Foster
Costume Design	Natasha Christie
Music	Christiaan Ercolano
Sound Design	Ron Mikalsen
Stage Manager	Simon Rayner
Lighting Operator	Kim Hunter
Sound Operator	Steve Marshall

Characters:

Lily – A conjoined twin. Ideal.

Rose – A conjoined twin. Un-ideal.

Clark – A flatmate. In love with Lily.

Gerald – Flatmate. Animal rights activist.

David Kurtson – Lily's boyfriend.

Clara – JISMCORP executive.

Philippe Mignon – A minion.

Manson – An axolotyl.

Tad Maniacal – A chat show host (recorded footage).

Some roles are doubled:
The actor playing Manson also plays Singer, Doctor, Woman and Gabrielle.
The actor playing Mignon also plays Mr Grant and Man.
The actor playing Clara also plays Mrs Grant.
The actor playing David also plays Erwin.

Staging:

Flexible staging, capable of representing a variety of locations. In the original production we made good use of levels, including a spiral staircase.

In act 2, when the twins are separated and there are more short scenes and scene changes, it is envisaged that Lily remains onstage a lot of the time in her JISMCORP office space off to one side, so fluid staging can be achieved by bringing up lights for her scenes rather than requiring her to enter and exit repeatedly.

Act 1: Stuck

Darkness.

Sudden light. Sudden music.

The cast sings and dances the JISM theme.

Performers: JISM!

> It's protein-packed, as a matter of fact
> You try it once, you won't ever go back
> It's got Vitamin A, an unusual bouquet
> It's the only thing to come between you and they
> It's not instant pud, it's not caramel crème
> It's the stain with the name, it's the cream with the
>   gene
>
> JISM!
> Just let yourself go
> JISM!
> Because it's you you should know
> JISM!
> So let your feelings flow
>
> I'm not talking about Optimism, Pessimism,
>   Joy Division, Seamen's Mission, Capitalism,
>   Communism, Television, Supervision, Catechism,
>   Antidisestablishmentarianism
> I'm just talking about JISM-ism-ism-ism-ism

All we are saying
Is give jizz a whizz

You can change your name, you can change your game
You can pull up the tracks and reroute your train
You can make a difference if you last the distance
And bust through people giving you resistance
So don't get trapped in all that crap
Don't listen when Frankie tells you to relax
(Re-re-re-relax . . .)
No, shoot for the stars and shoot it straight
Don't listen to the dribble, just ejaculate!

JISM!
Catch that buzz
JISM!
Don't make a fuss
JISM!
Get drowned tonight
In liquid love

It's got the pheromones for your danger zones
It's got the feel that's real and you know in your bones
That you were that sperm when it was your turn
Then you met an egg and you really learnt
That cell number one isn't so much fun
You've got to get it together and you've barely begun
If you want potatoes you've got to dig some dirt
You can't live your life like Ernie and Bert
And the thing about growth is it comes in spurts
(Uh-oh, it hurts)

JISM!
Just get on top
JISM!
And just don't stop
JISM!

Because that's your precious essence
Going drop by drop . . .

But if you want to be funky . . .
DO THE SPUNKY MONKEY
DO THE SPUNKY MONKEY
DO THE SPUNKY MONKEY

So don't forget . . .

JISM!
It's coming your way
JISM!
Making decadence pay
JISM!
In bottle
Or spray

JISM!

*Mignon bounces on, proud of the performance. He is
followed by Clara.*

Mignon: So what do you think, Clara?

Clara: It blows.

Mignon: It blows?

Clara: It sucks. It sucks and it blows.

Mignon: But it's got everything you wanted. It's got the style,
the excitement—it's got the monkeys in there . . .

Clara: There's never been a perfume like JISM. To advertise
it we need something just as unique. One-off.
Freakish.

We need the two sisters.

Mignon: But I've tried the sisters. They won't do it.

Clara strokes Mignon menacingly.

Clara: Oh, they'll do it. They'll do it. Come.

They exit.

A lone singer narrates Clark's arrival on a bus.

Singer: I wanna stick together
Stick together
Stick together with you
I wanna stick together
Stick together
Stick together like glue

What stops you falling apart
What makes you think you are
What you think you are

I wanna stick together
Stick together
Stick together with you
I wanna stick together
Stick together
With soul superglue

There's two sides to every story
Now Clark's coming home
He's still got his door-key

Stick together
Stick together
Stick together with you

He thinks he knows what he's coming back to
He thinks he's safe from any attack
He's through with that
He's cured in fact
Feels so complete
He's coming round the corner
Now he's walking up the street

Stick together
Stick together
With soul superglue

It's still the same—that's what he'll say
But the home that he knew grew legs
And it walked away

Stick together
Stick together
Stick together with you
Stick together
Stick together
Stick together like glue

There's two sides to every story
Two sides to every heart
Just get it together
Before it tears you apart

Clark, carrying a large rectangular package, reaches the flat and comes in the door.

Clark: The old flat. Still the same. Filthy. Lily? Rose?

Gerald appears with a large 'HAPPY BIRTHDAY' banner.

Gerald: Happy birthday to you,
Happy birthday to you,
Happy birthday, dear . . .

He sees who it is.

Clark.

Clark: Hi, Gerald. I'm back.

Gerald: So I see.

Clark: I specially wanted to be home in time for Lily's birthday.

Gerald:	Back from hospital. How long's it been?
Clark:	Six months now. Where's—?
Gerald:	Experience any brutality?
Clark:	Any what?
Gerald:	Brutality.
Clark:	No. So where's—?
Gerald:	Electric shock?
Clark:	No.
Gerald:	Injections?
Clark:	No.
Gerald:	Straitjackets? Sleeping restraints?
Clark:	No. No.
Gerald:	Padded cell with single stained mattress?
Clark:	No.
Gerald:	Oh.
Clark:	Where's—?
Gerald:	Lobotomy?
Clark:	No.
Gerald:	Still—you'd be the last to know, wouldn't you?
	Pause. Clark laughs.
Clark:	It's great to be back in the old flat. I've really missed the four of us here, together. My little family. Are you still working for the SPCA, Gerald?
Gerald:	We had an ideological conflict.
Clark:	Is Lily alright?
Gerald:	Fine. As is Rose.
Clark:	She never wrote to me.

Gerald:	Rose?
Clark:	Lily.
Gerald:	So Rose did write to you?
Clark:	No.
Gerald:	Perhaps she was busy.
Clark:	Rose?
Gerald:	Lily.
Clark:	Has she been busy?
Gerald:	No.

Pause.

Clark:	Do you think she missed me?
Gerald:	She did say something about missing you.
Clark:	She did?
Gerald:	It was either 'I really miss Clark' or 'I don't miss Clark at all'. I can't remember which.

Pause.

Clark:	The old flat, eh?

Gerald hears something.

Gerald:	Here they come. Quick. Grab this.

They hold the banner up. David Kurtson enters.

Gerald/Clark: HAPPY—!

Another letdown.

Gerald:	You haven't met David Kurtson, have you, Clark?

Clark goes to shake hands—

Lily's boyfriend.

Clark freezes. David looks at Gerald.

Gerald:	The missing flatmate.
David:	Oh.
	He removes his hand from Clark's.
	Where's Lily?
Gerald:	Rose took her shopping.
Clark:	Look at that.
David:	What?
Clark:	Dirt. Everywhere. I was always the only one who worried about cleanliness.
Gerald:	Don't excite yourself, Clark.
Clark:	How long have you been going out with Lily?
Gerald:	About five months.
Clark:	I'll get my brush and pan.
	Gerald stops him.
Gerald:	Listen. It's them.
	They man the banner. Mignon enters.
Gerald/Clark/David:	HAPPY—!
	Mignon recoils in fright.
Gerald:	Not you again.
David:	They told you they're not interested in doing ads.
Mignon:	It's the perfect opportunity for them. A new perfume, an all-media advertising campaign. They could become—
David:	Tell it to Lily and see how far you get.
	David turns away.
Mignon:	I understand your protectiveness—
Gerald:	This perfume hasn't got any whales in it, has it?

Mignon: Of course not.

Clark: Lily's not stupid, you know.

Gerald: What about civets, polecat and musk? You're not one of these bastards who goes around squeezing the anal glands of innocent woodland creatures, are you?

Mignon: JISM is completely new. Whales, rodents—they're all passé. What we—

Clark: They're home!

Gerald drags Mignon in behind the banner. Rose half-enters, carrying a parcel, and gets stuck in the door, talking to Lily behind her.

Rose: Look, just don't give me any aggravation. Birthday or no birthday.

Lily enters, carrying a bunch of roses and some birthday cards. Lily and Rose are conjoined twins, connected on one side from the hip up to the chest. They share a heart and one lung. They are arguing.

Lily: It's just a couple of cards, for God's sake. Stop making a big thing out of it.

Rose: Twice as many!

Lily: It doesn't mean anything!

Gerald/Clark/David: HAPPY BIRTHDAY TO YOU!!

Lily is thrilled; Rose less so.

Lily: Gerald, it's wonderful.

Clark comes out from behind the banner.

Clark!

She hugs him.

You don't have to go back?

He shakes his head.

	What a lovely birthday present.
Rose:	Hi, Clark.
Clark:	Hello, Rose.
Rose:	Did you escape, or what?
Lily:	(*to David*) Hello, you.

They kiss.

The roses are beautiful.

Rose:	Very suss if you ask me, coming from someone who works in a mortuary.
Lily:	Nobody asked you, Rose.

(*to David*) She's been like this all day.

Mignon comes forward.

Mignon:	The charming sisters.

He kisses their hands. Unsure of whose he has kissed, he ends up doing all four.

I had no idea I was taking part in your birthday celebrations. Happy birthday, Lily. And happy birthday to you, Rose.

Rose:	It's not my birthday.
Mignon:	(*not understanding*) Ah.
Rose:	We didn't want to share, so we split the dates up.
Mignon:	Fascinating.
Rose:	Of course, I didn't get a banner when it was my birthday.
Lily:	Rose.
Rose:	I'm just stating a fact, aren't I? Nobody made me a banner, that's all.
Lily:	Just don't start.

Rose:	It's a simple observation. Your birthday, everyone acts like it's Christmas; mine they all look like the dog died.
Lily:	That's not true!
Rose:	Well, don't get upset about it. Sensitive people round here. You can't say a thing.
Gerald:	Perhaps I don't like you as much, Rose.
	Rose is amused by this.
Rose:	You're a really weird guy sometimes, Gerald.
Mignon:	I don't wish to intrude, but I feel I didn't explain myself last time we met.
Lily:	Oh, I think you did. You've got a new perfume and now you're looking for a two-headed monster to advertise it.
Mignon:	I've been authorised to increase the offer.
Lily:	The money doesn't matter.
Rose:	How much?
	Lily looks at her.
	Just interested.
Mignon:	We can now offer you founding shares in JISMCORP.
Rose:	(*derisively*) Shares?
Mignon:	As well as the fee I mentioned earlier.
Rose:	Oh.
Mignon:	Plus 40 per cent.
Rose:	Oooh.
Lily:	Look—
Mignon:	Please. You can't decide without at least trying it.

He takes out a bottle.

JISM represents an entirely new aesthetic in the scent industry.

He dabs a bit on Rose's wrist, then on the wrist of the slightly reluctant Lily.

Its main constituent must remain completely secret for the moment. But I've been given special permission to tell you what it is.

Rose: What?

Mignon: Guess.

They sniff.

Rose: Doesn't really smell very strong.

Mignon: As it warms, the complete aroma emerges.

Rose: It's almost like . . . compost or something. Like grass on a hot day. Something else. Something really familiar. I know it . . .

Lily: Just smells a bit mouldy to me.

Rose: I give up.

Mignon looks at Lily.

Lily: Alright then, what?

Mignon looks at the others.

Mignon: Is there somewhere we can speak privately?

Everyone exhales exasperatedly. Mignon sees he is losing them.

(*loudly*) Monkey semen.

Pause.

Gerald: What?

Mignon: JISM is made up of the semen of monkeys.

Rose: You mean I've got monkey come on my arm?

Lily: Eugghhh.

Mignon: JISM operates on the deepest erotic centres. It doesn't disguise, deflect or insinuate. It *is* sex—in a bottle.

            Lily holds her arm away.

Lily: How disgusting.

Mignon: Your answer's still no?

Lily: You don't think I'm going to help you sell . . .

Rose: Spunk. Spoof. White Christmas.

Mignon: Clara will be very disappointed.

Lily: I'm sorry.

Mignon: She'll take it out on me.

Lily: Could you please go?

Mignon: She may want to see you herself.

David: She said *go*.

            Mignon goes.

Lily: I have to wash this off.

Rose: I think it's quite exciting—rubbing monkey spunk all over yourself.

Lily: You're being revolting for the sake of it.

Rose: Imagine diving into a vat of it.

Lily: Rose.

Rose: I still don't see why we can't do the ad.

Lily: Because we're not circus freaks to be gawked at.

Rose: Speak for yourself. We get gawked at for free every time we walk down the street.

Lily: Don't start all that again. It's my birthday. I just want to get this . . . stuff . . . off me and relax.

Rose: Go and have a wash. I'm staying here.

Lily: Don't be difficult.

Rose: If you're so worried about it, why don't you lick it off? Or get someone else to do it.

Lily: Stop it. Now.

Rose: Come on, you guys—who wants to lick Lily?

Lily hits her. Rose hits Lily back. They fight, toppling to the floor and rolling back and forth. Lily ends up on top of Rose.

Lily: It's my birthday. On your birthday, you get it your way; on my birthday, I get it my way.

(accentuated by thumping Rose against the floor)

That's . . . the . . . rule.

Rose: We're not kids anymore.

Lily: No, we're adults—who can resolve our differences with reason and compromise.

Rose: So take your hands off my throat.

Lily does.

David: I'll get a cloth.

He exits.

Rose: Do you want your present now?

Lily: Why not?

They get up, all tensions resolved.

Rose: Quick. While David's gone.

She gives Lily the present. Lily starts to open it.

Hurry up. You can't let him see it until later.

Lily pulls out a black negligee.

Rose: You didn't guess, did you?

Lily: I thought it was pyjamas.

Rose: You peeked!

Lily: Just enough to know what department we were in. It's beautiful.

Rose: I thought I'd get something you could both use.

Lily wraps it up again. Clark gives her his present.

Clark: Happy birthday, Lily.

Lily: Thank you, Clark.

She unwraps it. It is a portrait of her.

Clark: I did it in occupational therapy. From memory.

Lily shows it to Rose and Gerald.

Lily: Look.

Rose: I was in motion at the time, was I?

Lily looks at her reprovingly.

              Well, is this supposed to be me? I look like a hump on your back.

Lily: I love it, Clark. I won't even sell it when you're famous.

Rose: For my birthday you can just do me a nice basket, okay?

David comes back in.

Lily: David—look what Clark's given me.

David: Nice.

              (*to Rose*) Where are you?

Rose: Didn't you see the wart in the corner?

David wipes Lily's arm, then goes to wipe Rose's.

Rose: I'll keep mine.

She sniffs at it loudly and shivers in mock-excitement.

Gerald: Happy birthday, Lily.

He hands her a gift-wrapped poster. She unrolls it. It is a gruesome antivivisection illustration.

Rose: Well, that'll certainly brighten up our room.

Lily: Thank you, Gerald. It's very—thought-provoking.

Rose lights a cigarette.

Rose: (*to Lily*) Don't look at me like that. You've got a lung all to yourself. I don't know what you're worried about.

Clark: How have you been, Lily?

Lily: We've all missed you, Clark. I'm sorry I didn't write.

Clark: That's alright.

David whispers in Lily's ear.

Lily: (*to Clark*) You can tell me all about it later on.

(*to Rose*) We're just going in the bedroom.

Lily and David go to the bedroom, dragging Rose after them.

Rose: Okay. See you later. You kids have fun now. Don't do anything I wouldn't do.

They've gone. Clark looks round.

Clark: Dirt. Everywhere.

He goes out. Gerald follows.

In the bedroom, David, Lily and Rose lie on the bed. David and Lily embrace. Rose takes a walkman out from under her pillow and prepares to play it.

Lily: Well, where is it?

Rose: Steady on. I haven't got my headphones on yet.

Lily: My present.

David: I didn't get you a birthday present.

Lily: Scumbag.

Rose: I'll say.

Lily and David look at her. She puts her headphones on.

David: I got you something else.

Lily: What?

David is watching Rose out of the corner of his eye. She puts on an eye mask and lies back. David takes out a ring box and gives it to Lily. She opens it.

David, it's beautiful.

David: It's not a birthday present. It's an engagement ring. I want you to marry me, Lily.

Lily: What?

David: I love you. And I want to marry you.

Lily: That's not very funny, David.

David takes her hands.

David: No, it's not. It's serious. I'm serious.

Lily: But what about Rose?

David: What about Rose? Always what about Rose? What about you? And me? I'm asking you if you want to marry me.

Lily: Of course I *want* to.

David: Then forget about Rose. Forget about everything else. Imagine there's just you and me. For the first time ever. Alone. I love you, Lily.

Lily: I love you, David.

David:	Then, please—be my wife?

Rose starts to sing along to the music.

Rose:	'Smoke on the water Fire in the sky . . .'

Lily jabs her.

Lily:	Yes. Yes, I will.

They kiss.

David:	I'll take care of you, Lily. Working as a mortician may not be much, but it's safe. When the economy goes bad, business usually picks up.
Lily:	I've always dreamed about getting married, but . . .
David:	Rose can still live her own life. She just has to learn to compromise. All that's important is that we're together.
Lily:	I want it so much I'm frightened.
David:	We won't say anything to Rose yet, okay? Let's just have this time.
Lily:	I'll put the ring on my right hand.

She does.

It's beautiful.

They embrace again. As they get more passionate, Rose starts to show signs of getting a bit hot and bothered— fanning herself . . .

Meanwhile Clark enters the bathroom and starts to clean it. He is unaware that there is a monstrous something in the bath. Suddenly it lunges at him. Clark screams. The huge thing is halfway out of the bath in its attempt to get at him. Clark runs out in a panic and bursts into the bedroom, jumping on the bed.

Clark:	There's something in the bath!

This completely startles everyone. David falls off the bed. Rose tears her eye mask and headphones off.

Rose: What?! What?!

Clark: There's a thing in the bath!

Lily: Clark, it's only Manson.

Clark: Manson!

Lily: Gerald's Mexican walking fish.

Clark: But it's huge.

Rose: Well, it's pretty big for a Mexican walking fish.

Lily: Gerald said a bowl would stunt his growth.

Rose: He said fishbowls were fascist.

Clark: It tried to get me!

Lily: Get you?

Clark: In the bathroom. Just now.

Lily, David and Rose look at each other.

Lily: It's been a long day, Clark. Perhaps you should lie down.

Rose: Or have a nice, warm bath.

Clark: No!

Rose: Just take Manson out and put him in the handbasin. Like we do.

Clark stares at her.

Lily: It's alright, Clark—we'll do it for you.

Clark: No. I'll leave the bathroom until later.

Lily: Clark, you're not cleaning again?

Clark: If I don't, who will? Someone's been really dirty while I've been away.

He goes out again.

David: What's he doing back here?

Lily: This is his home.

David: He's a dangerous loony!

Rose: Clark?

Lily: They wouldn't have let him out unless he was better.

David: You call that better?

Rose: He's starting it all again. The midnight cleans . . . It'll be Mickey Mouse next.

David: How did you get him in the first place?

Lily: We put an ad in the paper.

Rose: Clark was the most pathetic, so Lily chose him.

Lily: Rose thought Gerald had that 'lean and hungry look', so she picked him.

Rose: He didn't mention he was a vegetarian until later.

Lily: You stay here. We'll go and get changed.

Lily and Rose get up. Rose sees the ring.

Rose: Hey, what's this?

Lily: David gave it to me.

Rose: There must be more money in dead people than I thought.

They exit.

Gerald has come back into the living area and is reading the paper. As he turns the pages we see that each one consists only of a large headline—'NO CLUES IN BUTCHER-SHOP BOMBING', 'VEGETARIAN VENGEANCE CONTINUES', 'ANIMAL AVENGER STRIKES AGAIN', etc. Clark enters carrying a dust-ball two feet in diameter balanced on his dustpan.

Clark: Look at this dust I found under your bed, Gerald.

Gerald: I've told you before, Clark. Don't go in my room.

Clark: I have to. To clean it.

Gerald: Don't clean it. Remember what happened last time.

Clark: Why does everyone think there's something crazy about doing a bit of dusting? You don't have to be insane to want to be clean.

Gerald: First it was the dusting, then it was the mice.

Clark: You can't have mice in your house. It's unsanitary!

Gerald: Mice are beautiful people, Clark.

Clark exits.

Lights up on the bedroom. David is sitting in bed. He hears a whirring sound. He looks over and sees Clark crawling along the floor with a dustbuster mini vacuum cleaner. To David's discomfiture, Clark starts to vacuum the bed.

Clark: You have to vacuum all beds regularly to get rid of the bedmites. Little crawly things. Scientists estimate the average bed has more than 50,000 mites in it.

David starts to scratch. As Clark gets closer with the dustbuster, David gets out of bed to avoid him. David exits. Clark starts doing the floor again, disappearing behind the bed. David enters the living area.

David: Have you seen Lily?

Gerald: I think she's somewhere with Rose.

David: He's—vacuuming the bed.

Gerald: To Clark, household dust is like cocaine.

David: He's got this delusion it's seething with crawly things.

Gerald: Why are you scratching?

David, embarrassed, laughs. He goes back to the bedroom. He can't see Clark anywhere, and gets back into bed. Lily and Rose enter.

Rose: Hi, stud.

Lily is wearing her birthday negligee. Rose has a long wincyette nightie and bedsocks on. They get into bed. The lights dim.

Lily: Now, where were we?

Rose puts her earplugs in. As David and Lily embrace, Rose remembers she hasn't put her cold cream on. She gropes round for it and smears it on her face. David can't help looking at her. She starts doing facial toning exercises. David struggles to concentrate on making love to Lily. Rose yawns cavernously. David breaks away from Lily in frustration.

David: I'm sorry. I just . . . It's her!

Lily: It's alright. I don't mind. Really. And I don't want you to worry about it. I'm just so happy.

They kiss.

Lily: Pass me my Moggies?

David: You don't need them.

Lily: I'll be waking up all through the night otherwise.

Reluctantly he hands the pills over. She pulls herself up to take them. Rose takes out her earplugs.

Rose: You don't need those.

Lily: Don't you start. You should know what I'm like without them.

Lily takes them and settles down to sleep.

Goodnight, honey. Goodnight, Rose.

Lily is quickly asleep. David and Rose lie awake.

In semi-darkness, Gerald reenters the living area with a suspicious-looking suitcase, then exits.

Manson slides out of the bath . . .

Rose and David are still awake, either side of Lily, staring at the ceiling. Rose lights a cigarette.

David: I bet you enjoyed that.

It's always a real highlight for you, isn't it? And thanks for the birthday present. About as subtle as a sledgehammer.

He gets out of bed.

I'd be alright if I didn't know you were lying there laughing the whole time.

Rose: Men and their willies.

David: I've got to get a hold of myself.

Rose: Be my guest.

David: It has to stop.

Rose: No skin off my nose.

David: (*rounding on her*) Lily deserves better. Better than either of us.

Pause. They look at each other.

Rose: So—are you getting in, or what?

She pulls back her bedclothes.

David crosses to her, jerks the cigarette out of her mouth and gets into bed with her. They make love passionately. The sound of a train is heard, distant at first, coming nearer. Clark's head pokes out from under the bed. Unnoticed, he crawls out and escapes.

Halfway across the stage, Manson leaps on him. Clark shrieks and struggles wildly. He breaks away, and Manson chases him into the bathroom. Trapped, Clark bludgeons the axolotyl with his dustbuster. Manson falls, writhing into the bath as Clark delivers the coup de grâce. By this time the sound of the train is massive, as if it's running through the room. Manson lifts his head to scream in a final death throe at the same moment as the train whistle shrieks and David and Rose orgasm.

The train dies away. Clark sobs.

Gerald crashes back into the flat. He is wearing a pig mask and is out of breath. He takes the mask off. Clark, trying to creep back to his room, runs into him. They both jump.

Gerald/Clark: What are you doing up?

Gerald/Clark: Couldn't sleep. Thought I'd just . . .

Gerald: Stretch my legs.

Clark: Have a drink of water.

They both yawn.

Gerald/Clark: Well, I'd better be . . .

Clark: What's that on your shoulder?

(*looks closer*) It looks like bacon.

With a shiver of revulsion, Gerald flicks it off.

Gerald: So it is. Well, how about that.

He gingerly picks up the bacon again.

Manson!

Clark: No! Don't wake him up. Fish need their sleep.

Gerald: He won't mind. Bacon's his favourite.

He moves towards the bathroom. Clark stops him.

Clark: It looks a bit fatty. He could get build-up in his arteries, and then a heart attack and . . . die.

Gerald pushes him aside and looks in the bath. He places

the bacon on the side of the bath, reaches in, pulls out a small dead Mexican walking fish, and turns back to Clark.

Clark: It . . . it was an accident, Gerald . . . I never meant . . . you see, he . . .

Gerald's unreadable demeanour suddenly lurches into a smile. He pats Clark on the shoulder.

Gerald: That's alright, Clark. These things happen.

I mean, when all's said and done, it's only a fish, isn't it? And people can do pretty much anything they like to a fish, can't they? It's not as if they've got any rights, is it?

Clark: No.

Gerald: No. So I'd forget it if I was you, Clark. Just put it right out of your mind.

Clark turns to go.

I hope you *can* put it out of your mind, Clark. Because we all care about you, you know. Remember how upset Lily and Rose were—and me, of course—when you were being tormented by Mickey Mouse because of all the mice you'd killed. I'd hate anything like that to happen again, Clark.

Night-night. Sleep tight.

Clark exits. Gerald's smile vanishes. Lights down to blackout.

The next day. Lily and Rose enter the living area.

Rose: God, I'm exhausted. Bloody job. We were better off on the dole.

Lily: Oh no, I'm not going back to that—watching you slop around all day in a dressing-gown, reading magazines.

Rose:	Miss Prissy.
Lily:	Let's have a cup of tea.
Rose:	No—sit down.

They collapse on the couch. Rose lights a cigarette.

Lily:	If you didn't smoke so much, you wouldn't get out of breath.
Rose:	Don't be so bloody smug. And stop looking at that ring all the time.

Lily takes it off her right hand and puts it on her left.

Lily:	Don't you think it looks better on this hand?
Rose:	Dream on. Hey, you don't think he stole it off a corpse, do you?
Lily:	What's so funny about being a mortician? He's got ambitions for after he's finished his training, you know. He says there are lots of openings in mortuaries. For someone who wants to get ahead.

Lily fiddles with the ring, admiring it on her wedding finger.

Rose puts her hand over Lily's.

Rose:	Stop it, Lily. You'll just make yourself sad.
Lily:	You do like David, don't you?
Rose:	He's alright.
Lily:	Well, couldn't you be a bit nicer to him?
Rose:	He just pisses me off sometimes. He's your boyfriend, not mine. But as far as that goes, we've done alright, haven't we? You've had boyfriends—
Lily:	Not that many.
Rose:	—I've had boyfriends—
Lily:	Too many.

Rose:	—and we'll have more. But you know and I know that this—(*picks up her hand*)—is not going to happen.
Lily:	But it has happened, Rose. David's asked me to marry him. This is my engagement ring.
Rose:	Eh?
Lily:	Last night.
Rose:	Then why are you wearing the ring?
Lily:	Because I said yes.
Rose:	You said yes!
Lily:	Don't spoil it, Rose. We just thought we'd wait a bit before telling you.
Rose:	What are you trying to do to me? You can't get married!
Lily:	That's what I always thought. But David doesn't care that we're joined. He wants to marry me anyway.
Rose:	(*struggling to control herself*) Lily—I'm not ready to get married.
Lily:	Nobody's asked you. You'll still be single.
Rose:	If you think you're just going to drag me up the aisle without even—
Lily:	I'd do it if it was you.
Rose:	Don't be ridiculous!
Lily:	I would! If you were ever with anyone for more than two nights, who you loved, and you wanted to marry him and have his children—
Rose:	Children?
Lily:	Haven't you ever thought about any of this?
Rose:	I'm still enjoying my life!

Lily:	David understands that.
Rose:	(*suddenly remembers*) Last night? He proposed to you last night?
Lily:	We would have told you, but David just wanted it to be special for the two of us.
Rose:	That bastard!
Lily:	Rose!
Rose:	Lily, you can't marry him. You can't! Don't you see what he's trying to do?
Lily:	He loves me.
Rose:	He thinks he can get two for the price of one.
Lily:	More than anyone else, when he looks at me—that's what he sees. Me. Only me.
Rose:	No.
Lily:	It's all so beautifully normal. He'll be my husband. I'll be his wife. You'll be his sister-in-law, Rose!
Rose:	No, Lily.
Lily:	He makes me feel like a real person.
Rose:	He's just one more guy who gets off on the idea of three in a bed.
Lily:	Don't you say that.
Rose:	It's true.

Lily becomes chillingly furious.

Lily:	Don't you ever say that. Never. You hear me? Never!

She is poised threateningly over Rose.

Rose:	Lily?

Lily starts to cry.

Lily:	It's just . . .

Rose: Lily.

Rose cuddles her.

Lily: I've been so scared I was going to lose him. And when he said he'd never leave me . . . I love him, Rose.

Rose: I know you do. I've known from the beginning.

Lily calms down.

Lily: Let's not talk about it any more. We'll wait until David's here.

They hug.

Lily: Rose?

Rose: What?

Lily: Isn't it romantic?

Rose turns her eyes upwards, helplessly. Clara bursts into the room, followed by Mignon (with a black eye) and Clark, who has obviously been unable to stop them coming in. Clara has a pistol.

Clara: In here? Ah yes.

She holds the gun on Lily and Rose.

Please don't get up.

Lily: Who are you?

Clara: I am Clara.

Mignon: I said she'd want to see you herself.

Clara: But how beautiful you both are. Exquisite skin.

Lily: Look—

Clara: Let's be friends. Let's send all these men out and just all be girls together. Go on, you men—out, out, out.

She shoos Mignon and Clark out.

There. Now, let's giggle and tell secrets. I'll go first.

She lights a cigarette with the gun and puts it away.

I've got some monkey spunk I want to sell.

Lily: Then do it. Without us.

Rose: What do you need us for, anyway? It'll sell.

Clara: You think so?

Rose: Yeah.

Clara: And you, Lily?

Lily: It's none of my business.

Clara: But it can be.

She takes out a bottle.

Do you know how explosive this is going to be?

Imagine the entire scent industry is the city of Hiroshima. This—is the bomb. And I want you to be my B52s.

Lily: We're not interested.

Clara: What a lovely face. I'd hate to see it scarred. By acne. You are using a good cleanser?

Rose: Are you trying to threaten her?

Clara: Don't be silly, dear. If I was going to threaten anybody, I'd tell them all about my friend who burns down houses for a living. With the people inside.

(*to Lily*) I could make you famous, admired, adored; get you out of this semi-furnished urinal.

Where's your ambition?

Lily: Oh, go . . . suck a monkey.

Rose cringes at Lily's attempt at profanity.

Rose: Oh, Lily . . .

Clara: You know, I like you. No, really, you're a couple

of swell kids. And that's what makes the rejection so much harder. I've always had a problem with rejection, since I was a little girl. It hurts me. And then it hurts everyone else. I've offered you shares, I've offered you fame, I've offered you a sum of money that makes my nipples hard just thinking about it.

But you reject me. So now I'm going to offer you one more thing. Twenty-four hours. To change your mind.

No, please—don't say anything. I don't think I could stand another rebuff. I might just snap.

She suddenly darts at Lily.

Look at the curve of that ear. Perfection.

David busts in with Mignon behind, trying to persuade him not to.

David: Lily!

Clara: Uh-uh—girls only.

She karate-kicks him in the crotch. He drops.

Lily: David!

Clara: Think. Carefully.

She exits, Mignon scurries behind her.

Lily: David, are you alright?

She rushes over to him, Rose in tow.

Did she hurt you? Where does it hurt? What?

David is winded and can't speak. He gestures towards his feet. Rose is standing on one of them, grinding her heel into it.

Lily: Rose!

Rose: Oh, I'm sorry. I didn't notice.

Lily:	Get him onto the couch.

Rose uses the opportunity to get in a few more sly pokes and hair-pulling. They collapse onto the couch.

	It's alright, honey, I'm here.
David:	What did she kick me for?
Lily:	She's just a very sick lady.
Rose:	With good aim.
Lily:	She was trying to persuade us to do that ad. We said no.
David:	Good. I'm not going to let anyone exploit the two of you like that.
Rose:	Don't you dare say that, you bastard. Don't you dare tell me who's going to exploit me and who's not.
Lily:	Rose!
Rose:	You didn't ask me if I wanted to do the ad, did you? I didn't say I didn't want to do it—you did. I might want to be on TV and be a star.
Lily:	Rose, stop being silly.
Rose:	I can do it—sing, dance and everything.
David:	What's going on?
Rose:	What about my trip to Argentina?
Lily:	You've never wanted to go to Argentina.
Rose:	I have always wanted to go to Argentina. Always!
Lily:	Perhaps we could go for a holiday.
Rose:	I don't want to go with him!
David:	You didn't tell her, did you?
Lily:	I had to, honey.
Rose:	I want to learn to hang glide!

Lily:	No, you don't.
Rose:	I do!
David:	I'll . . . give you a moment.
	He exits hurriedly.
Rose:	And I want to go to university. In Paris. You can't deny me an education.
Lily:	Calm down . . .
Rose:	I've got my whole life ahead of me.
Lily:	It's alright, Rose.
Rose:	What about me?
Lily:	If you're so worried—call Dr Mary.
	Rose freezes. They stare at each other.
Rose:	I will.
	Lily marches them over to pick up a diary. She finds a phone number.
Lily:	Here you are. Ring her up. Tell her we want the operation.
	Rose stares at the number.
Rose:	I will.
Lily:	Well, go on.
Rose:	I will!
	Pause.
Lily:	Still here?
	Rose puts the book down. They sag onto the bed.
Rose:	You're just lucky I haven't got the money.
Lily:	Hey, don't even joke about it. God, what a day.
	Rose hands Lily her pills—Lily takes a couple as they

undress.

Lily: Wonder where David's got to? I'm exhausted.

          They get into bed.

Rose: I'll tell him you couldn't wait.

Lily: It'll be alright, Rose, you'll see.

          They lie down. Lily goes to sleep.

          Clark enters the living area, a bit agitated. He stops and listens. Noises from the bathroom; the shower curtain moves . . . David gets out of the shower and comes into the living area, wearing only a towel.

Clark: Did you hear something just then?

David: No. What?

Clark: Nothing.

David: Nothing?

Clark: I didn't hear anything either.

David: Right.

          He starts to cross to the bedroom.

Clark: I don't hate you.

David: Sorry?

Clark: It's nothing personal.

David: Okay.

          He creeps into the bedroom.

Clark: I just like things clean.

          Clark exits.

          David goes to slip into bed, hoping Rose is asleep.

Rose: You bastard.

David: Sshh. She might not be properly asleep yet.

Rose: You crawling maggot.

David: Alright, I know you're angry.

Rose: You think you've got me now, don't you? Every night until death do us part. You think you've scored the only wife in the world with the bit on the side already built in.

David: That's got nothing to do with marrying Lily. I love her!

Rose: So much so that you screwed me on her engagement night.

David: You weren't complaining.

Rose: You didn't tell me you were her fiancée!

David: What's the difference?

Rose: It makes a difference to me!

David: I didn't tell you because it was the last time. It's not going to happen anymore.

Rose: Who do you think you're talking to? Do you expect me to believe that we're going to lie here every night for the next 50 years with her zonked out between us and nothing is going to happen?

David: It *can't* happen.

Rose: Oh, you've cut it off, have you?

David: How do you think I feel?

Rose: I don't care how you feel. (*gestures at Lily*) That's the other side, remember?

David: I love Lily. She's everything I want. I don't even like you. You think I can understand it?

Rose: It's all your fault for starting it in the first place.

David: You started it!

Rose: I'll tell you something right now. There's not going to be any marriage.

David: You can't do that.

Rose: She thinks she's going to talk me round. No chance.

David: You haven't got any right—

Rose: I've got every right. I'm not sticking my neck in the noose. And I'm not going to let Lily do it, either. Somebody has to look out for her.

David: Don't make me laugh. You screw your sister's fiancée and then tell me you're looking out for her interests?

Rose: I didn't know you were her fiancée!

David: You've never been interested in me. I bet every one of Lily's boyfriends got the same reception after lights-out.

Rose: You shit.

David: You know what it is? You know why you do it?

Jealousy. Simple spiteful jealousy because you can't stand to see her happy.

Rose: That's not true!

David: It is true. You have to hurt her behind her back to get even.

Rose lashes out at David. They struggle. They stop, panting.

David: Oh, Christ.

Rose: Fuck it. We can't make it any worse.

They make more passionate love.

You know what I'd really like? Just once to be able to get on top.

Suddenly Rose freezes.

Stop!

She's struck by a dreadful creeping realisation.

. . . She's awake.

David: What are you talking about?

Rose: She's listening to us!

David looks at Lily, who shows no change.

David: She's sound asleep.

Rose pushes David away.

Rose: Get out. Get out, get out.

David: It's just you—

Rose: GET OUT!

Pushed out of bed, David steps back, puzzled. Rose turns to the still unmoving Lily.

Lily? Please, Lily—it doesn't mean anything. It's all a stupid mistake. You can get married. Of course you can. I'll take sleeping pills too. Please, Lily, please . . .

Lily strikes. Clamping both hands on Rose's throat, she strangles her. Her fury is terrifying and totally silent.

David: Lily!

He tries to pull them apart. Lily kicks him in the balls and he lets go. Lily and Rose roll off the bed and into the middle of the floor, Lily still implacably holding on, Rose fighting for her life . . .

The lights go down to a single spot on them. Rose goes limp. A few seconds later Lily releases her grip. Rose is semiconscious. Lily starts to shriek and jerk herself away from Rose as if trying to tear them apart.

Blackout.

A loud burst of the JISM theme music, abruptly cut off. Clara's voice is heard.

Clara:	Too loud.

The music comes on again, not as loud, then is cut off again.

That'll do. Where are the lights? What's going on down there?

The lights come up. Lily and Rose are standing, not looking at each other while people put up a jungle set around them.

Come on, kiddies—let's hustle. We should have had three takes in the can already.

Monkeys! Where are my monkeys?

People in monkey suits emerge and practise jumping about.

Places. Places, everybody. Ready Lily?

Lily nods.

Rose? Okay. Quiet! Cameras! Playback.

The JISM theme starts to play.

And . . . action!

Lily, Rose and the monkeys lip-sync and dance to the recorded soundtrack.

Playback:	JISM.
Lily:	Feel twice the woman.
Rose:	Get twice the attention.
Playback:	JISM.
Rose:	Feel twice the woman.
Lily:	Get twice the attention.
Playback:	JISM.
Lily/Rose:	Feel twice the woman. Get twice the attention

All: JISM!

One of the monkeys seems unsure what he is doing,
especially in the finale.

Clara: Cut! Back into positions.

You! Monkey number two. Get it right.

That's good, Lily.

Rose—you're losing the sync. And how about putting
some life into it?

(*more distant, off-mic*)

She's a bloody liability, that one.

The dissident monkey breaks away and climbs to a
vantage point.

What's that monkey doing?

The monkey takes off his mask. It is Gerald.

Rose: Gerald!

Clara: Get him down from there!

Activity and confusion as people attempt to get him
down.

Gerald: Stop this oppression! This perfume is made from the
results of enforced animal orgasms, purely for the
sake of vanity. The vanity of the capitalist animal-
hating human classes!

Have you seen JISM's laboratories, where innocent
monkeys are kept in cages with their private parts
dangling through holes—every hour on the hour,
being wanked against their will by third-world
women wearing rubber gloves?

How would you like it? A tube over your dick being
agitated all day?

Stop this madness! End the wanton wanking of our

animal neighbours!

Gerald is dragged off his perch and beaten up.

Rose: Leave him alone, you bastards! He hasn't done anything to you. Who do you think you are?

Clara: Get rid of him.

Rose makes to go towards Gerald.

Rose: Lily, do something.

Lily ignores her. Gerald is dragged out.

Clara: Okay, let's go for another take. Places!

Rose starts to cry.

Oh, for God's sake—not again. Makeup!

The lights go down to a single spot on Lily, staunch, and Rose, sobbing. The jungle set is taken offstage. A Doctor comes out.

Doctor: There we are. Now, you pop back in there, dear, and you'll feel much better.

Lily and Rose get into the bed, now a hospital bed.

Rose: I'm so tired, Dr Mary.

Doctor: Perhaps you could have a sleeping pill tonight?

Rose: No! She'd do something to me. She'd try to kill me.

Lily: You see what I have to put up with?

Rose: She won't let me sleep. You think she doesn't talk to me, but she does. When we're alone she says things to me. Awful things.

The Doctor doesn't know what to think. Lily smiles at her.

Doctor: Here's Mrs Grant, back from radiation.

Mrs Grant is wheeled in.

Mrs Grant: Morning, girls.

Lily: Morning, Mrs Grant.

The Doctor exits. Mrs Grant is engrossed in an electronic game.

Rose: Lily, please, let's go home now? You've made your point.

Lily ignores her. Rose tries to be jovial.

Hey, I'm not complaining, but isn't a heart–lung transplant going a bit far?

No reaction.

TALK TO ME!

Rose reaches out her hand.

Lily, talk to me.

Lily does something quick and vicious to the hand, biting it or stabbing it with a pen.

Even if you could make me sign your stupid consent form, you're never going to get a donor! You've wasted all your money getting here, but it's pointless. Pointless!

The Doctor pokes her head in.

Doctor: Visitors!

Clark and Mr Grant enter.

Lily: Clark!

Clark: Hello, Lily. Hi, Rose.

Lily: Are you getting enough sleep, Clark?

He looks a bit haggard.

Clark: Gerald . . . couldn't come. But he sent you a card.

Lily opens it. It's another homemade, pasted-up, gory animal torture picture. She reads various scrawls on it.

Lily:	'Down with Animalism'. 'Death to all Animalists'. 'JISM money is blood money'. 'Lynch the JISM sisters'.
Clark:	He means well. Any news of a donor yet?
	Lily shakes her head.
Lily:	Why don't people die when you want them to?
Clark:	Please come home, Lily.
Rose:	You tell her, Clark. Tell her! She wants to kill both of us!
Clark:	Rose says you want to kill both of you.
Lily:	I can't speak for anyone else, but I intend to live.
Rose:	You're sick. Know that? Sick.
Clark:	You're sick.
Rose:	You're talking about major surgery.
Clark:	You're talking about major surgery.
Rose:	Just because I screwed your boyfriend.
Clark:	Just because she screwed your boyfriend.
Lily:	Fiancée.
Rose:	I didn't know he was your fiancée! Except for the last time.
Clark:	She didn't know he was your fiancée. Except for—
Lily:	I can't be with you anymore.
Rose:	Lily . . .
Lily:	I CAN'T!
	Mrs Grant's husband chokes on a hard-centre and dies.
Mrs Grant:	Jeff! Jeff! Oh my God. Someone get the lolly! And the doctor!

The Doctor rushes in.

There's a lodged lolly!

The Doctor struggles to revive him. She pulls a lolly out of his mouth.

No, not that one. It was a caramel.

Too late. The Doctor stands up slowly.

Doctor: I'm sorry, Mrs Grant.

Mrs Grant: That's alright—just have another go.

Doctor: I'm afraid there's nothing more I can do.

Mrs Grant: Well, get someone else then.

Doctor: There's nothing more anyone can do.

Mrs Grant realises.

Mrs Grant: Oh Jeff . . . Jeff . . . you were the best.

Rose: Gross-out.

Lily: I'm so very sorry, Mrs Grant. Doctor . . . if you've got a moment . . .

The Doctor comes over. Lily whispers to her.

Mrs Grant: He'd do anything for you. Anything.

Doctor: Mrs Grant . . . is your husband's heart of any particular sentimental value to you?

Mrs Grant: He had a big heart.

Doctor: Enlarged?

Mrs Grant: No. Generous.

Doctor: Have you met Lily and Rose?

Mrs Grant: Yes, lovely girls. They're on that ad. But they're not at all stuck up.

Doctor: They need a heart.

Mrs Grant: My Jeff's heart?

Doctor: Would do very nicely.

Mrs Grant: But he's a man. Surely that's not right?

Doctor: It's a new technique.

Mrs Grant: Oh. Well, I suppose that's alright then.

Lily: Mrs Grant . . . I don't know what to say . . .

Rose: I do—

Lily: We'll never be able to repay you.

Mrs Grant: He gave his heart to me. Now I'm giving it to you.

Doctor: Lovely. That's settled, then.

Rose: Wait a minute—

Doctor: Oh. And the lungs. They sort of go as a set.

Mrs Grant: Help yourself. It's as if God willed it, isn't it?

Doctor: No time for a trolley. Speed is essential.

Mrs Grant: He didn't even like caramels.

Doctor: (*to Clark*) Here, give me a hand.

Mrs Grant: He only ate it to please me.

The Doctor and Clark grab a leg each and exit, dragging Mr Grant.

Doctor: See you in theatre.

Rose: No, wait—I don't believe this is happening.

Lily produces the consent form.

Lily: Sign.

Rose: No. I'm going home.

She struggles to get up. Lily holds her back. She speaks slowly and deliberately.

Lily: I'll push you in front of a bus. Or a train would be better. Then whatever bits of you are still attached, I can get trimmed off me later.

Rose stares at Lily in horror.

She snatches the form, scribbles her signature on it and falls back on the bed, sobbing. Mrs Grant is wheeled out. She stops by the bed.

Mrs Grant: You won't cry when you've got Jeff's heart in you. He was a soldier once. A brave, brave soldier.

She exits.

Lily: I think we're ready for our injections now, nurse.

The lights around the bed dim to an unearthly green. Strange figures approach with various knives and implements and begin to operate on Lily and Rose. Among them, Manson is recognisable. The electronic beeping of a heartbeat is heard.

Clark runs on to the other side of the stage in a panic, hands over his ears. He is back at the flat.

Clark: No, you can't come in here.

He takes his hands away slowly and listens. A soft voice is heard. The voice of Donald Duck.

Voice: Clark.

Clark: No!

Voice: Clark.

Clark: You're not real.

Voice: It's me, Clark. Donald. Murderer!

Clark: No!

Voice: You have to pay. Pay for your crime.

Clark: I had to do it.

Voice: 'When you wish upon a star . . .'

Clark: Lily!

Voice: Fantasyland—the happiest kingdom of them all.
            (*starts to laugh*) Wak-wak-wak. Wak-wak-wak-wak.

Clark: Get out! Leave me alone!

            Gerald enters.

Gerald: Are you alright, Clark?

Clark: Can't you hear it?

Gerald: Hear what?

            The laughter dies away.

Clark: It's all my fault. I did it. I swapped Lily's pills for
            some of mine.

Gerald: Did you?

Clark: That's why she woke up. That's how she found out. I
            wanted her to. I couldn't let her marry him. But now
            it's gone wrong. I could be a murderer.

            *The sound of the Donald Duck laughter creeps in again,
            growing louder.*

            You know me, Gerald. You know I wouldn't hurt a
            fly.

Gerald: What about a fish?

Clark: Tell him I'm not a murderer.

Gerald: Tell who?

            *The beep of the heartbeat abruptly becomes irregular.
            The surgical team's activity is frantic.*

Clark: They're dying! They're dying—and it's all my fault!

            The laughing becomes very loud.

            Stop it! Stop it! Stop it!

            Clark runs out. Gerald takes his hand out of his pocket.

He has a remote control. He turns the Donald Duck voice off.

He points the remote control after Clark and presses it. The Donald Duck voice is heard offstage, followed by a scream from Clark. Gerald starts to laugh. The voice is Donald Duck's.

Gerald: Wak-wak-wak. Wak-wak-wak.

He exits.

The surgeons begin to separate Lily and Rose. As they are stretched apart, their garment stretches with them. The doctors strain. The sound of the heartbeat staggers. Lily and Rose seem semiconscious, writhing. It is like a macabre birth. The twisted material joining them splits and tears audibly. Blood soaks their sides. Separated, the two bodies convulse in sync. Lily and Rose scream and collapse. The heartbeat sound goes dead. The lights go down on the surgeons desperately applying CPR to both of them.

Blackout.

End of Act 1

Act 2: Unstuck

Lights up to reveal Lily sitting quietly, looking at a photo album. She looks up, notices the audience and speaks directly to them.

Lily: Oh, hi. You know, things have really changed for me since the operation. But there are times when I just like to sit here and look back on my life with Rose. I guess any woman with a sister knows how close that bond can be. Laughter, tears, those little secrets—sisters share it all.

But there's something more intimate to a woman than even her sister. Her perfume.

She stands up.

That's why I use JISM—because it's natural, delicate and so alluring. JISM actually works on your own individual scent, heightening and personalising it.

There's no alcohol, no chemicals in JISM—just the pure, healthy, stimulating ejaculate of specially selected African monkeys.

And you couldn't get more natural than that, could you?

She holds her smile. We hear Clara's voice.

Clara: And . . . cut.

Lily's expression changes. Moodily, she lights a cigarette. Mignon enters.

Mignon: Wonderful, Lily, wonderful.

Lily: Who wrote this crap, anyway?

Clara enters.

Clara: This 'crap' is what moves product. It's what makes you a celebrity. And I wrote it.

Lily: It'd be better if you just let me make it up myself.

                Clara laughs.

Clara: Mignon, did you hear our little Lily? She wants to be
                creative!

                We're in the business of toilet-training, darling—not
                free expression. Your job is to shit in the potty like
                everyone else.

Mignon: I think what Clara means—

Lily: They buy it because of me. Isn't that what your
                market research is showing? Now the novelty's worn
                off, I'm the selling point.

                Clara throws a glance at a guilty-looking Mignon.

                I know what they want to see.

Clara: JISM's been good to you, Lily. You're a rich girl:
                young, single. Adored. Don't push it.

                Clara exits.

Mignon: Be careful, Lily.

                *Lily turns to exit. A woman in a white coat enters with
                a tray of perfume samples.*

Woman: Would you like to try some of the new samples?

Lily: I'm sure they're fine.

Woman: Just have a sniff.

Lily: I don't have a sense of smell. Not since the operation.

                *Lily exits. The woman crosses to Mignon, who sniffs
                and gives his approval. The woman exits. Rose enters,
                dishevelled, half-hysterical.*

Rose: Where is she?

Mignon: Rose . . .

Rose: Come out, you bitch!

Mignon:	Rose, you know you're not supposed to come here.
Rose:	Lily! Lily!
Mignon:	You're not part of JISMCORP anymore.
Rose:	Tell her I'm here. Tell her I want to see her.
Mignon:	There's no point, Rose.
Rose:	You could make her. She likes you.
Mignon:	Rose, she won't see you.
	Rose collapses crying.
Rose:	Lily, I need you.
Mignon:	You've got to stop this. Drinking. Taking drugs. Look at yourself.
Rose:	I can't!
Mignon:	Lily's gone. Find something to replace her.
Rose:	Why doesn't *she* need *me*?
Mignon:	Come on. Get yourself together.
Rose:	(*angry*) That's what I'm trying to do!
Mignon:	Security!
	Security man enters, cap pulled down.
Security:	Sir.
Mignon:	Show Rose to the gate. And don't let her back in.
Security:	Sir.
	Mignon exits. The security man tips his cap back. It is Gerald.
Gerald:	Hello, Rose.
Rose:	Gerald! Where've you been?
Gerald:	Underground.
Rose:	The police are after you.

Gerald:	And the Butchers' Guild. They've put out a contract on me.
Rose:	What are you doing here?
Gerald:	Seeing what Babylon looks like.
Rose:	Why did you do it, Gerald? All those butcher shops?
Gerald:	For the animals, Rose. For the animals. I blow things up for those who can't blow things up themselves. For the porpoises. For the mice. For the eagles. For every pure creature uncontaminated by human vice.
Rose:	It must be good to believe in something like that.
Gerald:	Oppression and injustice make me strong. Can you hear them, Rose? The million agonised cries of animals tortured, imprisoned, slaughtered for the sake of a sick human pleasure? Listen.

Gerald listens.

Do animals need possessions? Do animals need anyone but themselves to survive? Do animals cry 'Who am I?'

Rose starts crying again.

Rose:	Gerald, you've got to help me.
Gerald:	Do you understand your own misery, Rose? It's the guilt of your animal-oppressing lifestyle eating you away.
Rose:	What am I going to do?
Gerald:	Rose, I've learnt something. Something incredible. We can change our destiny. It's a difficult path, Rose—but if you follow it, you can come to realise, as I did, your true identity. That you, too, are an animal.
Rose:	An animal?
Gerald:	Pure, perfect; in harmony with your life. Isn't that

what you want, Rose?

Rose: Yes.

Gerald: Then come with me. There's an army of us living underground—away from the tainted humanist power structures. I'll teach you, Rose.

He holds out his hand.

Come.

Rose grasps his hand. He leads her out with a last poisonous look round the JISMCORP headquarters.

Blackout.

A TV screen flickers into life. The music and titles appear for a double-entendre chat show.

Voiceover: It's *Innuendo*! With your host Tad Maniacal!

Tad: And tonight's guest, ladies and gentlemen, the spunkiest woman in the western world—put your hands together, please—for Lily!

Applause. Lily appears.

Hi, Lily—so glad you could come.

Lily: Good evening, Tad.

Tad: Lily, you're riding high on the crest of the JISM wave at the moment, and that must give you a pretty warm feeling.

Lily: Yes, Tad, it's been a real thrill to see JISM shoot up as high as it has.

Tad: And certainly JISMCORP has done anything but monkey around. First there was the swelling rise in the company's fortunes, a vigorous entry into the marketplace coupled with a determined thrust to the top of the share index, and the result, as we all know, has been a truly awesome liquidity.

Lily, where to now?

Lily: Well, Tad, I'm predicting a market rollover, requiring
          a completely new position on our side.

Tad: What about the rumours of marital disharmony
          in the company? Do you feel you're still capable of
          having a mutually satisfying relationship with the
          directors of JISMCORP?

Lily: Certainly, Tad. As with any relationship there's bound
          to be one or two sticky patches. It's just a matter of
          putting your head down and getting stuck in. I'm
          sure we can lick anything that comes up.

          Tad searches for a witty retort—unsuccessfully.

Tad: And Lily, I understand you've single-handedly made
          smoking fashionable again. And that you're about to
          launch your own brand of cigarette.

Lily: Yes, Tad.

          She shows the packet.

          Lilywhites.

Tad: And the slogan?

Lily: 'Die with Style'.

Tad: 'Die with Style'. That's great. One last question, Lily.
          Has there been any recent news of Rose?

Lily: As far as we're aware, she's still with the Animal
          Liberation Army.

Tad: As a hostage or voluntarily?

Lily: We don't know.

Tad: Maybe Rose is watching at this moment, if there's
          any message you want to send . . .

          The camera zooms in on Lily.

Lily: No. No message.

Tad:	Okay—looks like we're out of time, anyway. Ladies and gentlemen—a big hand-job for Lily!
	Applause. The picture freezes. Lights up to reveal Gerald, Gabrielle and Erwin putting Lily's image on trial.
Gerald:	I bring this session of the Revolutionary Court of the Animal Liberation Army to order. Who is this woman?
Army:	The enemy of all animals!
Gerald:	What does she reek of?
Army:	Monkey semen!
Gerald:	What crimes is she responsible for?
Gabrielle:	Thousands of monkeys dead from exhaustion!
Erwin:	Thousands more caged, reviled, abused . . .
Gerald:	Is there anything that can be said in her defence?
Army:	Nothing!
Gerald:	What is the verdict of this court?
Army:	GUILTY!
Gerald:	And what sentence do you recommend?
Erwin:	Instant fine.
	Gerald and Gabrielle look at him.
	Death?
Army:	DEATH! DEATH! DEATH!
Gerald:	This woman represents the acceptable face of animal exploitation. She gains money and power from torment, then tries to remove herself from the filth and degradation she creates.
Gabrielle:	I'd like to see her stripped of her fancy clothes and forced into a cage.
Erwin:	Or raped by a gorilla. It's only just.

Gabrielle: I'd have her covered in offal and flogged.

Erwin: Caged and abused day after day.

Gerald: The pain of all mutilated animals rests on her.

Gabrielle: Her!

Erwin: And when she'd beg I'd flog her harder. 'Does it hurt, Lily? Does it hurt?'

Gerald: She must die.

Gabrielle: Die!

Erwin: Die!

Army: DIE! DIE! DIE!

The chant turns into a cacophony of bloodthirsty animal noises. Suddenly there is a burst of barking from behind a door to one side.

Gerald silences the other two. He turns the TV off. They wait, tense. Rose enters, pushing a blindfolded man with his hands tied. She is holding a cordless drill to his neck.

Gerald: Any problems?

Rose: No sweat.

Man: Where are we?

Gerald: You weren't followed?

Rose: Of course not.

Man: Let me go now and I won't tell anyone about it, okay?

Gerald: We'll have to consider you initiated after this, Rose.

Gerald goes to take the man's blindfold off.

Rose: Gerald . . .

Gerald motions to her that it's okay. He takes the blindfold off.

Gerald: Well, well—who's been a naughty boy then?

The man puts on a ghastly smile.

Man: Look, if it's about the dogs . . . I explained everything to the police. I wasn't fighting my dog. I wouldn't do that.

Rose: Don't try and bullshit us. You forced your pit bull terrier to fight and kill other dogs. For sport!

Man: You can't prove anything. They threw the case out of court.

Gabrielle: You scum!

She launches herself at the man, biting his cheek.

Gerald: Get back, Gabrielle. Back! I'm in command here.

He turns back to the man, who is bleeding. Gerald tenderly mops up some of the blood on the man's face with the blindfold.

Whatever happened to your dog? What was his name?

Man: Jellimeat.

Gerald: That's right. Jellimeat.

Man: He was impounded. And destroyed.

Gerald smiles. He crosses to the door, opens it quickly, throws the bloody blindfold through and closes the door again.

Barking breaks out again behind the door, which shakes as Jellimeat throws himself against it.

Man: You mean, that's Jellimeat?

Rose: We saved him.

Gerald: A daring midnight raid. No, please, don't thank us.

Man: You'd better let me go right now. Jellimeat's trained to protect me. He'll tear you to ribbons.

Gerald:	I think he'd tear anything to ribbons at the moment. He's been in there a week. And I haven't fed him yet.
Rose:	What? Gerald, you—
Gerald:	A necessary step to break down old allegiances, to transform him from a slave into a soldier.
Man:	You're all bloody crazies!
Gerald:	Gabrielle.

Gabrielle holds the man.

Gerald:	Erwin.

Erwin goes to the door.

Gerald looks the man directly in the eye.

Gerald:	Dog. Killer.
Rose:	Gerald, what are you—
Gerald:	(*friendly*) Ever read *Nineteen Eighty-Four*?
Man:	No.
Gerald:	That's alright. Don't worry about it.

Gerald throws the man to the floor, drags him over to the door and jams his head in it. The man kicks and screams as the dog eats his face off. When he is still, Gerald opens the door further and the body is dragged through it.

Thank you, Rose.

Rose:	You're completely mad, aren't you, Gerald?
Gerald:	That's not a very nice thing to say. A giraffe wouldn't have said that.
Rose:	YOU'VE KILLED SOMEONE!
Gerald:	I've killed nothing.

Gabrielle and Erwin fall back to cut off Rose's retreat.

Any microorganism you care to name is morally
more pure than him! Or you. Or me. Only animals
deserve to live on this planet, Rose. Only they're good
enough. And animals don't feel remorse.

Rose: Well, I do!

Gerald takes out a knife.

Gerald: Erwin?

*He gives Erwin the knife. Erwin's eyes gleam as he looks
at Rose.*

Kill the dog. Every revolution needs its martyrs.

*Erwin faints. Gabrielle goes to his assistance. Furious,
Gerald picks up the knife and goes through the door.
Rose seizes the opportunity and runs out. The barking
starts again, then suddenly stops.*

*Cross to Lily, sitting alone in her office at night. Slowly
she covers one eye with her palm, then the other.*

Clara enters, Mignon behind.

Clara: What do you think you're doing?

Lily: Good evening, Clara.

Lily lights a cigarette.

Clara: I've just spent the entire day watching a complete
film crew—40 highly skilled, grossly overpaid
people—fiddling with each other whilst they wait for
you to show up.

Lily: Yes. The ad.

Clara: This had better be good, Lily. Very good. Where were
you?

Lily: I think the world can survive another day without me
telling them 'Nothing says I love you like a splash of
JISM'.

Clara laughs.

Clara: Look how far we've come. From Sunday paper oddity all the way to prima donna. Let's get this straightened out once and for all—when I shout, you jump.

Lily: The ads are crap, Clara.

Clara: And if I tell you to paint your bum pink and walk like a baboon, then you do it.

Lily: No. Not anymore.

Clara: You're not refusing to do this ad, are you, Lily?

Lily: That's exactly what I'm doing, Clara.

Clara smiles triumphantly.

Clara: Oh, thank you. You have made me so very happy. You're fired. Mignon!

Mignon hurries forward.

(*to Lily*) Be honest—you didn't think I'd do it, did you? And I've been looking forward to it for so very long.

Mignon lays a document in front of Lily.

Your resignation. 'Dismissal' always looks so tacky, I think. You say here you're leaving due to creative differences, but you bear absolutely no ill will towards JISMCORP. Just sign on the bottom. And get out.

Lily: I was in a meeting today, Clara.

Clara: Too late to make excuses now, darling. You're out.

Lily: A meeting of the board of directors and major shareholders.

Clara: Surely you can think of a better one than that. I'm on the board of directors.

Lily: Yes, it was you we were talking about. It was felt you posed a bit of a problem.

Clara: Don't be ridiculous. I'm returning record profits. They practically wet themselves with glee every time they see me.

Lily: They noticed there was a lack of available information about exactly which species of monkey were being milked. Well, they noticed when I pointed it out to them.

Clara taps her nose.

Clara: Trade secret, darling.

Lily: Yes, but I did manage to dig up some information.

She produces a document—Clara snatches it.

Clara: Where did you get this?

Lily: That doesn't matter.

Clara: I said, where did you get it?

Lily: I've got it, that's the important thing. And I'm sure I don't need to draw your attention to number three on the list. The Green Monkey. A particularly dirty little bugger.

Clara chuckles.

Clara: A waste of time, I'm afraid, sweetness.

Lily: Oh, I don't know.

Clara: Nothing can survive the purification process. JISM is clean.

Lily: You know and I know that the truth is irrelevant. It's what it looks like that counts. If anyone finds out about this, the hysteria will annihilate JISMCORP overnight.

Clara stews.

Clara: You've got copies, I suppose?

Lily: Stacks of them.

Clara tries to think of a way out. There isn't one.

Clara: Well, well, well—little Lily. Alright, keep your job.

She turns to go.

But I want you on that set tomorrow so bright and early you'll think you've died in your sleep.

Lily: Oh, I'll be there, Clara. But you won't.

Clara stops.

The board agreed it would be better if I took over your position. After all, the focus groups are unanimous.

Who produces JISM? Lily.
Who markets JISM? Lily.
Who is JISM? Lily.

She hands a document to Mignon.

Your resignation. You say you're not leaving, you just feel it's time to step back in favour of someone younger—

Clara lets out a strangled cry.

—with new ideas and a better awareness of what the public wants.

Clara is rigid, fists clenched, eyes and cheeks bulging. She is making a weird keening noise.

What's she doing?

Mignon: I think she's holding her breath till she goes blue.

Clara throws herself on the floor and starts to pummel it with her feet and fists, shrieking.

Lily: Clara?

Clara: No! No! I won't! I won't! You can't make me!

Lily: Come on now . . .

Clara puts her hands over her ears.

Clara: I can't hear you! I can't hear you!

Lily: Don't you want to know what your new job's going to be?

Clara: Noooooo!

Lily: We're putting you in charge of inspecting the bottles.

Clara suddenly jumps up and pulls out her gun.

Mignon: No!

He flings himself between Clara and Lily. Clara relaxes slightly.

Clara: You're quite right, Mignon. It would be foolish of me to kill Lily. You're always so loyal to me. Any idea where she got that list?

She shoots Mignon in the arm. He hits the floor, then struggles up again.

Mignon: That's it—I resign!

Clara shoots him in the other arm. He hits the floor again.

Clara: I accept your resignation. I always knew you were going to be a phenomenon, Lily. Your image is perfect. Nobody ever gets to see the real person behind. But we know why that is, don't we? Because there's nothing to see.

She runs out. Lily sits, staring. Mignon tries to crawl to her.

Mignon: Lily . . . are you alright?

He falls back on his arm, hurting himself. Lily is oblivious. She touches her side . . .

Lights cross fade to—

Clark sitting on a bench. He is throwing bread at a

duck decoy. Rose enters. She is fat. She stuffs the last bit of a chocolate bar into her mouth, drops the paper, then approaches Clark.

Rose: Clark?

Clark: Rose. Has Lily come?

Rose: No, Clark. Just me.

She sits down.

They said you don't have many visitors.

Clark: I wrote a letter to Lily. She never replied.

Rose: Yeah. Me too.

Clark: You look strange all by yourself. Did you fall over when you tried to walk?

Rose: Only the first hundred times. How do you stand it here, Clark?

Clark: It's not so bad.

Rose: It gives me the creeps.

Rose takes his hands.

I want you to come and live with me, Clark. I'll take care of you. You won't have to worry about anything. We can get married. I don't care that you're not the full quid. I mean . . . I mean it doesn't matter.

Clark: What about Lily?

Rose: What's she got to do with it? She never wrote back.

Clark: I still love her.

Rose: Okay. No problem. We just won't have sex. We won't get married. We'll just live together. We'll be like a . . . team. You can still love Lily. But I'll support you—I've got some money—and I can work. And you can . . . need me.

Why are you shaking your head? Don't do that. I'm offering you the chance to get out of here.

Clark: I like it here, Rose.

Rose: You like it!

Clark: It suits me. I've sort of come to terms with myself here. You see, being mad doesn't really bother me. Just as long as I'm not the odd one out.

Rose: You can't turn me down. You're halfway to being a vegetable. I'm making a big gesture.

Clark: Out there I always feel like I have to make an effort, that I've got to try all the time to be sane. And that's what really drives me mad.

Rose doesn't know whether to laugh or cry.

Rose: Are you using that bread?

She takes what's left of his bread and eats it compulsively.

Clark: You can't be like Lily, Rose. Just be yourself.

Rose: Who?

Clark: Yourself.

Rose: That is the worst advice I have ever heard, Clark. I think Mickey must have told you that one.

The sound of a gong is heard.

Clark: Lunch. What's today?

Rose: Tuesday.

Clark: (*happily*) Macaroni cheese.

He gets up.

I'll see you later then, Rose.

Rose: Yeah. Bye.

Clark goes.

Rose sits moodily.

Christ. Jilted by Clark. How low can you go?

She glances round, then gets down and picks up all the bread round the decoy, stuffing it in her mouth.

JISM music. Lights up on Lily. Pause as she gazes directly out.

Lily: Love me. Buy my product.

Lights down.

Lights up on Gerald's hideout. He is alone. He has become very animal-like, moving around on all fours, lapping water from a bowl. He turns round and round like a cat before settling to sleep.

Clara enters. She looks at him then taps him with her foot. He springs away, back arched, hissing. He looks desperately round for a weapon or escape.

Clara: Nice pussy. I've been looking for you. Wanted to have a little chat.

Gerald straightens up.

Gerald: I know who you are.

Clara: Congratulations. You're one of the few. I know who you are, too. You're the one who sends us those very nasty letters saying what you'd like to do to Lily. Your handwriting is appalling. However I've always given you an A for imagination.

Gerald: What do you want?

Clara: I want to find out if you're serious. See whether you've got the guts. You don't look like much. This is supposed to be an army, isn't it? Where is everyone?

Gerald: We had some problems with discipline in the ranks. I had to have a court martial. Two, actually.

Why do you want Lily dead?

Clara:	[That's] My business.
	(*the other meaning*) My business.
Gerald:	Your business is death and degradation. It—
Clara:	SHUT UP! Not when we're conniving. Please.
Gerald:	I could kill Lily at any time. I don't need your help.
Clara:	Things have changed a bit down at JISMCORP since you so easily slipped in and slipped out again with Rose.
	Oh yes, we have very efficient security arrangements now. Lily insists on them. But I could get you to her. And I'm the only one who can.
Gerald:	Why worry about Lily? Why don't I kill you instead? You started it all.
Clara:	Because even a terrorist has to have some sense of PR. You kill the one who's identified with the product— not the one who's actually guilty.
Gerald:	It's true. You have to be practical.
Clara:	Good. I'll be in touch.
Gerald:	One thing: Rose will also be executed. As a deserter.
Clara:	You're sort of cute really, aren't you?
	She exits.
	A Doctor's surgery. The Doctor comes in, followed by Lily buttoning up her blouse.
Lily:	Well?
Doctor:	I can't find a thing wrong with you, Lily.
Lily:	But my heart . . .
Doctor:	Lily, your heart is performing magnificently.
Lily:	There's something wrong with it. There must be. Why don't I have a sense of smell? Why can't I taste

anything? Why am I going blind?

Doctor: Lily, you're not going blind. You have trouble distinguishing colours, that's all.

Lily: It's getting worse.

Doctor: Hundreds of thousands of people are colourblind. It can have a physical basis, or in some cases it can be psychological. These other symptoms—loss of appetite, sleeplessness, no interest in sex—they're all classic signs of stress, Lily. We've just been working too hard, haven't we?

Lily: It's this heart you gave me. It's not right.

Doctor: I've never seen a healthier heart. It hasn't shown a single sign of rejection. It's the best transplant I've ever done.

Lily: To reject it, my body would have to recognise it as being different to me, wouldn't it?

Doctor: Yes.

Lily: And for that to happen, there'd have to be a 'me'—an identity—a . . . soul?

Doctor: You've lost me.

Lily: What if there was only ever one—person—between us, and it had to make a choice? Me or Rose?

Doctor: That's just silly, Lily. (*giggles*) 'Silly Lily'.

The Doctor writes on a notepad.

I'm going to give you the name of a therapist.

She hands it over.

Lily: Suppose I was right . . .

Doctor: You're not right, Lily.

Lily: Suppose it was true. And suppose I found Rose, and I made it up with her . . .

Doctor:	That would be nice, wouldn't it?
Lily:	Couldn't you join us together again?

The Doctor stares at her.

Lights cross fade to—

Rose, very fat, trying to hang herself.

Rose: This'll fix you, Lily. When you find out about this you'll be sorry.

God, I'm starving. I don't want to die hungry. Maybe I should have a little snack first? No, that's right—I ate everything in the house. Maybe I should go down the shops and get something? But I haven't got any money. This is all your fault, Lily!

She steels herself to do it.

I read somewhere that when people hang themselves their bowels empty. Gross-out. Maybe I should take some laxatives and get rid of it all first? No, that's right—I ate them all. Maybe I should go down the chemist and get some more? But I haven't got any money! Damn you, Lily! Damn you!

She really looks like she's going to do it. Gerald bursts in with the drill.

Gerald: Hold it right there, Rose. One move and you're dead.

Rose slowly puts her hands up . . .

Blackout.

The television comes on in darkness. It is Innuendo; *same opening music, titles.*

Tad: It's been a while since she was on the show, but now she's back by popular demand. The woman who's not only thrown a spanner in the works of the whole perfume industry, but given many a monkey a wrench at the same time.

That's right, folks—will you welcome, please, Lily!

Applause.

Tad: Lily, you're even more phenomenally successful now than when I last spoke to you. You've done more with a simple flick of the wrist than anyone I can think of.

I was particularly impressed with that last ad of yours where you just sat there for 30 seconds and said . . . nothing. You've brought honesty back to advertising. And there's no doubt about it—in the public imagination, you *are* JISM.

Lily: Do you use JISM, Tad?

Tad: Everyone uses JISM, Lily.

Lily: Then let me tell you something about it.

Tad: Shoot.

Lily: JISM is made up in part of Green Monkey semen.

Tad: Green semen? Sounds a bit off to me, Lily.

Lily: The Green Monkey is the species which is thought to be the source of the AIDS virus.

Tad: AIDS?

Lily: Which, as you know, is spread through blood or semen.

Tad: You're saying you use AIDS-infected semen to make JISM?

Lily: Quite possibly.

Tad: Oh my God.

Lily: Don't worry. There's no danger.

Tad: No danger? Your perfume is contaminated with a killer disease! I've been wearing it every day for a year. Get it off me! Someone get it off me!

I'm doomed, I'm going to die. And it's all your fault.
You bitch!

*He attacks Lily. A floor manager in headphones runs
on and tries to drag the hysterical Tad off Lily. The end
music starts.*

You knew! You knew all the time!

He lets go of Lily.

Oh my God, I've cut myself. I'm bleeding. AIDS is
mixing with my blood.

*He faints. The picture swerves downwards as if the
cameraman has run away.*

*Lights up to reveal David Kurtson in his mortuary,
watching the TV (which is sitting on top of a coffin). He
turns it off. He is wearing a bloodstained apron. He goes
back to his work, painting the fingernails of a shrouded
corpse.*

Lily enters and watches him. He looks up and sees her.

Lily:	Hello, you.
David:	Are you alright? That thing on the TV . . .
Lily:	I'm fine. Well, I'm in a better state than all the JISM buyers will be.
David:	Why did you do it?
Lily:	It was the only way I could get away. I had to ruin JISM before I became JISM. There's more to me than just a symbol, isn't there? You see it, David.

She puts her hand on his arm.

David:	Lily . . .
Lily:	I found you in the Yellow Pages. Kurtson's Mortuary. I always knew you'd get your own business.
David:	It hasn't been easy. I've got an outrageous mortgage.

That's why I'm working late. Have to grab all the overtime I can.

So you think JISM's finished?

Lily: There'll be a public investigation. JISM will be given a completely clean bill of health. And nobody will ever buy it again.

David: You understand it better than me.

Lily: I don't want to understand it. I want to forget all that. Go back to being how I was.

David: You can't sew Rose back on.

Lily: No. But there's you. Do you remember all the plans we made? We would have done anything just to be together.

David: I remember.

Lily: I never loved anyone else, David. I want to have all that again.

David: Lily—

Lily: Just kiss me. Please.

         They kiss.

         You're married, aren't you?

David: And we've got a baby. But that's not it.

Lily: Are you happily married?

David: No. I'm . . . ordinarily married. That's the difference. What we had, it was too perfect. We all loved you— me, Rose, Clark, even Gerald in some bizarre way. Somehow you managed to be all things to all of us. And that's not real, is it?

         When we kissed then, it was just like it used to be. Beautiful. But not a real kiss. Not one with lips and tongues and teeth.

Lily:	And with Rose? When you kissed her?
David:	You were always too good to be true, Lily. Rose was more like the rest of us.
Lily:	I'd better let you get on with your work.
David:	She came here, you know.
Lily:	What did she want?
David:	The same thing you did.

Lily turns to leave.

	You've got to come down to earth sometime, Lily.
Lily:	You've got your wife and your baby to hold you down. And you've got yourself. I'm weightless.

She exits. David stares after her.

Lights up on JISMCORP. Lily enters and sits down, gazing blankly. She senses something.

Rose?

Gerald comes out of hiding. He has Rose gagged, bound and tied to one of his arms. He has a bomb attached to himself, the detonator of which he holds in his free hand.

Gerald:	Very perceptive, Lily.
Lily:	How have you been, Gerald?
Gerald:	Up and down.
Lily:	Thanks for bringing Rose back.
Gerald:	No trouble. Stay where you are.

With the hand bound to Rose he writes on the wall with a spray can, 'I AM AN ANIMAL'.

Lily:	It's all over, Gerald. JISMCORP will be bankrupt. There'll be no more factories. No more monkeys.
Gerald:	You can't get out of it that easily, Lily. You've committed crimes against animals. And justice must

be served.

He finishes writing.

Do you love Rose?

Lily: No.

Gerald: Then leave now. Go.

Lily: I can't.

Gerald: I'm going to die tonight, Lily. And one of you is going to die too. It's a pity Clark isn't here. He loved it when we all did things together.

Lily: Let her go, Gerald.

Gerald: I will. After you've done what I tell you to.

He looks round at the large steel vat of JISM.

So the JISM empire crumbles. But there's still time for one last batch.

He looks at Lily.

Get in.

She doesn't move. Rose whines and strains against the ropes. Gerald raises the detonator.

Get. In.

Lily goes to move towards Rose.

Lily: Rose—

Gerald: No. No touching.

Lily: Rose, it's right. It makes sense that it's me. You got the heart. It's something to carry on with.

Gerald raises the detonator again.

Gerald: Please.

Lily walks slowly to the vat and lowers herself into the boiling JISM. Rose is beside herself.

Lily: It's alright, Rose. I don't feel anything. Not anything.

She vanishes. Gerald turns the mixing machine on. Lily is minced up into the JISM. Rose gets her arm free and pulls the gag off.

Rose: Lily!

She collapses. Gerald switches the machine off, then turns a tap to draw off some of the JISM. It is red.

Gerald: The ads are true! Lily is JISM!

He anoints Rose. She makes a grab for the detonator. He catches her hand and dances her around.

Dance! Dance!

He holds the detonator out of her reach.

Is this what you want? Is this what you want? Do you want to press it? Do you? Do you? Then press it!

She does. Nothing happens. Again and again. Nothing. Rose collapses, moaning. Gerald is astounded.

Give me that.

He takes it and presses it.

It doesn't work. Bloody doesn't work.

He tries to check all his wiring but is hampered by Rose. He cuts her free. Clara enters.

Clara: Aren't you finished yet? What are you doing?

Gerald: (*fiddling*) It doesn't work.

Clara: What?

He crosses over to her.

Gerald: It doesn't work!

Clara: Just hurry up. I've got a plane to catch. Is Lily dead? That's something. Look, it's this thing on your shoulder. It's come apart.

She quickly pushes the connection back together.

There—try now.

Gerald pushes the button. They are blown away.

Blackout.

Birds tweeting.

Lights up on Clark, sitting on the bench, asleep.

Lily enters. She is blind, dressed like Snow White, a cardboard bird on one finger. Without moving or opening his eyes Clark says hello.

Clark: Hello, Lily.

Clark/Lily: Hello, Clark.

Lily sits down.

Clark: How are you feeling?

Clark/Lily: I'm feeling better. Better and better every day.

Clark: You don't mind my changes?

Clark/Lily: No. I'm happier this way. And you think it's for the best, don't you Clark?

Clark: I do, Lily. I really do.

He takes her hand.

Isn't the sun beautiful?

Lily: The sun is beautiful.

They sit in silence. Rose, no longer fat, enters with a suitcase.

Rose: Clark? How are you, Clark?

Clark: Rose. Lily's here.

Rose: Lily?

Clark: She comes to visit me.

Rose: Lily's dead, Clark.

Clark:	That's right. I'm the only one she visits now.
	Rose sits down on the other side of Clark.
Rose:	I came to say goodbye. I'm finally off. Parts unknown.
Clark:	That's nice.
Lily:	Listen . . .
Clark:	Why are you going?
Rose:	I don't know. To find myself? Just to have somewhere different to look, really.
Lily:	I can hear it.
Rose:	You still don't want to go home?
Clark:	No more than anyone else.
Lily:	My heart.
Rose:	Why is it, Clark, that whenever I come here I feel like asking you the meaning of life?
Lily:	Beating.
Rose:	You used to be such a jerk and now I feel like you know more than the rest of us.
Clark:	It's being crazy. It gives you a lot of street credibility.
	Rose takes his hand. The three of them sit there for a while.
	Rose?
Rose:	Hmm?
Clark:	Lily wasn't perfect, you know. I thought she was. But when she started coming here, after she died, I just noticed a few little things. I changed her a bit. I thought she should be a little more like . . . Snow White. I'd change her back but I can't quite remember exactly how she was. It worries me sometimes. I think that one day there'll be nothing of

Lily left. It'll all be me. And then she'll really be dead.

Rose: Or perhaps she'll live happily ever after.

The sound of the gong is heard.

Clark: Lunch. What's today?

Rose: Friday.

Clark smiles.

Clark: Macaroni cheese. Goodbye, Rose.

Lily: Goodbye, Rose.

Rose: See you, Clark.

Rose hugs him.

Clark: Lily says goodbye too.

Rose: Oh. Right.

Clark stands up and exits. Rose stretches and feels a jab of pain in her side.

Ow!

Lily reaches out and touches Rose's side. Rose relaxes. She thinks of Clark and laughs quietly.

Snow White.

She collects herself.

Come on, Rose—this is not the place to talk to yourself. They'll have you in the canvas pyjamas in no time.

She stands up, breaking contact with Lily. She walks to her suitcase and picks it up. She hesitates for a moment.

Bye, Lily.

Rose smiles at her silliness and exits.

Lily sits alone on the bench as the lights go slowly down.

The End

JISM Outtake

The Legendary Lost Third Act:

Well, it's not that legendary, since even Rebecca had forgotten about it. Not exactly lost, either, as it's just been sitting in a box along with the first draft. But perhaps it's of interest to any theatre historians or *JISM*-obsessives, if they're out there. It centres on Clark's madness and Rose's growth towards becoming a whole person—what was only an abortive offer by Rose in the staged play is enlarged on here as she sets up house with Clark in an effort to find a role and connection in the aftermath of Lily's death. Pregnant, she imagines she's going to give birth to Lily. The Punch-and-Judy motif always had a strong appeal for me—a show I saw as a kid obviously went quite deep . . . I'm pretty sure that putting all and sundry through a mincer and making sausages out of them would not be thought appropriate for the littlies these days (though I'm grateful I got to see it). Limited running time and some insanely ambitious production demands of this third section quite rapidly saw the play contract to two acts.

Act 3

Note: During the interval between acts 2 and 3, a Punch and Judy puppet show is performed in the foyer.

The plot of the puppet show is an old standard in which Punch, left to babysit, kills the baby when it won't stop crying. To cover up this crime and to avoid punishment, he then proceeds to kill every individual and symbol of authority who comes to apprehend him, starting with his wife and ending with the Devil. However he is eventually eaten by a crocodile which has periodically appeared at his window.

A distorted room. From a low back wall (so that anyone coming in has to bend down to get through the door) the room splays out, with a long roof sloping up and walls spreading out at an angle. The set has a cardboard two-dimensional look. There is a window in the side-wall, stage-left, behind it a flat matte blue sky.

A couch. A table where Clark is sitting, staring blankly.

On the table is a carry-cot. A baby can be heard crying incessantly.

Rose passes the window, then enters. The crying stops immediately. Rose is pregnant and is wearing a jazzercise leotard.

Rose: Hi.

           Clark doesn't move.

           I've brought a couple of people home. From the class. Do you mind?

           She goes out the door again. The crying starts immediately. Rose re-enters with two more pregnant women in leotards. The crying stops immediately.

           Jinny, Ann-Marie . . . Clark.

Jinny/Ann-Marie: Hiieee!

           Jinny and Ann-Marie gasp. Jinny hobbles straight over to admire the curtains. Ann-Marie does the same for the lounge suite. They ooh and ahh, change places, ooh and ahh again. Rose is kept busy discussing colour, pattern, etc.

           In the midst of this, Ann-Marie wavers and bursts into tears.

Ann-Marie: It's no good. I can't do it.

           She collapses on the floor. Rose and Jinny rush to comfort her.

Rose: Of course you can.

Ann-Marie: I'm a failure as a mother already.

Rose: You're not.

Ann-Marie: You saw me.

Rose: Just because you can't do a pelvic tilt, doesn't mean you're a failure as a mother, Ann-Marie.

Ann-Marie: It's alright for you. The instructor said your hip-thrusts were perfect.

Rose: She was just trying to be encouraging.

Ann-Marie: No, she wasn't. You always get everything right. It's so depressing.

Jinny: Ann-Marie.

Ann-Marie: Well, it's true. She's always perfect. I feel like the third world.

Rose: I think—that your baby is very very lucky to have you as a mother. I think that when you see her and hold her in your arms, you'll think she's perfect. And she'll think you're perfect too.

Because you are.

Ann-Marie looks at the floor.

Ann-Marie: This is nice. Did you put it down yourself?

Rose: That's the spirit.

She helps Ann-Marie up.

Ann-Marie: I suppose I must seem silly to you.

Rose: Yes.

They laugh.

Go on. I'll see you next week.

Ann-Marie attempts a few pelvic tilts. Laughing, Jinny and Rose join in.

Ann-Marie: Bye. (*to Clark*) Byeee.

She exits.

Jinny: You're really lucky having Clark. He seems so supportive.

She exits.

Rose sighs. She sets the table and dishes out some Chinese takeaway. She puts a knife into Clark's hand, brings the toaster over and pushes Clark's hand with the knife into it. She flicks the wall switch, shocking him.

Rose: So how was your day, dear?

Clark: It's not really you, is it?

Rose: What?

Clark: All this nurturing. Supporting. Taking care of everyone.

Rose: Ann-Marie's all right. She just needs a bit of reassurance now and again.

Clark: Why did you marry me?

Rose: I think it was your happy-go-lucky personality.

Clark: You can't be her, you know.

Rose gets up.

Rose: Remember, I've got a meeting tonight . . .

Clark: She's dead.

Rose: I know that! I'm the one who—

She stops herself.

Clark: She was kind to everyone.

She could afford to be. She had you to balance things.

Rose: Let's just change the subject.

Clark: She used you like that. To stop people getting too close. You used her.

Nobody used me. I was useless.

Why didn't she want me?

Rose puts her head in her hands, tired.

If you use someone, it's a sign that you love them.

Helping them—that's the opposite.

Rose loses control.

Rose: Just shut up! I don't want to hear it.

It's my house. My money. If you don't like it you can go back on the ward with all the other salad vegetables.

She calms down.

I'm sorry. I'm sorry, Clark. I didn't mean that.

You're my husband. I'll take care of you.

Clark: (*not really having noticed anything*) She was so kind to me, I knew there was no hope.

She was kind to everyone. I would have liked to have been the exception.

Rose: I've got to go.

Clark: Rose. Shouldn't you feed the baby? He's been waiting all day. He's been good, just lying there—gurgling away.

Rose: Clark. I haven't had the baby yet.

This is a hot water bottle.

She takes it out of the carry-cot and gives it to him. He looks at it.

Clark: A hot water bottle?

Rose looks at her watch.

Rose: Oh God, I'm late.

She goes to the door, then turns.

Rose: Why did you say 'he'?

Clark: What?

Rose: He? What makes you think it's a him?

Clark: Isn't it?

Rose: Are you crazy?

She exits. Clark places the hot water bottle on the table. The sound of the baby crying begins again, louder. Clark tries to ignore it, but finally picks up the hot water bottle and cuddles and soothes it. He falls asleep. Lily enters, halfway through turning into Snow White.

Lily: Open your eyes, Clark.

Clark: I don't want to.

He opens his eyes.

Lily.

Lily: No. Just a memory of Lily. Already changing into something else.

Clark: Snow White.

Lily: Looks like it.

Clark: I'm sorry you're dead, Lily.

Lily: Only the transplant heart died. My heart's still beating.

Clark: In Rose?

Lily: No, in a chimpanzee. Of course in Rose.

Clark: Sorry.

Lily: Don't apologise to your own imagination, Clark. It's a sign of madness.

Clark: Lily . . . things don't look the same to me anymore.

Lily:	Or me.
Clark:	I'm afraid, Lily. I'm afraid I'll get so lost I'll never get back.

You're the only one who can help me.

There is the sound of galloping outside.

Lily:	That'll be my ride.
Clark:	Don't go! Tell me what to do.
Lily:	Be yourself, Clark. Be yourself.
Clark:	Myself?

Lily exits.

That's the worst advice I've ever heard.

The crying returns as Clark 'wakes up'.

You're not a baby. So stop crying.

The crying gets louder.

Pull yourself together. You're a hot water bottle.

Louder.

I'll throw you out. I will.

He goes over to the window and opens it, then turns back to the hot water bottle.

This is your last chance.

Right.

He seizes the hot water bottle and goes to throw it out. A large crocodile suddenly appears in the window. Clark cries out and recoils in fright. The crocodile disappears. Clark stands, staring at the window. The lights fade on him—

—and come up on Rose in bed with Dr Chance.

Chance:	Where did you tell Clark you were going?

Rose:	To a tactics meeting of our radical PTA splinter group.
	It happens to be true, actually. They're discussing whether violence is acceptable in reforming the kindergarten system. And I'm supposed to be there.
Chance:	You're a little early, aren't you? The baby's not even born yet.
Rose:	Somebody's got to take an interest.
Chance:	Then let it be someone else for a change. You can't be everywhere at once; you can't please everybody. You're doing too much, Rose. As your obstetrician, I'm telling you you have to slow down.
Rose:	That's your advice, is it?
Chance:	That's part of it.
Rose:	And what's the rest?
Chance:	Leave Clark and come away with me.
Rose:	Where?
Chance:	What?
Rose:	Come away with you to where?
Chance:	Well . . . I've got the practice to think about, and hospital work . . . We might be able to get to Sydney for Christmas.
Rose:	So you want me to divorce my husband and move three blocks down the street on the off-chance of a week in Kings Cross?
Chance:	It was a mistake to marry Clark. You admit it was only pity.
Rose:	Something like that.
Chance:	And you said yourself he'd hardly notice you'd gone.
Rose:	But I might.

Chance:	Rose, it's my baby you're having.
Rose:	Is it?
Chance:	Well, isn't it? You came to me for infertility.
Rose:	And the treatment was thorough, I'll give you that.
	Sometimes I think it might be nothing to do with you. Or Clark.
	Or me.
Chance:	What do you mean?
Rose:	Nothing.
	She sighs.
	Slim, I can't leave Clark.
Chance:	But you have to.
Rose:	No. Don't push me. I can't and that's it. He needs me.
Chance:	But I need you.
Rose:	You've got me.
Chance:	I want all of you—not pieces.
Rose:	Pieces are all there is.
Chance:	No. Rose, I love you. Leave Clark—don't be afraid to be yourself.
Rose:	And who's that?
Chance:	The loving, kind, perfect Rose that I know so well.
Rose:	There's a logical error here somewhere.
	She gets up and starts to dress.
	I've got to go. I've got an appointment.
Chance:	I should get the gender test back any time now.
Rose:	Uh-huh.
Chance:	Don't you want to know what it is?

Rose: I know who it is.

Chance: When will I see you again?

She kisses him.

Rose: Come to my party.

The lights fade and come up on Clark sitting once again with the hot water bottle. He goes to put it on the table. The crying starts. He tries again, with the same result.

Clark: It's just mind over matter. Mind over matter.

He puts the hot water bottle on the table, gets up and starts to tiptoe away. The crying starts again, loud. Clark rushes back, picks the bottle up and shakes it angrily.

Be yourself! Be yourself!

He grabs a carving knife and starts to stab it.

You're a—hot—water—bottle!

The crying stops abruptly. Clark is relieved. He picks up the hot water bottle and blood leaks out. He puts his fingers into one of the slashes and, horrified, pulls out some guts. The crocodile appears in the window behind him. Ragged, choking breathing is heard. The hot water bottle heaves in Clark's hands, then lies still. Clark gasps and, turning to the window, recoils from the crocodile, which snaps at him.

The lights fade and come up on Rose with Edith, her psychiatrist.

Edith: Rose—before I can help you, you have to be able to admit to yourself that your nurturing compulsion, your overwhelming desire to support and encourage, is a response to certain traumatic events in your past. By being nice to people you're seeking to suppress guilts, anxieties and even hostilities in yourself. You're denying yourself access to your own life.

Further therapy will be pointless without this kind

of admission from you, Rose. And, frankly, I think you're stalling.

I know that to recognise these kinds of things, to bring them out in the open, can be very difficult. I've experienced the same reluctance to face some things in my background.

Rose: Like what?

Edith: Well, that's not the point at the moment . . .

Rose: Just as an example.

Edith: My . . . relationship with my father, for instance.

Rose: How do you mean?

Edith: He always seemed to me to be cold, distant, judgemental. Then he died at a time when I was possibly just getting to know him as a person, with the result that I was never able to express certain feelings I had towards him.

           But that's not what we want to talk about today . . .

Rose: It must have been very hard for you.

Edith: There are times when I feel it's getting on top of me. I feel, like a pressure rising inside of me, you know, like pressing up into my throat, as if I'm only just stopping myself from screaming out, 'I hate you, I hate you, Daddy, I hate you!'

Rose: You should.

Edith: I suppose it's a case of 'physician—heal thyself'.

           It's so . . . difficult to break through that barrier.

           I know in my head, but . . .

Rose: Go on—there's only us here.

Edith: I feel embarrassed.

Rose: You know you've got to do it.

	Come on—speak to me. Imagine I'm your father. What do you want to say to me?
Edith:	I . . .
	No, it's no good, I can't do it.
Rose:	Edith, you're a disappointment to me.
Edith:	What?
Rose:	Why can't you be like other girls? Do something with yourself. Straighten up—don't slouch.
Edith:	I'm not slouching.
Rose:	And take that whine out of your voice, for God's sake.
Edith:	You're always picking on me.
Rose:	That's enough of that, my girl. If you're going to act like a child then you'll be treated like one. Now go to your room.
Edith:	I hate you.
Rose:	I beg your pardon!
Edith:	I hate you!
Rose:	Louder.
Edith:	I HATE YOU! I HATE YOU! DADDY, I HATE YOU!
Rose:	Good.
Edith:	You don't love me! You never loved me!
Rose:	I do.
Edith:	No! Nothing I did was good enough. I tried and tried but you didn't care. You never cared about me. And I don't care about you. I hate you!
Rose:	I did love you, Edith. But I couldn't show it. I could never show it.

And now there's no way of telling you how much I love you, because I'm dead.

Edith: No.

Rose: Yes. I'm dead, Edith. I'm dead.

But I'll always love you. Very much.

Edith bursts into tears and throws herself into Rose's arms.

That's it. That's it. There you go.

Rose takes out a handkerchief and wipes away some of Edith's tears. She smiles at her.

Come to my party.

The lights fade on Rose and Edith and come back up on Clark, sitting with his back to the window. The crocodile appears at the window. Clark looks around. The crocodile disappears before he can see it. Clark turns back. The crocodile appears again. Clark whips round, but is too late again. He turns back. Mignon piggybacks Clara past the window. There is a knock at the door. Clark looks under the table suspiciously. Another knock. Clark cautiously puts his hand on the teapot lid.

Clark: Who's there?

He whips the lid off the teapot and looks inside. He puts the lid back on.

Must be bloody kids.

The door opens. Mignon staggers in with Clara and shuts the door again.

Mignon: I'm . . . sorry . . . to just barge in. But we're desperate.

Clark: Did you hear a knock on the door just then?

Mignon: Yes. It was me.

Clark goes to the door, yanks it open and looks out.

Clark:	Damn.
	He closes the door and goes back to his seat.
Clara:	Mignon—put me down.
	Mignon lays Clara down.
	Did we lose him?
Mignon:	I think so.
Clara:	Check the window.
	Mignon does.
Mignon:	Nothing. Your ankle?
Clara:	Twisted.
Mignon:	(*to Clark*) I never would have believed that shareholders could be so vindictive.
	At the last JISMCORP meeting, after the reading of the notice of bankruptcy, they all voted to put out a contract on us.
	They didn't even wait for General Business.
Clara:	We knew Rose would hide us. We're old friends.
Mignon:	We won't be any trouble.
Clara:	Just go about your normal business.
	Mignon waves a hand in front of Clark's face.
Mignon:	I think he is going about his normal business.
	Mignon turns to Clara.
	There's no chance of her letting us stay.
	She probably blames us for what happened to Lily.
Clara:	Where else can we go? We've worn out our welcome everywhere.
	The door is kicked in. The Marmoset, a professional hitman, enters.

Marmoset: Surprised? No one expects the Marmoset.

Mignon: The Marmoset?

Marmoset: Something funny?

Mignon: No.

Marmoset: All the good names were already taken. The Jackal, the Fox, the Panther . . .

Clara: Perhaps we can make a deal. How much are you being paid to kill us?

Marmoset: I'm going to pretend I didn't hear that. I happen to be a hitman of integrity.

Now, line up—the sooner we get this over, the sooner we can go home . . . I can go home.

Mignon: We didn't do it. It's all a mistake. It wasn't us who started the AIDS panic.

Marmoset: It wasn't?

Mignon: No.

Marmoset: Okay. Now—who's first?

Clara: Wait! Have you seen any money yet?

Marmoset: What do you mean?

Clara: Payment. For this job.

Marmoset: I haven't put in my bill yet. It's strictly COD.

Marmoset/Clara/Mignon: Cash on death.

Clara: But what's going to happen when you do put in your bill? JISMCORP is bankrupt. You'll just be one more in a sea of creditors, having to wait your turn like everyone else. You might get 20% of the full amount—in five years—if you're lucky.

Marmoset: You're joking.

Mignon: She's an expert.

Marmoset:	Well, of all the . . . They're not going to get away with this, I can promise you that. No one tries to screw the Marmoset.
	As soon as I've killed you two I'm going straight round there to sort this out.
Mignon:	But if you kill us, you'll be helping them rip you off.
Clara:	And you'll lose your bargaining position.
Marmoset:	Thanks, but it's okay. I'll kill you on my own time.
Mignon:	But why?
Marmoset:	I'm a Taurus. Once I get something in my head— that's it.
Clara:	You mean you're going to kill us for no money?
Marmoset:	Yeah—a freebie.
Clara:	What about union regulations? That'd make you a scab.
Marmoset:	No one calls the Marmoset a scab!
	He points the gun at Clara.
Mignon:	But if you shoot her you will be a scab.
	He points the gun at Mignon.
	If you shoot me, you'll be a scab.
Clara:	That's right. I'm declaring this an official picket line. If you lay a finger on us, the union'll black you for life.
	Clara and Mignon link arms and start singing We Shall Not Be Moved. The Marmoset wavers uncertainly.
Mignon:	You'll never work again.
Clara:	Everyone'll shout 'scab' after you in the street.
Mignon:	Scab! Scab!
Clara:	Blackleg! Strikebreaker!

Mignon: Don't do it, brother.

Clara: Don't cross the line.

Mignon: Solidarity. Stand with us, brother.

Clara: Join us in the fight against the filthy executive class.

Mignon/Clara: Join us! Join us!

> *The Marmoset links arms with them. They sing another chorus of We Shall Not Be Moved.*

Marmoset: Wait a minute. I haven't got a union.

Clara: You're affiliated to the clerical workers. Not many people know that.

Marmoset: I don't like tricks.

> *He raises his gun. Rose enters, carrying groceries.*

Clara: Rose!

Mignon: At last!

> *They dash over and crowd behind her.*

Clara: You look wonderful!

Mignon: It agrees with you.

Clara: Positively blooming. You must tell us everything.

Mignon: From the beginning.

> *Rose puts down her groceries and goes over to the Marmoset.*

Rose: Who are you?

Marmoset: Ever heard of the Marmoset?

Rose: Oh, yes. I love the way you swing from branch to branch with your tail.

Marmoset: I'm a hired killer.

> *Rose points her finger like a gun at him. Instantly he is on guard.*

Rose: Come to my party.

The lights fade down. A cigarette glows in the darkness. It is Lily. Clark comes over.

Clark: You shouldn't smoke, Lily. It's bad for you.

Lily: Listen, can you hear it beating?

My heart. In Rose.

Clark: I loved you, Lily.

Lily: Sshhh.

Clark: I did. You were the only one I could talk to.

Lily: You're a fool, Clark. Don't you realise?

All that time when Rose was cruel to you, hard or unsympathetic—she spoke for me.

Clark: No.

Lily: Yes. And I spoke for her. It was the same heart.

Clark: Rose isn't the same as you. You're better. I want you, not her.

Lily: Clark, you're really starting to piss me off, you know that?

The very worst aspect of your stark raving *boring* insanity isn't Mickey Mouse, or Donald Duck, Punch and Judy or even Snow White.

It's me. Your obsession with me.

I may be dead, I may be some kind of twisted memory come schizophrenic hallucination, but I don't have to take this kind of crap!

If you bother to recall, I was getting married to my fiancée—not to you. Never to you.

When it came to husband material I was looking for someone who wasn't two sandwiches short of a picnic. Whose elevators went all the way to the top floor.

Clark: Lily . . .

Lily: Just because I was half a woman didn't mean I wanted half a man. Someone with all the lights on and the music playing but nobody home.

           Don't you understand? Rose was guarding me from you. She always did.

Clark: No.

Lily: Yes. That was the double-act. The hard bitch and the soft touch. Different voices. The same heart.

Clark: Lily . . .

Lily: Rose.

           The lights come up on the birthday party. Rose is at the head of the table, surrounded by Chance, Edith, Clara, Mignon and the Marmoset. They are all looking at Clark.

           What are you doing?

Rose: Come and sit down, Clark.

           Clark stares at Lily for a moment, then crosses and sits down. The lights fade on Lily until she is a silhouette.

Chance: I would like to propose a toast. To Rose—the most caring person I have ever met.

Edith: The wisest, and most understanding of other people.

Clara: Who never forgets her old friends.

Mignon: And is always ready to help.

Marmoset: Cheers.

           They drink.

Chance: And another toast.

To the future. To the birth of Rose's—and my—son.

Rose: What?

Chance: I don't care who knows it anymore, Rose. It's got to
            come out some time.

Rose: Son?

Chance: The test came back. It's official.

Rose: No.

Marmoset: Come on—sing!

Everyone: Happy birthday to you
            Happy birthday to you
            Happy birthday, dear—

            Rose gives a cry of loss and despair.

Rose: LILY!

Marmoset: Happy birthday—to—you.

Edith: Rose?

Rose: She's gone.

Chance: What's the matter? Is it the baby? How do you feel?

Rose: Light.

Mignon: Light?

Clara: Light-headed, stupid.

Chance: Give her a bit of room.

Edith: You give her a bit of room, she needs me by her.

Mignon: Here—try and drink this.

Clara: Have a bit of cake. It's your birthday after all.

Rose: No.

Chance: She doesn't want the cake.

Marmoset: I'll have it.

Rose: It's not my birthday.

             When we were kids we wanted a day we didn't have
             to share. It only needed one of us to change dates,
             but we both did in the end. Neither one of us would
             let the other keep the real birthday.

             It's a boy?

Chance: A boy.

Rose: I want my real birthday back. I want to celebrate on
             the day I was born.

             I'll remember I had a sister who was born on the
             same day, who died. And I'll be sorry about that. But
             I won't be trying to carry her around inside me any
             more.

             I've got to teach this heart not to want more than me.
             I've got to be enough now.

             She goes to Clark.

             Clark, I'm leaving. I'm sorry. I thought marrying you
             might help something, somewhere . . . I don't know
             what . . .

             Chance takes Rose's hands.

Chance: It's the right thing, Rose. I promise you that.

             Lily comes up behind Clark.

Lily: Tough break, Clark. Looks like it's back to the rubber
             palladium for you.

             Rose shakes her head.

Rose: No, Slim, I'm leaving you too.

Chance: Rose, you can't. I need you.

Rose: I'm sorry.

Chance: Alright—forget Sydney. Hawaii. We'll go to Hawaii.

Rose:	Wherever it is I go, you can't come. None of you. Because I'm going alone. For the first time ever.
Edith:	'Going'? What do you mean 'going'?
	You can't set yourself up as my father-figure and then just walk out. It's not ethical. It's what my real father did!
Clara:	What about us? We came here so you could hide us.
Mignon:	She's right. There's no point if you're not here as a cover.
Clara:	We'll end up dead and it'll all be your fault.
Chance:	Rose, I need your support. I've got a particularly heavy week coming up.
Edith:	I'm at a crucial stage in my therapy.
Rose:	Pull yourselves together, for God's sake. Live your own lives.

Chance/Edith/Clara: YOU BITCH!

Marmoset:	No. It's a particularly wise decision, if you ask me. Personal relationships are nothing but trouble. I should know—I've had to settle enough of them.
	Bon voyage, pretty lady.
	He puts out his hand. Rose goes to take it. He grabs her and pulls her in front of him.
	Nobody moves, right? I can break her neck with one twist. You two—back against the wall.
	Clara and Mignon move back. The Marmoset takes out his gun.
Clara:	Remember the Clerical Workers' Union. You kill us and they'll have something to say about it.
Marmoset:	I'm not going to kill you.
	He is.

He puts the gun into Clark's hand, pulls him to his feet and points him at Clara and Mignon.

Marmoset: You shoot them, or I kill your wife. Understand?

Clara: Ex-wife, Clark. She's left you.

Mignon: Deserted you.

Clara: She doesn't care.

Marmoset: Shoot them.

Clara: It's not fair—there's two of us, only one of her.

Lily stands in front of Clara and Mignon.

Lily: Well, Clark—I'd tell you to make up your mind, but you'd probably only put lipstick on your forehead.

Marmoset: You got five seconds before I take her out.

Lily: I've got an idea. Why don't you ask Mickey what to do?

She starts to laugh, and moves towards the door. She pauses in front of Rose and the Marmoset.

(*still laughing*) Never mind, Clark. Just remember—you're the only one with any standards.

Clark has followed her with the gun. He shoots. A moment of stunned silence. The Marmoset falls. Lily continues on to the door and exits.

Clark and Rose stare at each other. The Marmoset tries to crawl across the floor. Clara and Mignon stand on his hands.

Marmoset: So dies the Marmoset.

He dies.

Clara: We'll be off, then. Before the police get here. No need to mention our names.

Mignon claps Clark on the back.

Mignon:	Fantastic shot, Clark.
Clara:	One in a million.
	Clara and Mignon exit. During the excitement, Chance and Edith have discovered each other.
Edith:	We'll be going too, Rose.
Chance:	Great party.
Edith:	But Slim and I have got a lot to talk about.
Chance:	Ciao.
	Chance and Edith exit.
Rose:	Well, who would have thought? A happy ending.
	She crosses to the couch and slowly sits down. She leans forward, takes off one of her shoes and pours blood out of it. The bullet has passed straight through her and into the Marmoset. The lights start to fade.
Clark:	Rose?
	Rose leans back and sighs. The sound of the baby crying begins softly, getting louder. The crocodile rises slowly into the window.
	Lily?
	He sees the crocodile and lets out a scream.
	Rose!
	He runs to Rose and shakes her. She is dead. The crying gets louder and louder. The gathering darkness is lit with flashes. The walls and ceiling seem to tremble.
	Lily! Rose!
	The crocodile reaches up and raises the mask off its head. It is Gerald. He is laughing. Clark searches wildly for the source of the crying.
	Don't cry! Don't cry! Where are you?

He realises the crying is coming from inside himself and starts laughing hysterically. The walls collapse inward and the ceiling shudders down, closing over Clark. It is a gigantic crocodile mouth, stretching across the entire set. The crying dies away.

The sound of a starter motor is heard, then an engine kicking into life. The eyes of the giant crocodile light up like headlights.

A light comes up on Lily and Rose sitting in a driver's seat on top of the crocodile. Rose looks at Lily.

Rose: I thought you were dead?

Lily: No sense of smell.

Pause.

Rose: Where are we going?

Lily looks at her and smiles. The lights slowly fade as they drive on through the night.

The End

The Temptations of St Max

The Temptations Of

Feminist or Fraud?

Somewhere in the cavernous
Vatican vaults reportedly lies a
mural of Pope John (855 - 858)
giving birth to a baby.
Yes, not only did a woman
in disguise attain the highest
office in the Catholic Church -
she also indulged herself
on the way.

BATS

#1 in a set of 4   book now!

Phone 384 9507 Sept 2 - 25

The Temptations Of

Piles of Piety?

St. Simeon Stylites
decided the best way to
get closer to God
was to sit on top
of a pillar ten feet high.
Not satisfied he raised
the pillar to sixty six feet
and proceeded to spend
thirty seven years perched
on top.

BATS

#2 in a set of 4   book now!

The Temptations Of

Flesh or Food?

Why is St. Agatha patron saint
of bakers and bell - makers?
The answer lies in strangely
shaped mounds she is depicted
as carrying on a platter.
Assumed to be loaves of bread,
they are in fact
her own breasts, cut off
by torturers.

BATS

#3 in a set of 4   book now!

Phone 384 9507 Sept 2 - 25

The Temptations Of

Saintly Sponsorship?

St. Clare is invoked against
diseases of the eye
and for good weather.
In the twentieth century
her ability to forecast
doom by clairvoyant vision
has granted her the title
of Patron Saint
of Television.

BATS

#4 in a set of 4   book now!

Ken:

You could argue that this was the one where it all went wrong. My previous plays—with Rebecca and without—had been on a steady track upwards, culminating in the Wellington hit that was *Blue Sky Boys*. Now my new play, *The Temptations of St Max*—written and directed by only me—was set to fly . . . Instead, reviews were uniformly mixed. They all liked some things but were baffled by others, and the majority of the (less than capacity) audience weren't sure what to make of it. This was the production where I paid all the actors' BATS bar tabs and that was their sole recompense.

Best to draw a veil over it?

No—this play was great. Not perfect. But wild, colourful and funny. It was a rampaging beast, not unlike the play's untidy and downright rude woolly mammoth-like representation of the Catholic Church, which the Pope rode crazily around the stage in the middle of proceedings. If the shrieking, skeletal pontiff barely had control of his mount, I think that I, as writer/director of *The Temptations of St Max,* had a more secure seat on my creation. There was method to the madness.

The inception of all this mayhem was a *Reader's Digest* article. The copy of *Reader's Digest* was dated 1975—one in a stack of back-issues in a doctor's or dentist's waiting room in perhaps the early 80s. I must have had it quite a long time before doing anything with it, the yellowing pages sitting in a drawer, slowly ripening. Do they even have *Reader's Digest* any more? Back then, it was as ubiquitous in waiting rooms as *National Geographic. Life's*

Like That, Humour in Uniform, Laughter: the Best Medicine—as a kid I would rack my brains for a comic anecdote that might earn me $100. Nothing ever occurred—I guess my life wasn't 'like that'. Anyway, I read this article about modern-day martyr Maximilian Kolbe, who sacrificed his life at Auschwitz to save another prisoner, and then I actually had to do that thing you see in the movies of tearing out the pages while pretending not to. I didn't make a habit of that, so why this story?

Because it bugged me. And that's the main cause of writing—plays or anything else. A grain of sand somehow drifts into your shell and it irritates you. It irritates you and you can't get it out again, so you start to build something round it. You go through a long process which produces something (hopefully) smooth and lustrous—a combination of that aggravating grain of life and your view of the universe—which swings your world back into balance. And, who knows, other people might see it and think it's a beautiful pearl.

I knew you couldn't strictly rely on the *Reader's Digest*—but even allowing for their slant on things, it seemed the basic facts of Max Kolbe's self-sacrifice were incontrovertible. A number of prisoners were arbitrarily selected to undergo horrible deaths by thirst and starvation—and Kolbe had stepped forward to offer himself in place of a man with children, Francis Gajowniczek. Kolbe's action was unsought, unexpected; it shone like a shaft of light in the darkness of Auschwitz. And something about it got under my skin. It was this: I was reading about someone who was undoubtedly a better man than I was or would ever be. I knew that if I had been in Max's shoes at the time of selection for the starvation bunker, I would have kept my head down and hoped for the best. I would have been grateful to have been spared. I definitely would not have offered up my life to save someone else—someone I didn't know. In doing so, Max Kolbe showed himself to be a superior human being to me. None of us like that sensation, but I could have accepted it if I didn't think everything that motivated Kolbe was wrong. Everything he believed in—his conception of life and death, where he was coming from and where he believed he was going to—I thought was a hopeless and tawdry fiction. His superpowers were based on his

belief in a lie (not even a very convincing one), and to swallow it
Kolbe must have been both credulous and naïve. And this made me
feel superior to him. In fact, when I researched him further, I found
that Kolbe's theology was made up of a particularly sentimental and
sticky mother-fixated devotion to the 'Immaculate' Virgin Mary.
God barely came into it.

So . . . cognitive dissonance; two truths that won't fit together
and cause friction, leading to story.

There was no way you could have convinced Maximilian Kolbe
he was wrong about the afterlife. He was impervious to logic or
anyone else's point of view. Only the evidence of his own senses
might crack his armour. So in my story, Max had to be dead, and
confronted by something very different to what he'd expected. I
wanted to demolish the creaky source of his power and see what
he would do then. If I could force his view of the universe into
alignment with mine, would he still do what he had done? Would
he still be a better man than me?

My mother's mother was Catholic, so as a baby I was baptised.
That's the full extent of my involvement. I never went to church, I
was not indoctrinated in a Catholic school, I was not beaten by nuns
or molested by priests. I don't believe in God or the Devil, heaven
or hell. Like most people, I have a sense of spirituality, but my only
interest in religion is from the point of view of human psychology.
I'm not an admirer of the Vatican or of many popes. I don't like
exploitation or preying on people's fears or vulnerabilities—but
there are plenty of institutions in the world that do that. All I'm
saying is, I don't have a personal bone to pick with the Catholic
Church. I'm interested in the here and now—how to live my life
and be some kind of fully functioning human being. So I wrote this
play to find out whether I was going to teach Maximilian Kolbe a
lesson—or whether he was going to teach me one.

My voice in the play is that of Ludwik/St Christopher—or so I
thought. He's the smart guy; he's got all the clever arguments and
the sharp one-liners. But his motivation is negative. He can't stand
to see someone with their faith intact. Scratch a cynic and you find
a disappointed idealist. Underneath it all, he hurts. His is a soul in
pain.

Already I was making discoveries . . .

Like Ludwik/Christopher, the other four rejected ex-saints have consistent personalities and drives, whether they are pretending to be Auschwitz inmates or demons, or dropping their disguises and revealing themselves. St Walburga/Zebrowski represents the corporal, the bodily; she's a seething, fleshly tub of appetites, pagan and primal, all the tidal urges that religion seeks to cauterise—which is precisely why she had to be purged from the canon of Saints. St Simeon/Howictz is a pedant. Self-centred and smug, he is a religious accountant, confident that, in following whatever manmade rules and regulations are put in front of him, he will do better than his fellow. He cares for nobody but himself; his religion is exclusionary and truly useless in that it benefits no one. St Rose/Kubit is a masochistic religious fanatic—full of sick fantasies and incoherent anger—whose aberrations are excused, tolerated and actively encouraged (for a time) under the banner of holiness. St Agatha/Stemler is all about fear of death—as a saint, she suffers torture rather than recant and faces death without fear. But this turns out to have been a lie: it never happened—instead, she is left terrified of her own mortality, of her tininess in an indifferent universe, of the futility of human life and death. These are all aspects of ourselves which we grapple with and which threaten to drive us to despair, which separate us from others, drag us away from the possibility of a communal life and bury us alone in our weaknesses. The saints express their particular human fallibilities—first, while pretending to be a companion of Kolbe's in the bunker, then again as the unacceptable, booted-out saints they really are. They make progress, they have their arcs, they work through their problems—their senses of rejection, betrayal and disillusionment. Ganging up to torment Kolbe proves to be therapeutic. Kolbe ultimately unites this disparate, disappointed bunch of wild things with new energy and direction—with faith.

And that was the best thing. The ending changed on me as I wrote towards it. I had begun to fear that my arguments—the arguments I put in the mouth of St Christopher—were so crushing that there would be no withstanding them. Poking holes in holiness was like shooting fish in a barrel. The deficiencies of organised religion were too numerous to itemise; the arbitrariness of human suffering blindingly obvious; Kolbe's attachment to his 'Immaculate' too Freudian for words; and all his obsessive self-sacrifice far too easily flipped on its head to show him striving towards his eternal reward in heaven and his sainthood on Earth. If that wasn't enough, history provided me with the killer blow; the massive and cruel cosmic irony that the man Kolbe sacrificed himself for did indeed survive Auschwitz only to have to confront the loss of his children— the children that Kolbe's sacrifice supposedly had been all about. Instead of a happy ending, Kolbe had delivered this poor guy into a purgatory of grief and guilt. Play that card right, and St Maximilian Kolbe was going to fold like a wet newspaper. And I did play it— via Christopher—with all the cunning, guile and exquisite timing I could muster. And it had the desired effect, except that I no longer desired it. It made me feel sick—and sad.

Kolbe needed help—I needed help. We found it at the still centre of the story. Not the blustering, brawling saints overcome by ennui, or Kolbe's mechanical cant (now in the dust anyway)—but in the humble old man who had suffered so much, who seemed to have lost all. In the end we looked to him to tip the universe this way or that, and held our breath . . . There was no denying Gajowniczek's misery, in the camp and after, his guilt and shame at his own weakness, his confusion in the face of greater powers, both temporal and universal, which made him a cog in their machine but robbed him of the sight and touch of his sons, leaving him childless to face his long, lingering dead-end. But in life, as in the play, that old man could smile. He knew what he had suffered, but he could still say of Father Kolbe the simple sentence that made all the difference: 'He gave me life. And life is beautiful.'

Life is indeed beautiful. And the human spirit, if not indestructible, is at least absurdly resilient. I learnt that by writing this play—and it answered something deep within me. I've heard that one key to understanding dreams is that you are everything in the dream. The same is true of plays. Every voice in *The Temptations of St Max* is mine—including the scarred smiling old man, and even (or especially) Max, who in the end chooses to believe just because; who chooses to have faith and help his fellow because that seems right to him; who believes that, whatever happens, life is beautiful.

I would say 'Thank God'—except I still don't believe in God. It wasn't that kind of a revelation.

The Temptations of St Max was written because I was awarded a playwright's bursary from the QEII Arts Council (now Creative New Zealand) in March 1992. I remember the award as being $16,000, and it was a huge break for me. It was going to support me for at least six theatre-dedicated months, and I knew I would be able to use that time to write more than one play. As well as *St Max*, I also wrote *John, I'm Only Dancing* that year. In the three years since *JISM*, there had been *Blue Sky Boys* in Wellington, but most of my writing life had been TV sketch shows and corporate videos. There were now also two kids at home. The bursary meant I could say no to a few things and relax back into writing for stage. I had been sharing an illegally sublet office space on Allen Street with Gary Henderson, but around this time I moved into my own office in the Hope Gibbons Building, on the corner of Taranaki and Dixon Streets. It's this space I associate with the writing and production of *St Max*. The office was at the back of the building, large and mostly unfurnished, with only one small window that overlooked an alley. A lot of writing came out of that blank-canvas room with its sun-faded orange curtains. It's now part of a flash gym, but I like to think I sweated as much as any of its subsequent occupants.

With *St Max*, though, I remember the writing as coming easily to me. I was happy to be following my nose and very much amusing myself with where that was taking me. I freed myself up to be irreverent, subversive, scatological—and also poetic. *Blue Sky Boys* had been naturalistic—more naturalistic than anything I'd written previously—and after the discipline of that, I wanted to get back to some juicy language. I wanted the visual images to be poetic—as befitted a play taking place in the afterlife—but also the spoken word to be flexible enough to descend to the gutter and soar to the heavens. I was a poet before I was a dramatist, and it was with a sense of release that I let the words flow.

To further lift the play away from naturalism, I also thought about song. The history of the Catholic Church gives you such great reference points—from the visual art it has inspired, to the language, to the music and singing. I heard a kind of music in the play, and with six multi-tasking actors, I decided it would be all about voice, a cappella singing—but not psalms, chants or any 'straight' church singing. So what could it be? In a somewhat tenuous thematic connection, I chose 70s music. Firstly, that was the period when the real Max Kolbe was being fast-tracked to canonisation—so, notionally, it was also when the action of the play was occurring. Secondly, the extravagant emotionalism of pop music of the time (including disco) seemed overripe and baroque to me in a way that reflected the excess of Catholicism and also the saturated intensity of style I saw this play as having on stage. Thirdly, I loved those songs. Tear-jerkers like *Wildfire*, *Daddy Don't You Walk So Fast* and *Green, Green Grass of Home*; the ornate Manhattan-hustle-isms of *Disco Inferno* or *More Than a Woman*; the faux R'n'B sincerity of *Float On*; and best of all, the opening number (not sung by the cast, but thundering through the speakers like armageddon), Hot Chocolate's overwrought *Emma*, as recontextualised by the Sisters of Mercy to become the gothic clanking knell of doom. That track was supplied readymade from an obscure vinyl B-side. I went on to place the other songs in contexts where they could simultaneously underpin the emotion and comment on it ironically; heart and mind tussling with one another in a way that spoke to the left brain versus right brain push/pull of our relationship with religion. Sincere feeling or manipulation—can't it be both?

Once *The Temptations of St Max* was written, I tried to set up a theatre company—Flying Wedge Theatre—to do locally written plays (including my own) and community theatre, and got a promise of funding from the Arts Council to support it. But that scheme crumbled away in the wake of the financial disaster of the season of *Blue Sky Boys* I supported in Auckland at the end of 1992. I lost what nerve I had for putting my money where my mouth was. Backing out of the larger plan for Flying Wedge, I was able to retain $8000 of the funding to put on *The Temptations of St Max* at BATS in September of 1993.

Okay, so this was now happening. And it was up to me, directing my own work for the first time since *Truelove*, to find the team who would attempt to cram heaven, hell and everything in between onto the earthly dimensions of the BATS stage.

Mick Rose, who first starred as the policeman in *Flybaby*, signed up for the titular role. Mick's family are Jewish, so he had to really think himself into the sandals of the uber-Catholic Max Kolbe. I remember, towards the end of rehearsals, going round to Mick's place in Island Bay one evening to talk about Max's track through the play. After two hours of intense discussion, we were only halfway— but Mick seemed reassured that I had at least thought the thing through and the character had some sort of interiority, rather than being 100% made up of religious mania. Emma Kinane brought the same commitment she'd shown in her axolotl costume in *JISM* to her role of Beerbaum/St Walburga, with all the carnal appetites and transgressive moments the role required. I'd known Jed Brophy for years through BATS shows, and he was the first actor to play the role of Don Everly when *Blue Sky Boys* was initially presented at the Playmarket Playwrights' Conference in 1988. Jed's physicality and verve made him perfect for the faith-scalding devil's advocate impact character of Ludwik/St Christopher. Bronwyn Bradley was not long graduated from Toi Whakaari, and brought a beautiful, weary decency to her role of Stemler/St Agatha—exemplified in the not-this-again way she dug a bullet out of her head and flicked it aside. Jeff Boyd was older and had been working as an actor in Wellington for years—I loved his smug pedantry as Howictz and his bafflement as St Simeon Stylites about why people might think sitting on top of a pole for 37 years was not a good use of time. He also pitched his Pope cameo brilliantly, and in rehearsal added 'Virgin cold-pressed' to the prayer to the Immaculate. I had also known Dra McKay for years, without us actually working on a play together. Dra's combination of serenity and energy was perfect to bring out both the barbed wire and the innocence in Kubit, and the loose-unit St Rose of Lima.

Next the task was to assemble the other creators, equally weighted with the actors, who would give the play the theatrical and transformative feel I envisaged. Set design was major—and Andrew Moyes was a lucky find. He designed and built a set of levels, one that could open out and out again. Framed in metal with a prison-like ceiling grille which was intermittently lifted on rattling chains to become the grim gates of heaven, and which were in turn cast crashing downwards by the transfigured Max, the set effectively conveyed the claustrophobia of a starvation bunker; the lurid underground of an imagined hell; the tedium of a light-industrial installation in a never-ending desert; and finally the rain and the greening of that same desert into a sense of expansive garden. Consider that as your challenge as you stand on the modest stage of an empty BATS, sizing it up. Andrew didn't blink and brought the whole thing off incredibly well. Murray Lynch told me recently that when he thinks about how much can be done in the BATS space, he thinks of *The Temptations of St Max*. We used the foyer as well as the upstairs dressing room, cutting what is now known as the 'suicide door' entrance through the wall and mounting lights in the dressing room to represent the final exit to heaven and beyond.

A key moment came when lighting designer Paul O'Brien queried whether it had to rain real water at the end of the play. He was rigging hell lights under the dais on the floor, and a regularly flooded stage was going to make life more difficult for him. I opened my mouth to answer, but Andrew got there first. 'If the director says it's gotta rain—it's gotta rain.' Paul shrugged and sealed up the dais so no one got electrocuted. Paul's lighting was another crucial factor in giving a sense of growth, transformation and widening out across the play. Things started dark, with slashes of white (and slide-projected titles), then sepia and grubby, with a shaft of sunlight in the bunker. Next was the thermal bubbling and broiling of hell, followed by the flat, uninspiring light of the desert of death, then bright beams of hope in the distance and the chlorophyll green-and-gold realisation of the script's final (impossible) stage direction, 'The desert blooms.' Helping that last transformation were beaten copper wall-washers constructed specially by Paul. At each point of change, the playing space, the set and the lighting expanded simultaneously. If the actors had failed to show up one night, the set and the lighting by themselves could have effectively told the story on an emotional level.

Kate Hawley's distressed and layered costumes also contributed to that sense of transformation. Actors could literally peel off a layer as their characters revealed themselves and find a different colour, tone and physicality beneath. The reveal of Kubit's barbed-wire girdle was particularly gory and effective. Tim Denton is credited as providing 'moving images', which meant he designed and constructed the large-scale creepy puppet of Mary and the Church Beast ridden by the emaciated Pope, with his skeletal, grasping arms. Everyone who saw the play seems to remember the Church Beast shitting gold—after everything else is forgotten, I think that will probably be the one image people retain. It was so gloriously inappropriate and unnervingly accurate in the way the soft, gold turds hit the floor and flattened—and also strangely cute, as the little stubby tail lifted and then waggled happily throughout.

Musical director Michael Williams, Emma Kinane's other half, created the choral arrangements for the songs and coached the cast through them, as did choreographer Sally Stopforth with some strategically placed dance routines. I also enjoyed working with Marty Roberts as PA/stage manager; anyone who has followed Marty's theatre career since will know he's no slouch as a theatre wizard himself. Taken all together, this was a seriously talented and imaginative creative crew, and they pitched themselves determinedly into tackling the challenges that the script threw at them. I knew at the time I was lucky to have this team (including the actors), but looking back I find myself marvelling at whatever crossroads of chance brought them all together to work with such expertise, invention and commitment on both my crazy idea and a low-paying BATS show.

Publicity was innovative and widespread. We produced a collect-the-set series of fliers, each with details of a dodgy saint. Our main poster image showed Mick as an ecstatic Max, lifting his face to the mercy of rain. It avoided—but only just—looking like an ad for a shower system. In the lead-up we had two teaser newsprint posters plastered up around town. To give some sense of the play's dialectic, one said 'Life Is Beautiful', the other, 'Eat the Priest'. Some time later, on TV, there was one of those regular 'behind the scenes' looks at prostitution, and in the background of an interview in a Vivian Street brothel, I was delighted to spot the 'Beautiful' poster. Someone had liked it enough to steal it. Couldn't see if they had the other one up, though . . .

A couple of peripheral things connected the production at BATS to my early days there. Colleen Foss, originator of the Bit Players, took care of front of house, and Rebecca performed *Polythene Pam* (directed by Simon Bennett) as a 6pm show before *St Max*.

We did 37% across the three-week run (according to my report to the Arts Council), incurred an overall loss of about $1100, and no one in the co-op got paid. But everyone brought their best game every night—heaven and hell—and no one complained. At least, not to me. All those guys were great—and still have my gratitude.

Also, five of us were nominated in various categories for that year's Chapman Tripp Theatre Awards, including me as a director for Most Original Production, so that was nice . . .

I think it was Elric Hooper whose main advice to New Zealand playwrights was 'Don't write about Nazis'. I didn't exactly do that—but *The Temptations of St Max* was a massive show on an unpopular theme. The big questions did not translate to big box-office takings. Maybe people weren't thinking and wondering about these things as they once had? We did a benefit performance for the Āwhina Centre, which supports people with AIDS, and some of the workers there were nuns. I was a bit concerned when these middle-aged to elderly nuns turned up in the audience that night, but interestingly they seemed to really get it; not necessarily agree with it, but certainly relate to what the play was talking about much more than other often younger BATS-goers, who assumed the whole thing was a giant pisstake that was mysteriously not funny at times.

Practically, I learnt a couple of writing lessons. One was that, in the small-scale BATS environment where doubling of roles had become common, some audience members assumed that the actors were playing different characters rather than pretending (to Max) to be different people, then stripping away disguises to reveal who they really were. If you miss that and the fact that the setting is not changing but also revealing itself, the play does indeed become fractured and baffling. I had not set up the transformative convention strongly enough in the writing—and fatally, in my direction of the play, I had resorted to doubling in one scene where Jeff, Dra and Emma played the Pope and two supposed recipients of miracles. All three wore masks, but nevertheless it was confusing.

Those are the kinds of things you learn in a first production—

you're trying to get so much up on that stage that inevitably you're going to win some and lose some. You take those lessons back into the writing and the next production will be all the stronger for it. Yet, as is so often the case in New Zealand theatre, there has been no further production of *The Temptations of St Max*. It's a pity, because we got so much right; so much light, colour, darkness, emotion and faith packed into that small container.

I've sat on this story and this script ever since. Now I think I understand something about it. It should be a musical. It wanted to be a musical back then but I didn't have the skill or the resources. Perhaps its true incarnation lies in reshaping the play with songs; songs which are a direct line to emotion, which can key into the already existing style but propel that further to reach escape velocity.

Could I—should I—come back to a script a quarter of a century later? Maybe that grain of sand is still in there somewhere . . .

The actors and crew were not the only ones stumbling away from the season of *St Max*, mumbling to themselves, 'I need to make some money,' and ruefully acknowledging that theatre was not the place to do it. A TV drama series was about to take over my life for the next few years, and when I found my way back to the stage, it wouldn't be this stage. There was one more play at BATS in 1995—*Horseplay*—but after that it would be 17 years before I had a show on there again.

Emma Kinane:

I thought *St Max* was a stunning play. It wasn't kitchen sink; it was ideas and beliefs and death and pain and laughter and horror and singing. It was so unreal it was more real than a real thing. *The Church Beast shat gold!* But it didn't make money. I don't remember why; maybe the budget was too high, maybe there wasn't a big enough audience. It certainly didn't feel like a flop—the season felt like a triumph. But for whatever reason there was no money for the co-op to divide afterwards, and Ken paid all our bar tabs, which was kind and in a way hurt more than not making any money. Theatre is hard.

As Zebrowski, I remember joyously leaping about the stage

morphing from a backing singer to a dying man, from a puppeteer inside the huge Church Beast to a saint clamouring to enter the gates of heaven. And all the while I watched the wonderful Mick Rose turn himself inside out as poor old serious, suffering Max. My God, he worked hard. So what if he got all the glowing reviews? I decided I definitely had the better deal.

The costume designer had drawn an idea for Zebrowski that excited and terrified me. The top half was almost totally deconstructed (read: non-existent) and my boobs were destined to flop around freely and visibly. Basically, I was going to be topless. Zebrowski's character was all about fleshly appetites, so it was appropriate, and intellectually I got all enthusiastic and personal growth-ish about it. I was still breastfeeding my son, plus I was overweight, so there was plenty of personal growth to be flung around. Thanks to the wonders of modern maternity bras, probably neither Ken nor the costumier realised just how much would be flung nor how low they'd swing without support. I tried not to think about how distracting it would be for the audience and how uncomfortable I might feel once we got to the crunch point of me actually having to take my top off in the green room, keep it off backstage and then walk out onto the stage. Topless. I just focused on how brave I was to even contemplate it. I was doing this for *theatre*. Character, schmaracter. Who had headspace to think about character when I was going to do a show topless? Me. Fat, unattractive, character roles-only me. It was all I thought about or talked about. When people asked me what project I was working on, I told them all about my upcoming boobfest. People must have thought *St Max* was a burlesque. I shudder at the memory of myself at this time. But then, for some reason, the costume design was altered. I have no idea if my uncomfortable hyperfocus was the catalyst, or if Ken and the designer merely changed their minds, but that boob-o-rama costume (or lack of it) never eventuated. At the time I remember saying I was disappointed and probably bored my castmates senseless bemoaning the loss of opportunity to challenge myself in this way, but the pathetic truth is that I was grateful.

I'm from an Irish Catholic background, so the concept of a play peopled with saints felt quite normal and cosy to me. The fact that they were all insane was likewise not beyond my experience. My grandmother's favourite saying, yelled skywards in martyred tones, was 'Jesus, Mary, Joseph and all the saints . . . Take note!', ending in a vicious point to the sinner or situation that was her current cross to bear. All quite normal.

Michael Williams, vocal arranger:

It was one of the stranger briefs I've been given. Write a capella vocal arrangements of 70s disco numbers for faux saints to taunt Max with. 'What was Ken thinking?' I wondered. But when I saw the show, it was like, 'But what else could it have been?' I wish I knew where those arrangements wound up . . .

Gary Henderson:

The Temptations of St Max was produced after Ken's Everly brothers play, *Blue Sky Boys* and was a real story about a real person from history. While *Blue Sky Boys* was a fairly conventional narrative with the added drive and excitement of live music, *St Max* seemed to be a return to the earlier style of Ken and Rebecca. The story could have been told in a straight-line biopic style. Ken, however, wrote and directed it in a symbolic world. The devil appeared as a real person; the choices of purity or martyrdom hung above Max in the form of two gymnasts' rings—he leapt and grasped both. In the most striking image, the Pope arrived cackling madly, riding on the back of the Catholic Church, a monstrous beast constructed by puppet maestro Tim Denton, which lumbered across the BATS stage shitting lumps of gold. Ken was again translating poetic images into physical ones.

The Temptations of St Max

by Ken Duncum

Originally performed at BATS Theatre, 2–25 September 1993

Maximilian Kolbe	Mick Rose
Zebrowski (St Walburga)	Emma Kinane
Ludwik (St Christopher)	Jed Brophy
Stemler (St Agatha)	Bronwyn Bradley
Howictz (St Simeon)	Jeff Boyd
Kubit (St Rose)	Dra McKay
Director	Ken Duncum
Set Design	Andrew Moyes
Lighting Design	Paul O'Brien
Costume Design	Kate Hawley
Moving Images	Tim Denton
Vocal Arrangements	Michael Williams
Choreography	Sally Stopforth
Stage Manager	Martyn Roberts
Publicity	Liz Byrne
Operator	David Harker
Assistant Stage Manager	Catherine Wilton

The Temptations of St Max

A Note on the Play:

The setting of the play does not change; instead it is progressively revealed to Kolbe as his perception widens. At first he is induced to believe he is still in the starvation bunker at Auschwitz, then that he is in hell. Finally he perceives the reality of the wide empty desert of Death around him and the fortress-like 'heaven' before whose gates he stands.

Similarly the other characters do not change; they cast off disguises and reveal themselves. They are all ex-saints, expelled from the church canon and therefore from a more comfortable existence in the 'heaven' outside which they still cluster. Bored and jealous of a new wave of saints, they band together to torment Kolbe at the point of his entry into the canon/heaven. First they pose as fellow Auschwitz prisoners in the starvation bunker, then as denizens of hell, finally revealing themselves as rejected saints. St Christopher—in the guise of Ludwik—is the ringleader in this attempt to mock and destroy Kolbe's faith. But dissension grows in the ranks, leading some of the saints to help Kolbe, sometimes by 'channelling' or seeming to become people who knew him, most significantly Gajowniczek, the man he saved.

Staging:

A raised rectangular dais protrudes from a structure comprised of grids. A wide circle encloses the dais and an area of floor to signify the circumference of the starvation bunker. A barred ceiling over this area is progressively lifted higher and higher, like a drawbridge, in short juddering bursts throughout the play. Once this is perpendicular to the back wall, it forms the gates of Heaven. Props lie scattered about in the shadows outside the circle.

Darkness. The Sisters of Mercy version of 70s angst classic 'Emma' is overpowering. In flashes of white light, the actors play out the stations of Maximilian Kolbe's martyrdom. He is selected with nine others for death by starvation in a bunker at Auschwitz. Passing through despair and suffering, comforted always by Kolbe, the others die one by one. At the last, Kolbe raises his arms for the lethal injection, forgiving the guard who carries it out. He dies.

The music has drowned out any sound, but titles have accompanied the action. They are:

1. Auschwitz, 31 July 1941
2. Following the escape of a prisoner . . .
3. . . . ten men are selected to be starved to death.
4. A Franciscan monk, Maximilian Kolbe, . . .
5. . . . volunteers to take the place of a man . . .
6. . . . who cries out for his children.
7. Over the next fifteen days, . . .
8. . . . in an underground cell . . .
9. . . . without food or water, . . .
10. . . . Kolbe leads the men in song and prayer, . . .
11. . . . helping each of them to die.
12. Finally Kolbe, the last survivor, . . .
13. . . . is killed by injection of carbolic acid.
14. 1982: Maximilian Kolbe is canonised.

The music is over. The twisted bodies of the dead lie strewn in the circle, which is the circumference of Max's prison. A dull, watered-down ray of light falls on the dais. A vision of Kolbe's mother/the Immaculate Virgin Mary approaches, crossing the perimeter of the circle.

Vision: Mundzio. Mundzio! Rise and shine, sleepyhead! Rise and shine. Saint Max.

            The Vision fades back over the line as Kolbe stirs, wakes.

Kolbe: Mother?

Kolbe touches his left arm, which is painfully stiff. He drags himself up onto his knees, where he is racked by a spasm of pain. He prays.

Dear little Mother. My Immaculate. You have given me to these poor souls—give me the strength that I do not fail them. Let them not feel how I tremble as I hold them, trembling.

He sees the body nearest to him, moves to it.

Kubit?

Before he can touch the body, a voice comes out of the darkness.

Ludwik: Dead.

Kolbe moves to the next.

Kolbe: Zebrowski?

The voice repeats.

Ludwik: Dead.

Kolbe goes to the next body.

All dead.

Kolbe peers into the shadows, straining his damaged eyesight.

Kolbe: Only the two of us left?

Ludwik: No. I'm dead too.

Ludwik moves painfully into the light.

If not this morning, then this afternoon for sure. Tonight in all certainty. Tomorrow morning beyond a doubt. Dead like them. Whether they wake up or not.

Kolbe touches his arm again. A memory flickers under

the surface.

Ludwik rouses the bodies.

WAKE UP!

The others begin to wake, groaning. Ludwik pushes Howictz, who collapses.

This one's on his way.

Stemler scrabbles away in fear.

Stemler: He's dying, isn't he? He's dying!

Ludwik returns to his corner.

Kolbe drags himself over to Howictz and, with an effort, raises him and supports his head.

Kolbe: Howictz?

Howictz speaks in a fading whisper.

Howictz: I'm so cold, Father.

Kolbe: There is a little sunlight. It will warm you.

Howictz: I can't—move.

Zebrowski: God, I'm thirsty.

Kubit: Shut up, Zebrowski.

Stemler: Water.

Kolbe tries to lift Howictz. He can't manage it in his weakened state. He looks at Stemler for help.

Kolbe: Stemler—

Stemler: Water.

Kolbe: Zebrowski—

Zebrowski: I dreamed of mountain streams.

Stemler: Water.

Zebrowski: Fresh and pure.

Kubit: Shut up, Zebrowski!

Kolbe half-lifts, half-drags Howictz towards the dais and the meagre shaft of light. He stops, exhausted, and looks up at Kubit, who is pacing restlessly, rhythmically flailing his arms against his sides, mumbling an indistinct rosary of disco lyrics.

Kolbe: Kubit—

Kubit looks Kolbe in the face, eyes shining crazily.

Kubit: We're the holy ones. We two. Only we understand what suffering is!

Kubit moves off. Kolbe looks towards Ludwik, who has been watching, silent.

Ludwik: Leave him. You'll no sooner get him up there than he'll cark, anyway.

Kolbe makes a superhuman effort and hauls Howictz up onto the dais. He lies there, gasping, beside Howictz, who squints up into the light.

Howictz: A little to the left would be nice, Father.

Kolbe moves him.

Zebrowski: God I'm hungry.

Kubit/Stemler: Shut up, Zebrowski!

Howictz: You will say a prayer, won't you, Father? We can't let the Day of the Assumption go unobserved.

Kolbe: The Assumption?

Howictz: You remember, Father? Yesterday was the vigil.

Kubit: You said a mass.

Kolbe: Of course.

He frowns.

After that—I can't [remember] . . . There was

something . . .

He touches the tender spot on his arm again—the site of the injection. He goes to push up his sleeve. Stemler grabs him by the arm.

Stemler: That man, Father, whose place you took . . .

Ludwik: Gajowniczek.

Stemler: Why him? Why not—me?

Kolbe: My son—

Stemler: No! You didn't know Gajowniczek! He was nothing to you!

Kolbe: His children . . .

Stemler: I've got eight kids! I'm a good Catholic!

Kolbe: He—cried out.

Kubit: Pansy.

Stemler: Don't you think I cried out inside?! But no, 'Be a man,' I thought! 'Don't give the bastards the satisfaction,' I thought!

Kolbe: I'm only one man.

Stemler: It should have been me! Why not me? Why do I have to die?!

Stemler collapses, crying.

Kolbe: I couldn't save you all.

Ludwik: Then why save any?

Zebrowski: I expect I was too fat to save.

Howictz: It's the squeaky hinge that gets the oil.

Kolbe: Stemler.

Stemler pulls away.

Stemler. We must accept our fate. And embrace

all our suffering in the knowledge that it is the fire which will purify us. The flame which will burn our souls clean.

Ludwik: There speaks a man with more than a passing affection for death. His own death.

Ludwik raises himself.

I bet you've been hopping into bed and snuggling up to your death every night for years—just like the rest of us do with our wives.

Kolbe: Don't despair.

Ludwik: The difference is you've had to wait all this time to consummate the relationship. To get a proper poke.

Zebrowski: God, I'm horny.

Kolbe: We have to believe that our sorrow—all this cruelty—is necessary.

Ludwik: Necessary for what?

Kolbe: For happiness. For the happiness of those who live after us.

Ludwik: Who gives a shit about them?!

Zebrowski: A shit.

Ludwik: I say let everyone else die. Let them die by the trainload! As long as I—I—I stay alive!

Zebrowski: There's nothing like a good shit.

Stemler: What if he's right? What if it's all for nothing!

Zebrowski: The innocent animal pleasure of dropping a log.

Ludwik turns away.

Kubit: Father, pray with us!

Howictz: Intercede with the Blessed Virgin for us!

Stemler: Pray for a miracle!

Zebrowski: Some of the best moments of my life.

Kolbe looks over at Ludwik.

Kolbe: Ludwik. Will you pray with us?

Ludwik moves back to his corner.

Zebrowski: Never to shit again. It's just too much!

He starts to blubber loudly.

Kubit/Stemler/Howictz: Shut up, Zebrowski!

Kolbe gathers them in with his prayer.

Kolbe: Our Immaculate, our little mother, bless us on this the most holy and happy day of your entry into Heaven. We, who so soon must follow after.

Stemler: Oh no!

Kolbe: Unite our souls here and let us each swear a holy contract with you. That we are willing to remain forgotten, comfortless, scorned and friendless in this terrible place, even though others return home.

Stemler: Oh no! Oh no!

Kubit: Yes, Father! Yes!

Kolbe: We are willing to die on this stone floor, surrounded by these stone hearts, abandoned by all, persecuted at every step—

Kubit: Yes! Yes!

Stemler: Oh no!

Kubit: Amen!

Howictz/Zebrowski: Amen.

Stemler: Ah! Ahh!

Kolbe takes Stemler by the shoulders, fixes him with his eyes and wills his strength into him.

Kolbe: Be brave a little longer, Stemler. Everything we see and suffer now will peel away. And we will stand in glory!

Stemler straightens. A look of determination comes into his face. He grasps Kolbe's arm.

Stemler: Amen, Father. Amen.

Kolbe sways a little, in pain and exhausted by the effort. He begins to recite the litany of the blessed Virgin Mary.

Kolbe: Holy Mary—

Others: Pray for us.

Kolbe: Holy Mother of God—

Others: Pray for us.

Kolbe: Holy Virgin of virgins. Mother of Christ, Mother of Divine Grace, Mother most pure. Mother most chaste . . .

As the prayer takes over, Kolbe straightens and a light comes into his face. The others cease the 'ora pro nobis' *and sing a Polish hymn, soaring with the sound of Kolbe's voice. Abruptly, the ceiling judders up with a clanking and crashing. The prisoners take it for signs of life outside.*

Howictz: It's the guard!

All except for Ludwik and Kolbe crowd desperately to the 'door', clamouring abjectly.

Howictz/Stemler/Zebrowski/Kubit: Water! Guard, please! Water! I beg of you!

Kolbe pays no attention and continues his prayer without faltering. The clamour of the others dies down as the guard passes by and disappears. The sight and sound of Kolbe still praying is felt as a reproach by them all.

Ludwik: So much for your holiness. If that guard had stopped to piss on you, you'd all have opened your mouths.

Howictz: And I suppose you've got a better idea?

Ludwik: Let's eat the priest.

Zebrowski: God, I'm starving.

Kubit/Howictz/Stemler: Shut up, Zebrowski!

Ludwik: Why not? He says he's here to help.

Zebrowski: Keep thinking I can smell—

Zebrowski sniffs, connoisseur-like.

Zebrowski: —hot sausage with mustard.

Howictz: Sausage.

Zebrowski: Or is it lemon meringue pie?

Stemler: Pie.

Ludwik sniffs.

Ludwik: Hey, who cut the cheese?

Stemler: Cheese.

They sniff the air and look over suspiciously at Kolbe.

Kubit: Forget about food. We can have all the food we want once we escape!

Stemler: Escape?

Kubit: It's simple. The next time the guard comes in, I'll drop on top of him and bite him to death. I'll shoot the other guards with his gun. We'll throw their corpses across the electric fence and I'll lie down across the barbed wire while you run over my body. Then we raid the officers' quarters, commandeer a staff car and, disguised as a high-ranking Nazi Glee Club, drive to the airstrip. We steal a plane, fly to Britain, retrain and re-arm, parachute back into Auschwitz, hand out guns and tanks to everyone, break out and win the war. So who's with me?

Silence.

Zebrowski/Howictz/Stemler: Food. Water. Water. Food. Food.

Kubit: You gutless bastards!

Kubit grabs Kolbe interrupting his prayer.

You'll help won't you, Father? You can get the guard in by creating a disturbance, and I'll tear his throat out!

Kolbe: Kubit—

Kubit: He'll never know what hit him!

Kolbe: We must be men of peace.

Kubit: Peace!

Kolbe: We must not hurt anyone.

Kubit: They're not anyone! They're Nazis!

Frustrated, Kubit is pacing, windmilling his arms into his abdomen.

Syphilitic, fornicating black-hearted Nazis!

Kolbe: We can't give in to hate.

Kubit: Coitus the Third Reich!

Howictz: Sshh.

Ludwik howls like a wolf, in concert with Kubit's curses.

Kubit: Oral sex to the SS!

Howictz: Ssshhh!

Kubit: You hear me, you Nazi nun-molesters!

Howictz: Don't make trouble!

Ludwik: We're being starved to death! What more trouble could we get in?

Kubit:	Intercourse Adolph Hitler up his droopy back passage!
Kolbe:	Kubit—anger and hatred can create nothing. Only love gives us creative power.
Ludwik:	Love! You can talk about love in here!
Kolbe:	A love without limits. Love, even for our torturers—
Stemler:	The SS!
Kolbe:	—who cannot harm us, but only betray themselves. Who only deny themselves the happiness of Heaven, which awaits us, which awaits all the oppressed peoples of this camp and of the world!
Howictz:	Well, not all the peoples—obviously, Father.
Kolbe:	Even here amongst the darkness and the smell of death, we can say we are invincible! Since we know the truth. A truth which guns, or lies, or cruelty are powerless to change.
Howictz:	I mean, Heaven hardly awaits the Jews.
	Kolbe looks blankly at him.
	Far be it from me to correct a Holy Father, Father— but the Church is quite clear on this point.
Kolbe:	This time would be better spent looking to our own souls.
Howictz:	I've done everything the Church asked of me. More! I daresay I can rely on my place in Heaven.
Kolbe:	There are many sins, but lack of charity is a grievous one.
Howictz:	Very good, Father! Or what are you saying? Some dirty, fornicating, Christ-killing Jew is going to waltz into Heaven ahead of me?
Kolbe:	I believe the Jews may know the Kingdom of Heaven.

Howictz gasps.

Howictz: Now that's heresy! I may not be in the priesthood, but I know black heresy when I hear it!

Kolbe: Howictz—

Howictz: I'll hear no more! Renegade priest! Wicked messenger!

Kolbe: Death approaches! It's here amongst us! What sense is there in arguing how many angels can dance on the head of a pin?

Howictz: Oh yes! Getting a bit worried now aren't we? Perfectly willing to stand there two minutes ago spouting stinking heresies by the yard!

Kolbe: Howictz—

Howictz: It's too late to back down now! The Church's position on hereticism is unshakeable! We'll soon see who goes spinning into the yawning jaws of Hell!

He draws himself up.

I'll be on the other side of the cell if anyone wants me.

He moves away a few steps, self-righteously turning his back on Kolbe. Zebrowski, who has gradually slumped semi-conscious to the floor, has begun twitching and uttering strangled sounds. Now he arches and gives out a long rattling exhalation.

Stemler: Oh no! He's dying! He's dying!

Zebrowski slumps limply.

Kolbe goes to him and cradles him in his arms.

Kolbe: Zebrowski.

Zebrowski opens his eyes dreamily.

Zebrowski: Father. I dreamed—I dreamed it was over.

Kolbe: I dream of nothing else.

Zebrowski: I was on a train. Going home. My mother and my father greeted me at the station. Everything was the same as when I was a boy.

Kolbe: *In nomine patris—*

Zebrowski: There was a band playing. To welcome me home.

Kolbe: *Et filie—*

Zebrowski: And I looked down the road—

Kolbe: *Et in spiritum sanctum.*

Zebrowski: —and there ran Mary.

The Mother/Mary 'vision' approaches again.

Vision: Mundzio!

Kolbe: Hail Mary, full of grace—

Zebrowski: Hair of gold and lips like cherries.

Unseen by Kolbe, who continues the Hail Mary, Kubit and Howictz step out of the circle where Kolbe can neither see nor hear them. Kubit and Howictz salute the Vision, singing 'Green, Green Grass of Home'.

She took my hand and led me around the other side of the train, where the crowd couldn't see us. She kissed me. I could feel her tongue in my mouth. She pulled up her dress, she wasn't wearing anything underneath.

Kolbe: My son—

Zebrowski has hold of Kolbe's clothes so he can't pull away.

Zebrowski: She was warm against me, rubbing me up and down. The train sheltered us from sight. But just as it was too late the wheels began to turn. The train started to pull out. I thought the carriages were full of cattle.

Kolbe: Zebrowski!

              Zebrowski clings on to Kolbe, pulling him down
              urgently.

Zebrowski: Then I saw it was people on their way to Auschwitz.
              Packed, standing up, naked. Hands pleading from
              every gap. Carriage after carriage of eyes.

              He squirms with humiliation.

              But I couldn't stop myself, Father. You know what I
              mean.

              The Vision retires. Kubit, Howictz, etc., are safely back
              in the circle. Kolbe has been too absorbed in Zebrowski
              to notice they have been gone.

Ludwik: You dirty bastard.

Zebrowski: Kiss me, Father! Kiss me!

              He throws himself on Kolbe in an excess of lust.

Kolbe: No, Zebrowski! No!

Zebrowski: At least we can scratch that itch! Give each other
              comfort!

              Kolbe escapes.

Kolbe: A man is a worm! The soul is all that is important!

              Zebrowski sits down and howls.

Zebrowski: He doesn't want me!

Kubit: You polluted flesh!

Kolbe: We're all in the hands of the Immaculate.

Zebrowski: One last bang! Is that too much to ask?

Kolbe: We live once. We die only once. It must be according
              to her pleasure, not our own.

Ludwik: And it's the pleasure of the Immaculate that you
              volunteered your life? To save this Gajowniczek? Any

idea what he's doing now? Out there? This man you 'saved'? He's starving himself to death.

Startled pause.

Kolbe: You lie.

Ludwik: I don't need to lie. I heard the guards laughing about it yesterday. Seems the guy feels so guilty about a priest dying in his place that he can't bear the thought of living any more.

Ludwik laughs. Stemler is shocked. He mumbles to himself.

Stemler: I shouldn't be here.

Kolbe: But he can't! It—

Ludwik: Makes a mockery of what you did? Makes it all seem futile?

Stemler: It's a mistake. It's all been a stupid mistake!

He rushes to the 'door'.

Guards! You can let me out! (*pointing at Kolbe*) He wants to die! Gajowniczek wants to die! That makes ten!

Kolbe: Stemler!

Stemler: Let me out! Let me out!

Kolbe: We must be steadfast! Remember our pact!

Stemler turns on Kolbe.

Stemler: No! NO! Don't make me feel guilty! I'm weak! I know I'm weak! Don't rub my face in it!

Kolbe: My child—I only want to make things easier for you—

Kolbe puts his hand out to Stemler. Stemler knocks the hand away.

Stemler:	No! Don't love me! Don't help me! Don't you see? I'd betray you in an instant to get out of here! Let you die; (*indicating Ludwik*) let him kill you! And eat you—yes, eat you!—to get you off my back!
Kolbe:	Eat me?
Ludwik:	Whoops—cat's out of the bag now.
Zebrowski:	Alright! Let's eat him! Drink him! Have sex with him! Something!

Kubit jumps forward to protect Kolbe.

Kubit:	He's a holy man! I'll kill the first bastard who touches him!

Howictz speaks up, still with his back turned resolutely.

Howictz:	I, of course, couldn't be party to cannibalism. The Church is quite clear on this point.

Ludwik shrugs.

	However, if I closed my eyes and someone were to place something in my mouth which they said was pork that they'd—found—well, it would be unchristian of me not to believe them.
Ludwik:	It's rare to find a man of your moral calibre.

Ludwik starts to move towards Kolbe.

Howictz:	He's a bit skinny, though, isn't he? What about Zebrowski instead?
Zebrowski:	NO!
Kubit:	Eat me!
Kolbe:	Ludwik, don't do this.
Ludwik:	The advantage of eating the priest—first—is that once he's gone, there'll be no one left to reproach us for doing it.
Kubit:	I offer myself as a sacrifice!

Ludwik: After that, we can revert to the law of the jungle and prey on the weakest until there's only one of us left.

Kubit: I'll start myself off if you like.

He starts savagely gnawing at his arm. The others ignore him.

Zebrowski: But won't that last one have to carry all the blame?

Ludwik: He can go mad and eat himself—that way we'll all be victims.

The others are impressed with this reasoning.

Kubit: Get back, you scum! None of you know what it is to be alight with holiness! With the suffering of God!

Kubit begins to work himself up, flailing his arms against his sides.

Like a burning sword! Piercing my flesh! My God hungers to be in me! Plunging into me over and over! I'm holy, Father!

He pulls up his shirt to show barbed wire wrapped round his waist, piercing his flesh. Old and new blood mingles in the wounds.

See how God infects me!

Kolbe is shocked at the pain and mutilation Kubit has caused himself.

Kolbe: My child!

He approaches Kubit, still proudly displaying his homemade torture device.

My poor, poor child! Let me help you. Let me take this away.

Kolbe tries to undo the wire. Kubit pulls away.

Kubit: No. It's my holiness, Father.

Kolbe: But you're in pain.

Kubit: God's pain. God's sweet sharp metal rain.

He begins to whack in convulsively against his sides again, hard and fast.

Hurting me. Hurting me, hurting me, hurting me!

Kolbe tries to restrain him.

Kolbe: No! You mustn't!

Kubit: Are you crazy!

Kubit breaks away from him angrily.

You want all the holiness for yourself! You're a greedy priest! You want all God's suffering!

Kolbe: Kubit—it is not God's will that you torture yourself!

Kubit evades Kolbe, moving back behind the others.

Kubit: You can't stop me! You can't stop me!

He seizes the barbed-wire girdle and savagely wrenches it back and forth. He gasps in agony and joy as blood flows freely down his waist. Kubit grins crazily at Kolbe.

You can't stop me being holy too!

Kolbe goes to step towards him, but Ludwik rises to block him.

Ludwik: Well, Father, would you like to say grace?

He advances slowly on Kolbe, Zebrowski having manoeuvred himself behind Kolbe. Stemler and Howictz studiously take no part, and Kubit watches.

Kolbe: Ludwik . . .Ludwik . . .

Ludwik and Zebrowski grab him. The three of them struggle, locked together.

For myself, I am prepared to die. I am prepared to sacrifice my life. I do not fear death. I fear—SIN!

He throws his attackers off and stands like a lion.

Kolbe: Your sin! That you should so corrupt and put
yourselves away from God. If I must, I will fight you
for your souls! Gratify your body with sin—and your
soul will starve to death within you!

The others pause, looking at each other.

Zebrowski: Well that puts a bit of a dampener on things.

*Ludwik laughs, genuinely amused. One by one the others
join in. The joke is not shared by Kolbe. There is a sense
of appearances being dropped, a conspiracy being sprung.
Kolbe is mystified and unnerved.*

Kolbe: Why do you laugh?

*The other characters move more and more freely and
energetically about the confined cell area, crisscrossing
around the alarmed and unnerved Kolbe. One by one
they cross the line and are gone.*

*Kolbe boggles. He spins around. Except for Ludwik, he is
alone in the cell.*

Ludwik: (*mockingly*) Mundzio!

Others: Mundzio!

Ludwik: Mundzio!

Others: Mundzio!

Kolbe: How do you know that name? Only my—

The Vision once more approaches.

Ludwik: Only your mother called you that.

Vision: Mundzio!

Kolbe turns and sees the Vision. He blanches white.

Whatever kind of man will you grow up to be?

Kolbe: (*almost whispering*) What is this?

Ludwik: Remember, Max? That time, as a child, you crept into the church to cry? So sad at disappointing her? How, as you knelt to ask our Holy Mother what kind of man you would become, you saw—standing in front of you—beautiful—smiling—so kindly . . .

Vision: Mundzio!

Two crowns appear.

Ludwik: And the two crowns she offered you—? One white for—

Vision: Purity.

Ludwik: The other red for—

Vision: Martyrdom.

Ludwik: The way she looked at you with such love, and said—

Vision: Mundzio, which will you choose?

Ludwik: Purity. Martyrdom. Martyrdom. Purity.

The others begin to sing 'Feel Like Makin' Love' by Bad Company. Kolbe looks round wildly.

Kolbe: It's the hunger. It's some sort of drug. The guards—they came and injected me with—

Ludwik: —carbolic acid. To end it. To kill you.

Kolbe grips his arm and rocks painfully.

Kolbe: No!

Ludwik: You lifted your arms to the needle and forgave the guard as he did it!

Kolbe: It can't be!

Ludwik: You're dead, Max! Dead!

Kolbe tears his sleeve off from the shoulder, revealing the ugly black bruise extending up his arm from the injection site, tracing the path of the acid to his heart. Kolbe is horrified.

Just as the Immaculate promised you as a boy, when she showed you the two crowns!

The Vision holds out the two crowns, clashing them together in the chorus of the song.

Ludwik: And asked you—

Vision: Mundzio, which will you choose?

Ludwik: And you replied—

Kolbe resists.

Kolbe: I can't be dead.

Ludwik: And you said—

Kolbe: How can I be dead? If this is not Heaven!

Ludwik: AND YOU SAID—!

Kolbe: I chose purity!

Ludwik: It's a sin to tell a lie!

Kolbe: Give me martyrdom!

Ludwik: Close but no banana! Child, child, I saw you! Alone in the cold church, in the half-dark of Poland, lost in the mud of a continent bent on revolution and war! Lonely, crying—sure your mummy and daddy didn't love you! Horses galloping in circles! The sound of hooves in your head! Purity. Martyrdom. Martyrdom. Purity. You said—

Kolbe: I will take—BOTH!!

He lunges upwards, grasping a crown in each hand. Completing the circuit, he is electrocuted, spasming. The song reaches a crescendo. The crowns rise up into the air, dragging Kolbe with them. He hangs above the scene, crucified, jerking with the voltage of his religious rapture. The song ends.

Kolbe hangs still and silent.

Ludwik: How greedy is the boy who will give you all of his
              cake and none of his holiness? Maximilian Kolbe—
              THIS IS YOUR AFTERLIFE!

              Come on down, Max!

              *Kolbe's grip fails. He falls and is caught by the others.
              The scene darkens.*

Kolbe: Where am I?!

Ludwik: Well, where the hell do you think?

              *Fire roars up—hot and brilliant—melting, fusing,
              transforming the scene into the (classic, much-loved and
              still-breathtaking-after-all-these-years) fires of hell. At
              the same time Ludwik/Devil and all his demons rocket
              into The Trammps* Disco Inferno—*production number
              in the first degree. The flames surge up to overcome
              Kolbe.*

Kolbe: NOOOOO!!!!

              *At the peak of Kolbe's torture, Ludwik calls an abrupt
              halt to proceedings.*

Ludwik: Stop!

              Everyone stops.

              God, this is so tedious!

              He turns to Kolbe.

              Is this your idea of what Hell is like? Lakes of fire?

Kubit: Tortures of the Damned?

Zebrowski: Demons dropping sulphurous farts in your face for
              eternity?

Stemler: What an original vision.

All: NOT!!

Ludwik: I blame Hieronymus Bosch. All those pictures of
              Hell, like a Disneyworld for the sado-masochistic.

Endless impaling, disembowelling, being eaten by demons. You can't tell me he didn't enjoy it.

He capers madly about.

Oo-oo! There's blackbirds flying out my arsehole! Oo-oo!

Ludwik clicks his fingers. The fires of Hell die down.

I suppose you think I'm going to tell you 'Hell is other people' or 'Hell is separation from God', or maybe one of those 'Teabreak's over—back on your hands' jokes? No. Hell is a place where it doesn't rain. That's all.

Ludwik claps the still-kneeling Kolbe on the shoulder.

Anyway, Max—have a look around, make yourself at home. Feel free to use any of the facilities.

Kolbe: Don't touch me, Satan!

Ludwik: Yeah, right, I'm Satan.

He makes scary hands.

Woooooo! I'm just having an off day.

Kolbe starts an exorcism-type prayer aimed at vanquishing Ludwik.

Kolbe: O Lord, let them be confounded and ashamed that seek after my soul. Let them be turned backward—

Ludwik breaks in.

Ludwik: Don't you get sick of those old prayers?

He gestures. Kolbe's prayer immediately becomes lyrics of a song.

Kolbe: Shake, shake, shake! Shake your booty!

Kolbe stops, and tries again.

I am Woman, hear me roar—

Gritting his teeth in fierce concentration, he tries yet again to recapture the holy word.

Kolbe: I command you in the name of—Shaft!

Others: SHAFT!

The steel machinery graunches into movement again, drawing everyone but Kolbe's attention, before it grinds to a halt once more.

Ludwik: We're wasting time.

Others move to the back, where they shed their prisoners' apparel, revealing their faded saints' regalia. From here on in they are the saints—Simeon, Rose, Agatha, Walburga—though Kolbe is still unaware of their identities.

Kolbe: You can choke the prayers in my throat, but I still feel them in my heart. I am not damned! I will not believe it!

Ludwik: No? It's impossible, for instance, that right down inside all that humility—well hidden, well buried, every track covered—you might have a certain arrogance of spirit that is repugnant to God?

Kolbe: I won't give up my soul without a fight!

Ludwik: And a fight you shall have!

He does a rock show intro.

One man against the full forces of darkness armed with a thousand ingenious enticements! Good evening, Purgatory! Are you ready to ROCK? Live on stage tonight, THE TEMPTATIONS OF ST MAX!

The others adopt the persona of smooth soul group the Temptations. They are singing and dancing to 'My Girl', now mutated into 'Max Kolbe'. Kolbe looks nonplussed.

Kolbe: These? These are my temptations?

Ludwik:	Oh, come on now, Max. We're on a bit of a tight budget. You'll have to imagine the white suits, the afros, the gleaming teeth . . .
	So what temptation would you like to start with, Max? Sex?
	The 'Temptations' move into Donna Summers' 'Love to Love You/I Feel Love'. Each of the women somewhat ineptly comes on to Kolbe, who remains deeply unimpressed.
Kolbe:	Exactly how low is the budget?
Ludwik:	Sorry, Max—forgot you're a Catholic priest. You're obviously gay.
	Now the Temptations start in on Mary Wells' 'My Guy'. Simeon reluctantly takes his turn as sexual temptation.
	Come on, admit it. It's a man's life in the priesthood. All those young men taking cold showers at five in the morning. Eh, Max? Eh!
Kolbe:	Devil, I hope you've got more up your sleeves than this.
Ludwik:	I'm not the Devil.
Kolbe:	Then fetch your master; you begin to bore me.
	Kolbe rejects them, casts them off and tries to drive them out.
	Scatter! Begone! Go!
	They flee, shrieking, but turn it into a game of father and children.
Agatha:	Catch me, Daddy! Catch me!
	Rose jumps up on to Kolbe.
Rose:	I love you, Daddy!
Ludwik:	How about this then, Max? Children!

The Temptations start into Daniel Boone's 'Daddy Don't You Walk So Fast'. Simeon jumps on Kolbe's back.

Simeon: Daddy!

Kolbe staggers under the load of the two affectionate children.

Ludwik: The children you could have had. The children who might have changed you.

Rose: Daddy!

Simeon: You're the best daddy in the whole world!

Kolbe tries to disengage himself.

Ludwik: Go on—turn your back on them again. Shut them out like you always did!

Kolbe: Do you think I didn't wish for children?

The song continues as Kolbe's unborn children pursue him.

Rose: Daddy, I'm so sad we were never born.

Simeon: We would have been good, and really behaved ourselves. Honest!

Rose: I would have made you so proud of me, Daddy.

Simeon: Daddy, don't leave us here!

Rose: Daddy!

Simeon: Daddy!

They rejoin the song.

Ludwik: You see, Max? That's really your sin. That's why you're here. You walked away from every true relationship you might have had—lover, children, kept your mother at arm's length . . .

Kolbe: It was not the will of God that I have a family. My path was different.

Ludwik:	You fought against your desires, your loneliness—
Kolbe:	I had a destiny!
Ludwik:	And the sin is that you won. You triumphed over yourself and became this sexless, loveless lump; an appendix to the human race. Like a hermit, you turned your face to the corner and painted yourself in with your prayers!
Kolbe:	That's not true!
Ludwik:	A man who could devote himself to strangers, to the sick, to the needy—but never to himself, or those who should have been closest to him.
Agatha:	Alright, we get the point.
Kolbe:	I had friends! My brother monks! They knew I loved them!
Ludwik:	You know how to join the human race, Max? How to make a connection? You learn how to take as well as give. How do you think your poor brother monks felt when you pushed your only crust of bread on them?
Agatha:	Lay off him now.
Ludwik:	When you slept on the floor, a smug smile on your lips, while one of them lay awake in the bed he'd wanted to give you, feeling about as holy as a bucket of shit?
Kolbe:	They didn't feel like that . . . you're lying!
Ludwik:	You know it's true!
Agatha:	Half-true!
Ludwik:	No one was allowed to out-sanctify you, were they? You made sure you could live your life as on a mountaintop—
Agatha:	There's another side—
Ludwik:	Alone, looking down, owing nothing to anyone,

swollen with the meaningless pride of it!

Your humility, your charity, was as cold and relentless as ice, and it burned everyone who stretched out their hand to you!

Kolbe: No! I loved—! I loved—!

Agatha puts on a cap, becoming Theo, and enters the circle. She lays her hand on the bowed Kolbe's shoulder.

Agatha: And you were loved, Father.

Kolbe looks up.

Kolbe: Theo?

Agatha: Are loved.

Ludwik: What do you think you're doing?

Agatha: Father, when I lost everything you became a true father to me.

Ludwik: Get out of there!

Agatha: I was from a beautiful home where 'love' was the key word.

Ludwik: Why are you helping him!

Agatha: But my three beautiful sisters, my mother, my father, grandparents—all perished.

Ludwik: What is he to you? To any of us?

Agatha: To be a child from such a wonderful home and then suddenly find yourself utterly alone, as I did at age thirteen, in that hell—Auschwitz.

Ludwik: Right—that's it!

He disappears.

Agatha: I was always trying to find some friend of my father's, a neighbour—someone in that mass of humanity who had known my parents so I would not feel so alone.

She turns to Kolbe.

And that's how you found me, Father—wandering around. With nothing. With nobody. You took me in your arms. You let me cry. And you wiped away my tears like any mother, like any father.

Kolbe and Agatha embrace.

Kolbe: Theo. My child. Yes—my child!

Ludwik returns, enters the circle and snatches the cap off Agatha's head.

Ludwik: Surprise!

Kolbe sees it is not Theo.

Kolbe: You!

He pushes Agatha away.

Agatha: He wants to stop you, Kolbe. Open your eyes. See!

Ludwik advances on Agatha.

Ludwik: I warned you!

Agatha stands up to him.

Agatha: You're afraid of the truth about him!

Ludwik: You can talk to me about truth after what the truth did to you?

Agatha: It still means something! If you're going to play this game, play it fairly!

Agatha walks away as if quitting.

Ludwik draws the gun.

Ludwik: See this?

Ludwik blows Agatha away. She falls, awkwardly sprawled, inert.

That's your fairness!

Kolbe is aghast.

Kolbe: You madman!

He goes to Agatha and holds her head. His hands come away covered in blood. He stares at them in horror, realising.

She tried to help me. She wanted to help me.

Ludwik: She always did get hot for priests. Though she's going a bit cold on you now.

Kolbe looks up at Ludwik, a slow-burning anger rising in him.

Kolbe: You are the Devil.

He stands and moves furiously towards him.

Foul and black in your murderous soul!

Ludwik uses the circle, skipping out and back, popping up behind Kolbe, who rages round the inside of his prison.

Ludwik: No point crying over spilt blood, I always say.

Kolbe: You will pay for this!

Ludwik: Do you take American Express?

Kolbe: You will pay in the name of all that is holy! In the name of the Immaculate—!

The Vision approaches once more.

Vision: Mundzio!

Ludwik: Your Immaculate? Here she comes now! Drawn by the smell of carrion.

Vision: Mundzio!

The Vision enters the circle and towers over Kolbe. Her eyes are open and blood-red. Her mouth is full of rotted teeth. As she moves, her robes part to reveal soiled rags.

Her breathing is loud and laboured.

Ludwik: Worship a woman if you like, Max, but this—this is hardly a woman!

Simeon and Rose sing 'More Than a Woman'.

Look at her! Look what you've done to your Immaculate!

Kolbe: This is a travesty! A depraved travesty!

The Vision snuffs the air.

Ludwik: At least the pagans with their pot-bellied goddesses worship fertility. But you've twisted yours into the opposite! Made her barren and bloodless! An eater of dead flesh!

The Vision moves towards Kolbe, drooling. He retreats.

Kolbe: Get away!

The Vision sweeps Kolbe aside and, to his horror, bends to Agatha's body.

NO!

Kolbe rushes the Vision and topples it, his momentum carrying it and himself beyond the perimeters of the cell. In a fury he pulls apart the apparatus of the Vision until it lies broken on the ground. Kolbe stands over it, panting. Simeon and Rose scatter to safety.

Simeon: Look out! He's dangerous!

Rose: Run away!

Walburga scrabbles out from the wreckage of the Vision in fright, throwing the blame squarely onto Ludwik.

Walburga: It wasn't my idea! It was him!

Walburga follows the others and climbs to a safe vantage point. Kolbe turns towards Ludwik, who scoops up the head of the vision and works the mouth, parodying

Kolbe's mother's voice.

Ludwik: Oh Mundzio! Whatever kind of man have you turned out to be!

Kolbe advances on him. Ludwik backs up.

I never wanted you! And you knew it! You knew you'd never get love from me so you turned to your precious Immaculate!

Kolbe continues towards him implacably. The Mother's tone becomes wheedling.

But now you're big-time, Mundzio, don't forget your mother, who loves you—who loves you, Mundzio— who gave you everything—

Kolbe strikes the mask down and seizes Ludwik by the throat.

Go on then! Commit a sin! Hit me! Hurt me!

Kolbe chokes him, bashing him against the bars.

Not that hard, you bastard!

Ludwik struggles but is powerless before Kolbe's implacable rage. He weakens, signalling desperately to Walburga, Simeon and Rose, who watch from above.

Do something!

They look at each other, then start to sing.

Walburga/Simeon/Rose: 'Sometimes—all I need is the air that I breathe . . .'

Kolbe wrings the life out of Ludwik.

Ludwik slumps.

Kolbe lets go and he slides limply to the floor. The lights come up to a general state across the full width of the stage for the first time.

Kolbe looks round at the vast emptiness, the flat

featureless country which he now perceives.

Kolbe: Where am I? What have I—?

He looks back at Ludwik's body with dawning horror.

No. No, I can't have—killed. Not me. Not me.

The ceiling begins to move again. Kolbe looks up in fear.

Oh please, God, don't leave me here. Don't turn your back on me!

The ceiling reaches perpendicular and stops with a crash like the slamming of a prison door. Kolbe drops to his knees.

WHAT HAVE I DONE?

Simeon, Rose and Walburga quickly clamber down and scurry out the back.

Kolbe is left alone with the bodies. Agatha stirs, moans and sits up.

Kolbe looks up dazedly from his misery.

Agatha: Ow. That always gives me such a headache.

She digs in her ear, removing a bullet which she flicks to the floor. Agatha sees Ludwik's body.

Who killed him?

Kolbe looks wretched.

About time someone did.

Kolbe: He wanted me to do it. He wanted me to damn myself.

Agatha: Don't look so tragic, Max. There is no Hell.

Kolbe looks at her.

No, and I'm not a demon either.

Kolbe stares round at the endless horizon.

Kolbe: You can't tell me this is Heaven.

Agatha: It's Death.

Kolbe: Death.

Agatha: Plain and simple. This is where you live when you die. Everyone. Whoever you are, whatever you do. No questions asked. No correspondence entered into.

Kolbe: This is another illusion.

Agatha: Game's over, Max.

              She nods at Christopher's body.

              I don't think he wants to play any more.

              Kolbe struggles to get his mind round the concepts.

Kolbe: No Hell? And no Heaven?

              Agatha looks at him.

Agatha: I didn't say there was no Heaven.

              She directs Kolbe's eyes up to the gates.

Kolbe: There? That's the gate of Heaven?

Agatha: Let me guess. You expected something more impressive? Take it from me—the longer you sit round here, the more impressive it gets.

Kolbe: For me, there can be no Heaven. God has seen what I've done.

Agatha: Lucky for you that God's not in charge of Heaven then, isn't it?

              Kolbe looks at Agatha in disbelief.

Kolbe: How can there be Heaven without God?

Agatha: Easily. Throw a few dead Catholics together and it was virtually inevitable. Don't worry, Max, no one's going to hold a little murder against you. They're creaking out the red carpet even as we speak.

A trumpeting sound is heard in the distance.

Here comes the welcoming committee now.

The trumpeting sounds again, louder.

Time to meet your maker, Max.

The trumpeting sounds again, accompanied by crashing. Kolbe looks towards the commotion with trepidation.

Your real maker.

The Catholic Church bursts onto the stage with a roar. It is in the form of a huge shambling beast, frightening and insatiable. Perched on top of it is a parched skeletal Pope, as if already embalmed.

The Holy Catholic Church!

The Pope speaks in a malevolent shriek.

Pope: Silence! It is I, your Pope!

Agatha takes cover. Kolbe stands back in amazement. The Pope notices Kolbe.

Ah, Maxy! Now there's a boy who knows about obedience! No head for politics—just shuts his mouth and does as he's told! Come here and kiss my ring!

Shy, eh? I like them shy. Let me be the first to greet you, Saint Maximilian Kolbe!

Kolbe: Saint?

Pope: I come hotfoot from your canonisation! And a lovely service it was, too. Bugger the expense!

Kolbe: Don't mock me! What saint has done this?

He indicates Ludwik's body. The Church Beast lurches towards it.

Pope: What's been going on here? Eh? Eh? What have these vermin been doing to you?

Kolbe: I've murdered!

Pope: Don't worry about this scum, Maxy. He doesn't
             count. No one out here does. Heaven awaits!
             Sainthood awaits! You're one of mine now. Whoever
             I say is in Heaven is in Heaven, whoever I neglect to
             mention—

Agatha: Or change your mind about.

Pope: —is shit out of luck! It makes for a more cosy
             atmosphere. Only popes, cardinals, saints, vatican
             officials and wealthy benefactors need apply.

Kolbe: This is not Heaven! Heaven is open to all!

Pope: Don't be like that, Maxy. After all the trouble I had to
             go to with your miracles.

Kolbe: Miracles?

Pope: You're confused, Maxy. The miracles required for
             your canonisation, of course. How could you forget
             poor Angelina Testoni?

             *The head, hands and shoulders of Angelina extrude out
             of the Church Beast.*

Angelina: Seven years I was ill with tuberculosis. Then you
             appeared to me in a vision, saying, 'Get out of your
             bed, Angelina. Go into the fields and work. You are
             cured. But don't forget to put some clothes on.'

Pope: Beautiful, beautiful!

Angelina: (*doting on Agatha*) I could never forget that angelic
             face!

Agatha: (*pointing*) That's Max.

Pope: And only a year later, you busy boy—Francesco
             Luciano Ranier!

             *Francesco extrudes from another part of the Church
             Beast.*

Francesco:	There I was, laid out in a coma. The doctor told my family I was dead meat and gave them a card for his brother-in-law, the funeral director. But I got down on my knees and prayed to you, and lo—I was a box of birds!
Kolbe:	You were in a coma but you managed to get down on your knees and pray?

Short pause.

Francesco:	It's a miracle!

Pope/Angelina/Francesco: HALLELUJAH!

Kolbe:	There were no miracles.
Angelina:	Such modesty!
Francesco:	So kind!
Pope:	It's fact, Max, fact. Vatican tests have proven it.
Kolbe:	There were no miracles—
Pope:	Shut up, you fool! Do you want to ruin everything?
Kolbe:	—only that God allowed me to fulfil his will!
Pope:	Gold? Did somebody say gold?

The Church Beast, which the Pope has trouble controlling, snorts, bellows, strains and shits out a fat yellow tube. The Pope is delighted, breathing deeply.

	Ah! The smell of fresh gold! Almighty Gold—all-powerful Gold—all praise to Gold!
Kolbe:	The true Church requires no wealth! Your gold should go to the poor!

The Pope shrieks at the very word and the great Church-Beast crashes about, trumpeting in alarm.

Pope:	Poor? POOR! Was it not our Lord who said 'The poor are always with us'? Do you propose to make him a liar by removing their poverty?

Be reasonable, Maxy. What would the dogs of the street do with money? It would only tempt them to the destruction of their souls with material pleasures. It is the Church's duty and responsibility to remove this temptation, to bear the heavy burden of this twenty billion dollars in stock, hard currency, real estate, and non-tax-paying Vatican banks on its own naked and bleeding shoulders—as Christ did with the world's sins. How often I wish my only worries were starving to death in Auschwitz and getting into Heaven.

Kolbe: I won't go to any Heaven you have a part in!

Pope: Careful, Maxy. You owe me. What kind of gratitude is that for kicking you upstairs? You belong to me, like a button stitched to a coat. And now you're nice and dead, I'm going to give you a shine and show you off!

The Church Beast lurches towards Kolbe, the Pope grasping for him with his withered claw-like arms. Kolbe evades.

Come on—come to Popey!

Ludwik stirs and sits up, rubbing his throat.

Ludwik: 'And lo, they saw a beast with seven horns.'

The Pope and Church Beast swing on Ludwik.

Pope: I know you, laddie. What ideas have you been putting in his head?

Ludwik: 'And on the horns lay the great Whore of Babylon.'

Pope: Shut it, you rabble-rousing scum!

Ludwik: Remember your scripture, Max?

Pope: I've dealt to you before! I can do it again!

Ludwik: 'And the beast was a great city.'

The Church Beast barges against Ludwik, knocking him down. He continues defiantly.

'And the seven horns were the seven hills of Rome!'

Pope: Trample him! Trample him!

Kolbe jumps in front.

Kolbe: No!

The Pope glares at him murderously for a long moment.

Pope: You're a new boy, Maxy—so I'll let you off this time. But remember—I made you. And I can break you!

As the Church Beast rampages out:

Ask your friends! SAINT MAX!

Kolbe: I won't be a saint in this place! I won't be a saint for you!

The Church Beast has gone.

Ludwik: Too late, Max—you're canon fodder. You heard the man. Now you're dead they can really start to use you. Like they used me.

Agatha: You didn't complain about it when you were in there.

She nods her head towards the steel gates of Heaven.

Kolbe: Then you—?

Walburga, Rose and Simeon approach, singing 'Float On' by the Floaters.

Agatha: None of us did.

Kolbe: All of you—?

Ludwik: All of us Max. All of us saints together.

Agatha joins the others dancing and crooning 'Float On'.

But where you're just beginning, we're already on the scrap-heap. Exiled, broken-down, has-been, senile. A ragged bunch of refugees who can't let go of what we were.

Each of the Floaters takes their solo.

Rose: Hi, I'm St Rose of Lima and my feast day is September the 13th. I pledged my body to Christ by scarring my face to make myself unattractive to men, burning my hands, starving myself and wearing a metal crown whose spikes pierced my skull. Canonised in 1215.

Simeon: Hi, I'm St Simeon Stylites and my feast day is January the 6th. I spent 37 years sitting on top of a pillar for God. My hobbies include flaying the skin off my back and encouraging maggots to breed in the wounds. Canonised in 856.

Walburga: Hi, I'm St Walburga, a decent Christian abbess whose feast day, May the 1st, got mixed up with an annual night of pagan debauchery. As a result I'm now a confused hybrid of Christian saint and heathen appetites. Canonised in 952.

Agatha: Hi, I'm St Agatha and my feast day is August the 23rd. Refusing to renounce my faith, I was tortured with rods, rack and fire. Finally I had my breasts sliced off, which I am depicted as carrying in front of me on a plate. This led to me becoming patron saint of bellmakers and bakers. Canonised in 1643.

The Floaters finish their song as Ludwik sums up, pointing them out in turn (Simeon, Rose, Walburga, Agatha).

Ludwik: The rejects and the unfashionable. Insane. Over the top. Corrupted by pre-Christian practices. And totally mythical.

Agatha: Three centuries of acting as a good example: brave, steadfast and true. But I wasn't brave at all. How could I be if I didn't even exist? Well, what's so great about being real anyway?

Simeon: What's wrong with sitting on a pillar? It was considered holy enough before this fad for helping people!

Walburga: It's not my fault I ended up as carnal as a shithouse door in a southerly—so why do I have to be punished for it?

Rose: I thought it was simple—if you loved God, you flogged yourself to death. Suddenly that's a bad thing. Suddenly I'm a sick girl. I don't understand!

Kolbe: (*to Ludwik*) And you? Who are you?

Ludwik: Don't you know me, Max? I was a giant. One of the greatest in the canon of saints. I moved with the times. I could adapt! Not like this bunch of cripples!

Kolbe: I—don't know you.

Ludwik: You know me! You've heard my story a thousand times! Told my story! How, as a pagan man, I lifted the infant Jesus on my shoulders, and for a moment felt the weight of the whole world that he carried. Name me!

                 Kolbe can't believe it.

Kolbe: St Christopher?

                 Ludwik stands tall with his staff, claiming his name.

Christopher: St Christopher!

                 He shouts up beyond Heaven's gate.

                 You hear that, you bastards?! St Christopher! Patron saint of travellers! Invoked against water, tempest, plague and sudden death!

Agatha: And fictitious. Same as me.

Walburga: Fired out of the canon.

Christopher: Let me tell you—Heaven used to be stuffed full of interesting people!

Simeon: Greek and Roman gods in disguise!

Rose: Mythical heroes crammed into haloes!

Agatha: Evil popes and madmen!

Walburga: People with the morals of a badger!

Christopher: Then all of a sudden we're supposed to move over for the new wave. For saints like you. Why? What makes you more holy than us?

Kolbe: You did all of this out of jealousy? Simple envy?

Christopher: Envy's never simple, Max. Particularly when it's about Heaven.

Kolbe: It was never my intention—

Others: (*by rote*)—to be a saint.

Kolbe: As God is my witness!

Christopher: God. I was wondering when he was going to crop up. In fact, we've all been wondering, haven't we?

Christopher turns away, leaving it to the others.

Kolbe: What do you mean?

They quickly look away, not wanting to get lumbered with the job.

Simeon: I'm not going to tell him! You tell him!

Walburga: No, you tell him!

Agatha: I had to tell him about Heaven!

Rose: I'll tell him! I'll tell him! Tell him what?

Agatha is forced to do it.

Agatha: About that 'God' thing, Max. It's just—we haven't seen him round lately.

The others shake their heads to support Agatha.

In fact—come to think of it—we haven't seen him—

Others: (*dismally*) Ever.

Rose: He might be hiding. Or in disguise!

Agatha: (*gently*) There's no God.

Rose: Or he could be a very, very, very small God! And we just overlooked him!

Agatha/Simeon/Walburga: THERE'S NO GOD!

Agatha: How many times!

Rose: (*crushed*) I just sort of miss him, that's all.

Agatha shrugs, looking at Kolbe.

Agatha: Sorry, Max. You'll get over it. We all had to.

Simeon: The first hundred years are the worst.

Kolbe: How can you believe that?

Rose suddenly points excitedly.

Rose: Hang on a minute—isn't that God over there now? Hah! Made you look!

Kolbe: You all had belief once. Every one of you. How can you just give up hope? How do you know this isn't one more step on our journey?

Agatha: Sure. That's probably what it is.

Rose, having wandered away from the others, now begins to sing 'Delta Dawn'. Kolbe looks round their dejected faces.

Kolbe: You poor wretches. Has none of you any faith left at all?

Simeon: How can we? With the evidence forever staring us in the face?

Kolbe: God may still stand beyond what we can see, waiting. Why can't death—all this—be only the final test of our faith?

Walburga: Oh yes? Which we've all failed I suppose?

Christopher: Give it up, Max. Any minute that gate's going to open, and you can go in and sit by the pool, sip a drink and forget about us, forget about God—forget about everything.

Kolbe: I can't!

Christopher: If it's one thing I can't stand, it's a bad winner. Someone who won't admit the truth even when it's in their favour.

Kolbe: I can't believe in a Heaven based on exclusion! I can't believe in a universe without God! I can't believe in chaos!

Christopher: Can't? Or won't?

Kolbe: There must be meaning. There must!

Christopher: Or what? You might actually have to feel the pain? Watch the world's suffering without being able to pretend it's only a hiccup on the road to Heaven? All that agony, all that grief—not the means you want it to be, but the end. The dead-end. Pointless and cruel.

Kolbe: It's pointless to believe in pointlessness! Cruel to believe in cruelty!

Christopher: That's the way it is!

He swings suddenly with his staff and hits Kolbe on his injection bruise.

That hurts, doesn't it? You're dead and it hurts, and it keeps on hurting and everyone keeps on suffering because that's the way of the universe!

Kolbe: No! We must be able to affect things! We must be able to make a difference! Even if Heaven is what you say it is—

Christopher: If Heaven is what I say it is, you'll buy it! Everyone buys it! Because all there is is the choice between that—and this!

Walburga: He's right. In there you don't care.

Agatha: You'll forget about us.

Christopher: Up there, Max, lies your reward. Sainthood. Heaven. What you spent your life working towards.

Kolbe: I never had ambition for myself.

Christopher: Don't be so modest, Max. You placed your bets well. You ran a good campaign. Look at that poor bastard Gajowniczek running round the world, scrambling on the hamster wheel of your holiness, just to make sure you got the promotion.

Kolbe: Gajowniczek? You said he starved himself. In Auschwitz!

Christopher stops, seemingly caught out.

Christopher: I didn't say he died of it.

Realisation dawns on Kolbe.

Kolbe: You didn't want me to know. I sacrificed my life for Gajowniczek, and he survived. I changed something! I had an effect!

Christopher: One man. Among millions.

Kolbe: It doesn't fit with your scheme of things, so you choose to ignore it!

Don't you see? God wanted him to live. He cried out for his children. It was a sign to me from God. And in return, God has given us this sign—has shown us proof of himself by bringing Gajowniczek alive out of the fire.

Christopher: It was luck. Good luck instead of bad.

Kolbe: If that's what you truly believe, then show me Gajowniczek! Show me the man I saved!

Christopher: Why?

Kolbe: For the truth!

Christopher scoffs.

Christopher: The truth!

He walks away.

Kolbe: What are you afraid of?

Walburga: He lived. What more do you need to know?

Kolbe: Help me find him. You'll see! Together we can rebuild your faith!

Simeon: He's not here.

Agatha: He's still alive.

Walburga: Still on Earth.

Rose: Fast asleep.

They look at each other.

Agatha: On the other hand . . .

Agatha/Simeon/Walburga: Dream sequence!

They go wavy, then move into a re-creation of the selection scene (already seen as the first image of the play).

Rose: 'Gajowniczek's Dream'.

Simeon adopts classic newsreel voiceover style.

Simeon: Another blazing hot afternoon in the glorious summer of 1941 here at Auschwitz, once a picturesque little village, now home to the world's largest crematorium.

And don't some of these chaps look like they could do with a sit down in the shade! They've been on parade all day, waiting for one of their pals who's decided to play hooky! I bet they'd like to give him a piece of their minds! Never mind, here's Lagerführer Karl Fritzsch! He'll sort things out.

Simeon falls in as Rose turns into Fritzsch.

Fritzsch: Pigs! Stand to attention!

Walburga: He walked down the ranks, staring every man in the face.

Simeon: You didn't know what to do. Look strong?

Agatha: Look feeble?

Walburga: Look him in the eye? He enjoyed it.

Fritzsch: You.

Walburga sags with a groan.

Kolbe: Gajowniczek?

He goes to Walburga, but gets no response.

Simeon: Fritzsch! He was the first to use Zyklon B, the rat-killing gas, on humans.

Agatha: Fancied himself as an innovator.

Fritzsch: You.

Agatha sags, stricken.

Kolbe: Gajowniczek? Is it you?

Kolbe is an unacknowledged ghost, trying to find Gajowniczek in each one of the chosen.

Walburga: The Lagerführer lived in a green garden in the centre of Auschwitz. His wife wore the silk lingerie of dead Jews.

Simeon: His boy and girl the clothes of children who'd died within their first hour in the camp.

Fritzsch: You.

Simeon sags.

Christopher: You thought you knew, didn't you, Max?

Kolbe takes his place in the ranks.

Agatha: Frau Fritzsch called her home an earthly paradise, said she'd live in Auschwitz till she died.

Walburga: So at least we had something in common.

Christopher: You thought Fritzsch was going to choose—

Fritzsch approaches, looks into Kolbe's face, but then suddenly stabs a finger out across the ranks.

Fritzsch: You.

Walburga: (*as Gajowniczek, cries out in pain at his selection*) My poor children!

Kolbe: Gajowniczek!

He tries to reach Gajowniczek but is prevented by Christopher.

Christopher: You couldn't believe it! It was meant to be you!

Kolbe: Let me talk to him!

Christopher: Then you saw the plan. What the Immaculate wanted you to do. And it was perfect.

Kolbe shrugs Christopher off and steps forward calmly and resolutely.

Kolbe: I want to die for that man.

Gajowniczek (Walburga) slowly turns, amazed and overjoyed. He holds a cap in his hands.

Gajowniczek: Father! Father Kolbe! I'm dreaming, I know, but it's wonderful to see you!

Gajowniczek kneels and kisses Kolbe's hands. Kolbe pulls him up.

Kolbe: Let me hug you. Let me feel you!

They embrace.

Gajowniczek: You're a saint now—as I prayed you would be!

Kolbe: And you lived! You survived the camp. This nonsense about starving yourself—?

          Gajowniczek is embarrassed.

Gajowniczek: Your friends told me that to carry on refusing my rations would be like spitting in your face. That you should be a saint, and a saint needs a witness. You died for me, Father—I knew I must live for you.

Kolbe: And for your family—your children.

          A shadow crosses Gajowniczek's face. He quickly smiles again.

Gajowniczek: Of course.

Kolbe: God was watching over you, my son.

          (*for the benefit of Christopher*) By his works so shall you know him.

Rose: Let me be Gajowniczek!

Simeon: No! My turn!

          Simeon takes the cap from Walburga and becomes Gajowniczek.

Gajowniczek: Four years I was in the camp after you died, Father. But I survived everything—the beatings, the malnutrition. When I caught typhoid, the camp underground hid me, got me medicine. You see, they knew too, Father. I was a living vessel—in me was contained your deed. Others died—thousands of others—but I had to live!

Kolbe: As long as you were in God's hands, no harm could come to you.

Christopher: You heard him! Men saved him, not God.

Gajowniczek: In the last days of the war I was taken out of the camp and death-marched with 500 others. At the end of two weeks, only 23 survived. But I was one of them!

Kolbe: By the grace of God!

Gajowniczek: Everyone said it was a miracle, Father!

Kolbe glances triumphantly at the others.

Kolbe: What more proof do we need of him?

Christopher: Haven't you had enough of miracles by now?

Kolbe: You returned home?

The shadow flits across Gajowniczek's face again.

Gajowniczek: Home. Yes.

Christopher: Don't forget Angelina and Francesco—the Miracle of the Bad Liars!

Kolbe turns on Christopher.

Kolbe: Your unbelief has become your religion! You cling to it like a drowning man! Because you're afraid to discover you can do good! That everything you've done, and not done, has meaning! That always you've held the universe in the palm of your hand when you thought it was the other way round!

              Gajowniczek knows. Let him tell you!

Simeon (as Gajowniczek) looks troubled. Agatha, sensing something is not right, looks on with concern.

Agatha: Let him sleep now, Max.

Rose: Let me! Let me!

Rose seizes the cap and turns into Gajowniczek.

Gajowniczek: I testified on your account, Father. I haven't lost a single opportunity to tell my story. About your saintly sacrifice—for me—a miserable man you hardly knew!

Kolbe: You had a necessity to live. You cried out not for yourself but for your children. God heard your cry. I was only his instrument.

The shadow drives the smile off Gajowniczek's face.

Gajowniczek: Father—

He falters.

Kolbe: And your family are well? Your children flourished?

Gajowniczek can't look him in the eye.

Gajowniczek: My—children . . .

Looking at him, Kolbe feels a chill of dread.

Kolbe: What? What?

Gajowniczek can't answer.

Walburga: Leave it now, Max.

Simeon: You've heard enough.

Kolbe shakes Gajowniczek.

Kolbe: WHAT?

Christopher: His children died.

A visible tremor comes over Kolbe.

Kolbe: Died.

Walburga: In the war. A month before he was freed.

Simeon: He never saw them again.

Gajowniczek: I was too late, Father. Too late.

Kolbe: No.

Gajowniczek: My wife moved Heaven and Earth to keep our sons together, to keep them safe. But one day when she'd gone searching for food, our village was caught in an artillery barrage. The boys thought they would be safer in the forest. They ran out and were killed by shells in the street.

Gajowniczek starts to cry.

I'm sorry, Father.

Kolbe: (*echoing dully*) Sorry?

Gajowniczek: I couldn't help them! I couldn't reach them!

Kolbe staggers away, sickened.

Kolbe: Don't tell me any more!

Gajowniczek: Father, I'm sorry!

Christopher: Can you believe it? He felt guilty. Guilty he couldn't give the world that moment. The moment of taking his sons into his arms that you'd laid down your life for.

Kolbe: Take him away!

Christopher: That he couldn't cry for joy and say it's all been for something. It has meaning.

Gajowniczek: Father, I—

Kolbe fends him off wildly, grabbing the cap and flinging it away.

Kolbe: NO! NO MORE! FOR PITY'S SAKE!

Gajowniczek reverts to Rose. Kolbe sinks down. Distraught, Agatha turns on Christopher.

Agatha: Look what you've done now. You should be ashamed of yourself!

Christopher: Ashamed! If he can't take the truth—

Agatha: I'm sick of your truth! I preferred his!

Kolbe: He was in God's hands!

Rose: Hands with holes. Some things just slip through.

Kolbe: Would it have been so much trouble to spare his children? Would the universe have tilted? Would rivers have flowed backwards!

Christopher: There's no one there, Max.

Kolbe's hands drop helplessly.

Kolbe: No God.

Agatha turns away in tears.

Christopher: Look for yourself.

Kolbe: And if I look, what will I see?

Christopher: Just another Auschwitz.

Kolbe: Where everything is the same. Nothing means
                anything. Good—

Christopher: Pleasure.

Kolbe: Bad—

Christopher: Pain. Unless, of course, your pain is my pleasure.

Rose: Or my pleasure is my own pain.

Christopher: And in there—the green walled garden where you
                can dress in the silks of the dead. The disappeared.
                Where the blood of the saints is always liquid and
                red, never believing it can dry to dust and the winds
                of change blow it away.

Agatha: It's not so bad, Max. In Heaven.

Simeon: You can rest there.

Walburga: You can get anything you want.

Rose: It's—nice.

*The gates of Heaven creak slowly open. Shafts of light
beam through them. An ambient voice is heard.*

Voice: St Maximilian Kolbe—boarding now. Boarding now
                through Gate 1.

Agatha: Prats. They've only got one gate.

Walburga:	Come on, Max.
Simeon:	It doesn't pay to keep them waiting.
	The light is brilliant behind the iron gates. The saints lift the floor grille to form a ladder going up to the open gates.
Kolbe:	Gajowniczek. What did I do to him?
Simeon:	Forget him.
Agatha:	Just for once take something for yourself.
Walburga:	Take the easy way.
Kolbe:	Why not? Why shouldn't I? I suffered—I worked all my life—for what? For this? Don't I deserve something!
	Kolbe starts to climb. He hesitates. The voice repeats its announcement.
Voice:	St Maximilian Kolbe—now boarding. Now boarding, please—St Maximilian Kolbe.
Kolbe:	I have to see Gajowniczek.
	He climbs back down.
Agatha:	What are you doing?!
Simeon:	There's no time!
Kolbe:	I have to speak to Gajowniczek. Please.
Walburga:	What can he tell you?
Kolbe:	He's given everything—but he must give more!
Agatha:	They won't wait for you!
Kolbe:	I can't go without his blessing!
	Christopher has quietly picked up Gajowniczek's cap.
Christopher:	*(as Gajowniczek)* I'm here.
	Kolbe turns to him. There is a sudden silence.

Rose: 'Gajowniczek's Dream'—a slight return.

Agatha: Don't trust him, Max.

Rose moves towards the front and starts to sing 'Wildfire' by Michael Martin Murphey. Kolbe steps towards Christopher.

Kolbe: Is it you—Gajowniczek?

Kolbe moves closer to Christopher.

Can you forgive me?

Christopher: I never blamed you. You wanted to help.

Kolbe: Did I do anything but bring you more pain? It's a stupid question, but—

Christopher: Ask.

Kolbe: Are you happy?

Christopher: Happy?

Voice: Final call—Maximilian Kolbe. This is your final call.

Kolbe: Please, tell me the truth!

Christopher: We have lost our children. My wife and I—we would rather have died a hundred times—if it could have saved only one. Yes, there were moments when I thought it might have been better if I had died. If you hadn't stepped forward.

Kolbe gazes at him hollowly.

Kolbe: I brought you grief.

Christopher: 'Mother' is always reminiscing about our sons. Even now there is no day passes without speaking of them.

Kolbe: (*brokenly*) I understand.

He goes to turn away. Christopher takes his arm.

Christopher: No, Father. We speak of them and we smile. Our memories are happy, and our sons still alive for us.

You understand, down there on Earth it's a cold night, but the bed is warm, and I am an old man at peace. You gave me life. And after all—

He smiles.

—life is beautiful.

Kolbe: Thank you. Thank you!

Overcome, Kolbe throws himself on his knees and kisses Gajowniczek's hands. The gates begin to close.

Agatha: The gates! They're closing!

The others seize Kolbe and pull him away. Kolbe climbs toward the gates.

Simeon: Speak for us in Heaven!

Walburga: They won't listen to him.

Agatha, Simeon and Walburga join Rose in the song. Christopher, still as Gajowniczek, smiles up at Kolbe as he pulls himself up and stands in the aperture of the closing gates.

Christopher: Farewell, Father Kolbe. It won't be long now till my family are reunited, together with you in Heaven.

Kolbe is struck by the sick knowledge that this will never happen.

Kolbe: Gajowniczek—

Christopher: Bye, Father! Bye!

Christopher spins, reverting to himself, and flicks the cap up to Kolbe.

At least his hat will get there.

Kolbe: Christopher. Why did you help me?

Christopher shrugs.

Christopher: Why should we all be miserable?

Christopher turns away. The gates are almost closed. Kolbe throws himself at the gap, straining to hold the gates apart, then force them further open.

Kolbe: No. No! NO! No more cruelties. No more exclusions. Everyone must be happy or no one!

Having forced the gates open, with a superhuman effort Kolbe now wrenches one of them off its hinges and sends it crashing down below. This is echoed by a rumbling of summer thunder.

Life is beautiful! We have to make Death more beautiful still! If not in this Heaven, then in a Heaven beyond. If we can't find God here, we will seek him further!

He tears the other gate loose and topples it down. The thunder sounds again, longer and louder. Kolbe stands before the breached gate, transformed and inspired.

On and on! I go running to my Lord—and as I run, I'm with him! Praise God, there is no end in sight!

He waves the other saints to follow him.

Storm Heaven! Storm Heaven! STORM HEAVEN!

With a shout, all but Christopher swarm up towards him. Dismayed and broken, Christopher backs away. The thunder continues. It begins to rain, drops spattering down, quickly turning to a downpour. Kolbe shouts down to Christopher.

Christopher! Come with us!

Christopher: I can't.

The others arrive at the top and stand, singing the climax of Wildfire. *Kolbe jumps down to Christopher. He resists.*

I was holy once. All I want is to be holy again. But I have no faith left!

Kolbe: Rain, Christopher!

Christopher: I'm too full of bitterness!

Kolbe is alight; an overwhelming, irresistible power of joy. He laughs with delight.

Kolbe: Rain!

Christopher: Let me go! I don't want your pity! Your charity!

Christopher stumbles away.

I don't want your love!

Kolbe: Then you'll just have to get used to it.

Christopher turns. Smiling, Kolbe shoots him clean through the heart. Hoisting Christopher across his shoulders, Kolbe climbs back up to the shattered entrance to heaven, where the others stand inspired and singing.

We go in search of our God!

Reaching the top, he stands triumphant.

Love without limits! Love without limits! LOVE WITHOUT LIMITS!

They surge forward into Heaven and disappear. The rain continues to fall through sunlight. The sound of birds. The desert blooms.

The End

Panic!

Ken:

Petra Massey hailed from Essex and was on an extended stay in Wellington while she busked her way around the world. She was pint-sized, strong-minded, used to organising things for herself, optimistic and resourceful. Come to think of it, she was everything Kiwis are supposed to be. As 'Pip the Hip', Petra busked regularly in town and had quite a following, but she fancied the idea of going indoors and doing a 'proper' show. Someone suggested she might perform *Polythene Pam*. Rebecca and I were curious and met Petra to chat—I'm pretty sure at my office in the Hope Gibbons building.

It was never going to be a great idea for Petra to do *Polythene Pam*—or even likely. That was Rebecca's show, and in fact Rebecca would perform a return season of it at BATS later that same year. Instead, I suggested the three of us collaborate on writing a show specifically for Petra—it would be nice for Rebecca and me to do something together again, and refreshing to have another voice in the mix.

There wasn't a lot of time, I remember, as Petra wanted to debut the show as part of the New Zealand Fringe Festival in late-March. She was equally clear that she then wanted to tour it across a series of fringe festivals in Canada. This idea appealed to me—work of mine girdling the globe while I stayed comfortably at home. But much depended on my impression of Petra on first meeting. I had nothing against buskers, but did she have the required attention span to do a solo theatre show? I liked her. She was funny, and underneath that I believed she was serious too.

353

Petra's timing was also good in that I was at a bit of a loose end. I'd emptied out my bank account on the *Blue Sky Boys* disaster of late-1992 and a TV job I'd been depending on to keep me solvent fell through, leading to what I remember as the Long, Dry Summer. I was within a week of signing up for the dole a couple of times but was scratching along from small job to small job. So, I had both the time and inclination to be one of three writers on a 50-minute play.

We went back to our original method of writing—scribbling separately to see what came up, looking for connections then selecting and shaping. Rebecca wrote about relationships, about hospital (which she'd seen quite a bit of), and fears and fantasies. Petra wrote stream-of-consciousness fables, poems, family stories and memories of moments in her life and the people she shared them with. I fictionalised more than the other two, writing stories of bike-boys, turkey violation and (after Petra telling me about tribes of Crusties) roving gypsy theatre artists, all from a female point of view. We quickly had a box full of stuff, much of which had to be dropped, as the thread which would connect the play swam into view. Things we really liked didn't make the cut.

Fear and loneliness amongst the detritus of life emerged as the theme. Following this came the character of Frankie, afflicted by nighttime fears and an inability to let things go. Hoarders weren't the recognised reality TV phenomenon they've become since— so someone surrounded by the trash of their life seemed literally and metaphorically interesting as theatre. The vignette of Frankie as a child being unable to walk past stones, feathers or bottletops without collecting them was a true description—with only the name changed—of my four-year-old daughter Katherine as she struggled with the difficult transition from afternoon to morning kindergarten. It was probably from this ongoing (and somewhat worrying) daily ritual that the whole rubbish-set and adult hoarder concept developed.

Performing in a theatre, acting other people's lines, was going to be a whole new thing for Petra—but I wanted to play to her strengths as well. These included physical dexterity (she was an escapologist, after all) and musicality, so we made sure there were some songs in the show, supported by Petra's ukulele, a comb-and-paper kazoo, and a suitcase which served as a drum. One of these songs—written once the theme of fear had shown itself—was 'Panic', which also eventually gave us the show title. I say 'eventually', because time was so short that Petra had to file her listing for the show in the Fringe Festival programme while we were still in the early stages of writing it. She gave the title as *All About Things*—which was probably the first thing to occur to her—so that's what it was known as during its first run. In that first incarnation it also ended with the Jethro Tull song *Skating Away on the Thin Ice of the New Day,* but for the second BATS season we replaced that with something original and more fitting.

Once we had a script, Petra asked me to direct the show. Actually, she paid me to direct it. With the aforementioned financial squeeze, that was the only way I could justify taking the time to do it. It felt a bit weird breaking out of the cooperative writing model to instead get a weekly cheque from one of my co-writers, but it was further proof of Petra's commitment to the enterprise. She was putting her money where her mouth was—and it was up to me to not let her down.

We rehearsed in Newtown in a space Petra rented from an Indian classical dancer. He was a bit tightly wound and complained about the junk we were leaving around the place. This 'junk' was our set. We assembled props from all over—the same way we'd assembled the script—and found ways to use them in the show. The plastic tulip lights and the flower music box; the little stainless steel rice-steamer, which could be a crystal ball or suggest an orgasm; a large green puppet ant-head which came in handy when Petra told the story of her father's nose. I cannibalised a surplus-to-requirements stuffed koala bear from home to create a convincing flattened and mummified rabbit. Throughout the show, everything chaotically strewn across the set was slowly shifted, shunted and assembled by Petra to create a boat in which she (notionally) sailed away at the end. This gave us the element of visual and metaphorical transformation, which powers the best theatre.

A lot of the junk came courtesy of Tim Denton, maker of large-scale puppets and stage illusions, who was helping us with design. He was also in charge of the other major coup de théâtre required for *Panic!*—the disappearing sleeper. What we wanted was simple to describe: there is a figure in the bed throughout the play, but when Frankie gets back in we see it's just her. But I had no idea how to achieve this. It was that 'impossible direction' every play should have. I passed the challenge to Tim, and he instantly knew what to do. He carved a lifelike figure, sleeping on its side, out of sponge rubber. All Petra had to do was lie on top of it and—hey presto—it disappeared; she was all alone in the bed. This worked brilliantly as both metaphor and as stage magic, once again seamlessly achieved within ten feet of an audience. And, to my chagrin, no one ever commented on it or asked how we did it!

There were a lot of props to set up which had to be arranged just so—but Petra learnt it all and was fearless. I wanted to start the show with a bang, so came up with the idea of Frankie taking a dive head-first off the bed and forward-rolling into a box amongst a pile of stuff which then collapsed cacophonously. Then, trapped under the overturned box, she would creep all the way downstage like a bizarre tortoise. I loved that—that I could say, 'Do you think you could . . .' and she'd say, 'Yep,' and do it better than I imagined.

Rebecca hadn't attended rehearsals, had probably come to a late run and had the novel experience of seeing how I'd directed her writing. I particularly remember her raising an eyebrow at the 'Gypsy Blood' sequence, during which Petra scrambled over, under and through the bed—a flurry of frenetic movement rather than the downstage-centre speech Rebecca might have imagined. I think she got used to it, though . . .

The short Fringe Festival season at BATS went well—good reviews, happy audiences—and *Panic!* was successfully brought back a few weeks later for a ten-night run, again at BATS. Having two bites at the cherry so close together was great. We were able to cinch up a few things and write the new song before the return season. More good reviews and happy audiences were had, and then it was time for Petra to bundle up a few key props and head to the other end of the planet.

Once again thrust back on her own resources, she had to work hard touring *Panic!* across the fringe festivals of Canada. Luckily Petra's resources, as always, were up to the challenge. She kept

Rebecca and I informed with hastily scrawled letters and packets of clippings. She received good press (articles sometimes described her as a 'native New Zealander'), mixed-to-good reviews, and the stunt Petra had evolved in Wellington of towing her bed through Manners Mall became her signature attention-getter. Edmonton was the big one on the festival circuit, and it was here that *Panic!* was recognised as a bona fide hit. Petra wrote joyfully to us of her success, relief and delight at the recognition she was getting from reviewers and audiences alike—and she was even making money. All the hard work had been worth it.

Petra later performed *Panic!* in London (to somewhat less approbation) and then it was put back in the cupboard. But Petra's original vision for it—to have her own show to take to Canada—had been fully and amply realised. My vision—to have fun writing and putting it on at BATS, and then to know that Petra was performing it in some little playhouse on the prairie while I was eating my breakfast—was also fulfilled. By the end, *Panic!* didn't owe us anything.

Petra went on to a theatre and TV career in the UK. She was in sci-fi comedy *Hyperdrive*—and not too long ago, I paused an episode of *Miranda* when I thought I recognised a familiar face . . . However she's most celebrated these days as a founding member of four-person physical theatre company Spymonkey, whose successes include performing for three years with Cirque du Soleil in Las Vegas.

But where did it start? Where did Pip the Hip, itinerant busker, first venture indoors to evolve into Petra Massey theatre artist? As with very many other writers, actors, directors and dreamers across the years—and as with Rebecca and myself—it was at BATS Theatre, Wellington, New Zealand. Wasn't it?

Petra:

I was in my early 20s and on the journey of a lifetime, travelling around the world performing solo street shows as an escapologist, when I found myself in windy Wellington. It was there that I wanted to realise writing and performing my burgeoning solo theatre show, and I set out looking for like-minded folk who might want to help. It was a naïve approach but that's always the best way. When you know too much, it can stop you moving forward. I knew little then, and not much more now.

Someone recommended I get in touch with Rebecca Rodden, who in turn put me in touch with her collaborator, Ken Duncum. We three met in a sunny white room and talked about ideas, things that excited us and the very dark sense of humour equally and unequivocally shared. (Although I have a vague suspicion that Ken might have thought Rebecca and I went a bit too far at times!)

I was particularly inspired by *Polythene Pam*, and originally it was thought to do a version with rewrites, but Ken and Rebecca rightly encouraged me to create something new. This was the catalyst for creating from real life experience, and thus *Panic!* was born. Working with two exceptional and very experienced writers was a 'Pinch me, I'm dreaming' moment. I just walked into a country I had never been to before, across the other side of the world. This was a golden wave. Patiently and with huge insight, Ken and Rebecca guided me through a new, vulnerable and thought-provoking process, setting me to writing verbatim stories which they would then squirrel away at, develop, colour and heighten, with wonderful comic aplomb and deep empathy, to build the imaginary world of a young woman trapped by fear. Indeed, Frankie was trapped by fear of fear itself, plus a whole bunch of treasure-shit that she couldn't bear to throw away until she got hemmed to her own bedroom hemming.

Once the story emerged, we all just started to write reams of stuff, both fictional and true. We all picked the golden nuggets and Ken tied the fragments together. Ken also directed the show, and Rebecca added her wisdom. This really was the beginning of my work, and it whetted my appetite for the resolutely absurd amidst what appeared to be normal. Ken and Rebecca gave me huge confidence to stick to my guns as both a writer and performer, and those early days have been instrumental to my work since. It's nice to finally tell them that, now aged half-a-century. (Gosh, they must be really old!)

As both Ken and Rebecca already had a strong relationship with BATS Theatre, it was an honour to be invited to perform the first run of *Panic!* at this warm and well-loved venue. I remember so many wonderful nights in the bar talking with other like-minded folk. It was such a hubbub of activity and friendly faces. This was my introduction to thespian world. Everyone at BATS was so supportive, and by the end of the run it was jam-packed. *Panic!* went on to tour all over Canada, and very proudly ended up in a fringe theatre in London, called Etcetera Theatre. I owe a lot to Ken, Rebecca and BATS Theatre, all of whom were the springboard for a lifetime dedicated to creating and making shows with good folk.

There is one other story. I even still have the newspaper cuttings! I was banned from Manners Mall for performing my street show, as the shop vendors complained that my crowds were too big and that I was stopping the public from spending money. I still recall, twenty-three years on, it was the man who sold the doughnuts and the Tandys record shop man who were the most resentful and used to shout abuse at me in the street. Never deterred, and with a solo theatre show to sell, I decided I would chain myself to the bed I used in the play and walk through the mall publicising the show. With *Panic!* posters plastered all around, and with my two staunch feminist friends both equipped with inflatable plastic hammers to protect me from the doughnut and Tandy men, it made the press. Headline: 'Pip the Hip shows too big and causing a fire hazard'. Then the first line: 'So come see her theatre show.' I thought that would piss off the vendors, but instead I got a free doughnut. Maybe I helped business or maybe it was just for being plain ballsy. Thanks, Rebecca. Thanks, Ken!

Panic!
by Ken Duncum, Rebecca Rodden and Petra Massey
Originally performed at BATS Theatre,
April 1993 (New Zealand Fringe Festival), and
April–May 1993 (return season).

Frankie	Petra Massey
Director	Ken Duncum
Illusions	Tim Denton

Panic!

Silence.

A dim light on the scene. A pile of boxes and other rubbish with a bed in the middle.

An unmoving lump in the bed. Beside it, sitting bolt upright, staring with speedy haven't-slept-for-seven-years eyes is Frankie.

She looks a couple of times at the lump, as if unable to believe it can sleep on, oblivious.

Trying not to wake her bedfellow, she switches on the plastic tulip lights beside her and reaches for a book. She accidentally drops it. She winces. The lump doesn't stir.

She retrieves the book, opens it and rustles the pages more and more noisily. No reaction from the lump. She 'accidentally' drops the book again, louder—then springs up as if suddenly woken by the noise. To no avail.

She reaches far over for her musical flowers, winds them a small amount, then settles back, still staring wakefully as they play. The music stops.

She reaches over, winding the flowers again. Then, stretching to replace them, she tumbles off the bed and into a box, which rolls into a pile of rubbish, which collapses in a crashing cacophony.

The flowers play on. The box is still.

It starts to move, working its way laboriously towards the front of the stage, where Frankie manages to flip it over.

She is stuck, shell-shocked.

She looks up.

Frankie:

I love this time.

The hour before dawn. When you don't know whether to be frightened of the night or scared of the day. The hour when all your rubbish cries out to be sorted.

I was in hospital once. Had the best bed in the whole ward, opposite the nurses' station. This was the time they'd wheel out the people who'd died during the night, rubber wheels squeaking on the lino, when everyone was deep asleep but me.

I didn't sleep at all. For one thing, I had a knee like a blood-filled pumpkin, and I was also coming off an addiction to tranquilisers.

The doctors said they wanted to get me off all prescription drugs. They were a bit concerned because the ones I'd been taking were usually reserved for large-mammal veterinary cases. Gave you a great night's sleep, though.

Although, they did have the slight side-effect of drying up all your spit so you walked around with your tongue superglued to the roof of your mouth.

I didn't really mind.

Well, that's the beauty of being on heavy-duty tranks, isn't it? You don't really mind anything.

But it did cause me a certain amount of unpleasantness in shops. I'd be standing in front of the counter, wanting a packet of tea and saying—

She imitates tongueless speech for 'Packet of tea. Packet of tea! Have you got a packet of tea, please?!'

—and the shopkeeper would shout, 'If you people want to live in this country, why don't you learn the bloody language!'

In the end I found it easier to steal.

But I only took things that I desperately, desperately needed.

I was eventually caught running out of a department store with an automatic golf-putting machine and a teddy bear in a top hat. The store detective chased me down the street, and, in a panic, I rushed out into the road. Luckily, just as he caught up with me I was run over by a car. Crushing my knee.

Even more luckily, it was a hit-and-run, and the driver drove off with the incriminating teddy bear impaled on his aerial. Then, as if to top off my good fortune, the store detective slipped over on my knee-cap, which had squirted out on the road. He banged his head, got concussion and couldn't remember anything. Owing to the lack of evidence, no charges were laid. Instead I was hospitalised, for months baffling medical science with my inability to walk, no matter how many operations or pieces of plastic they inserted in my leg. Cuddled, coddled, not even responsible for my own bowels. Always someone just a buzzer-press away to take care of my rubbish.

She touches a few pieces of her collection.

Rubbish. Even as a little girl I couldn't walk past a feather without picking it up. A scrap of shiny paper. Stones and driftwood from the beach. And look, Mum—a pink balloon full of snot. A what? Aaaaggghhh!!!! Wash wash wash! Bath bath bath!

I cried about that dirty old Frenchy, though. See, I couldn't bear to part with any of my collection. It all had to be there, from grasshoppers' legs down to bottle-tops, or I couldn't live my little kiddy life.

I'd lay it all out and check it every day, had to be able to lay my hand instantly on the smallest crusty bogey—I kept all them, too, in a matchbox. And if anything was missing, or I only thought something was missing, or I was just suddenly struck by the thought that I hadn't checked it today, even though I knew I had, I'd feel my—

—heart beat—

—chest tighten—

—breath pant—oh my God, I'm gonna die—

She grabs her ukulele and starts the 'Panic' song.

> I'd start to panic
> I'd start to panic
> I'd start to panic
> I'm in the P-A-N-I-C
> Icy grip of panic
> My heart's gonna burst, my head's gonna blow
> There's something going on that I don't know
> It's panic!

Like at school, they were always asking me questions:

'Frankie, what is the—'

I don't know! How would I know?! What are you asking me for?!

'I haven't even told you what the question is yet.'

Why pick on me? I don't know anything! Trust me!

'It could be a perfectly simple question'

Simple questions! They're the worst! What is 'truth'? How are you today? What's this puddle under your desk? Every time, I'd just start to—

> Panic
> I'd start to panic
> I'd start to panic
> I'm in the P-A-N-I-C
> Icy grip of panic
> My palms are wet, I'm in a cold sweat
> Gonna die any minute if I'm not dead yet
> It's panic!

Phobias. Some people collect stamps, I've got every phobia in the book. Fear of heights, fear of bites, fear of losing all my sight.

Fear of falling, fear of bawling, fear of people who come calling.

Fear of phones, fear of bones, fear I'll put on five stone.

Fear of snakes, fear of rape, fear of men who say 'She'll be jake'.

Fear of flying, fear of dying, fear of babies who won't stop crying.

Fear of car wrecks, bad sex, shouting out 'Nigger!' during *Malcolm X*!

I'm so bad I've got a phobia phobia. The fear of getting a fear
of something. You know, like that one where you suddenly find
yourself standing in your pyjamas in front of a—crowd—of . . .
Oh my God, I think I'm starting to—

> Panic
> I'm starting to panic
> I'm in the P-A-N-I-C
> Icy grip of panic
> What's my name? Well, I forget
> Gonna do something any minute
> That I'll always regret
> It's panic!

I looked up panic. It comes from Pan, the goat god of irrational
fear. When he couldn't stand it anymore, he'd dig a hole and
scream into it—

Frankie screams loudly into the hole of her ukulele.

—then he'd quickly cover it up before the sound could get out.

I tried that. My mum thought it was dogs digging up the lawn and
shot them with a BB gun.

The neighbours thought I was vomiting into the holes; jumped
to the conclusion I was pregnant and enlisted their son in the
merchant navy.

Everywhere my dad stuck his gardening fork, horrible screams
rocketed forth. They infected the air so that the birds became afraid
of heights and just huddled together on the ground. When we
put our canary outside for some sun, he just became seized by a
crippling terror of public speaking. Eventually the whole section was
riddled with my screams and you didn't know where to step without
the brittle crust breaking and plunging you down into the whirling,
pent-up boiling vortex of my panic—of my panic . . . of my . . .

WHERE'S MY FUCKIN' UKULELE!

> You always thought I was such a sweet kid
> But now you see what panic done did
> My voice is calm, my smile is wide
> But look at what I hide inside
> It's panic
> Pure panic
> Sheer panic
> You're in my panic!

She repeats mantra-like to herself, then states—

The only thing we have to fear is fear itself.

And, of course, that we get so drunk at a party we climb onto a table and masturbate.

Well, everyone's got that fear, haven't they?

When I realised that was my idea of bad form at a social gathering, I got scared it'd work subliminally. You know, self-fulfilling prophecy. One minute I'm standing around discussing astrology and home jewellery making, the next I'm up on the chips and dip table, playing with myself. Fingering my genitalia, full-colour, head back, laughing—figuring I'm being rad and seriously erotic. Mmmm—everybody watching—you're watching me. All acting casual, pretending you go to parties all the time where people fiddle with their diddles. Sooo sophisticated.

I probably got that fear from a rather traumatic experience I had with my first boyfriend. We went to this party once where he got so drunk that he had sex with a frozen turkey.

He was left alone with it in the kitchen and he said one thing just sort of led to another.

It's not the kind of thing your mother prepares you for, though, is it? Walking into the kitchen and finding the man in your life raping a naked, tied-up headless turkey.

I couldn't help but lose a little respect for him.

I said I never knew he felt that way about large game birds. He got all indignant and said what sort of a pervert did I think he was— he wasn't attracted to live turkeys.

Here was a man who wasn't even prepared to enter into a relationship with a turkey in full command of its faculties! The fact that it ended at the neck meant he didn't have to look it in the eye afterwards!

Of course, he broke down and said he was sorry—he was the innocent party; the turkey led him on.

He said his relationship with me was totally different. Much deeper.

But as soon as I opened the door and saw him with that turkey on his dick, I knew—I could never eat Christmas dinner with him again.

After that, I fell in love with a Frenchman—called Eric—who looked like a stunted version of Mel Gibson. He didn't know much English, so we didn't talk a lot—in the four years we lived together.

Eric had big green eyes, short cropped hair, a smile that gaped from ear to ear, and only half the amount of teeth most people have. He was tiny but perfectly built—my small Mediterranean hunk. He was probably the happiest, kindest, most generous person I've ever met. It all ended one morning when I panicked and made the ultimate Freudian slip at breakfast. I meant to say, 'Could you pass the butter please, darling?' but ended up screaming, 'Get the fuck out of my life you toothless leprechaun bastard!'

He left without even passing me the butter.

I knew I should never have taught him English.

But Eric's English was definitely his most exciting feature. The first time he met my father, Eric shook his hand and said—just like I'd taught him to—'Hello, please may I put my willy in your hole?' He was so sweet. One Easter, we promised each other chocolate bunnies. He was late coming home, so I ate his. But when he did arrive, it was with a small cardboard box which he gave to me. Inside was a tiny breathing bunny with soft brown fur and eyes as liquid as Eric's. I looked at it and thought, 'Oh, don't tell me I've got to look after a sodding bunny for the next ten years of my life!'

He saw the look on my face, so I quickly said, 'Oh, Eric—it's beautiful.' I was touched, I admit. I started to warm to the idea. This could be the image I was looking for. I could take the bunny everywhere on my shoulder attached to my ear with a gold chain.

I took the bunny out of the box and immediately noticed that it wasn't breathing right. It couldn't hop and its legs shook.

I knew it was dying, and once again I wished it was just a chocolate shell full of flowing caramel.

Eric started to get a bit upset, but I told him it would be alright and rolled the bunny up in one of his old cardigans for comfort. Sure enough, the next morning the bunny had died of hypothermia. Eric had gone to every pet shop in town and only found the right bunny in the one farthest away. It had taken him an hour to walk back in the cold.

We buried the bunny in the park on Good Friday. Eric blamed himself and cried the whole time, saying over and over, 'I snuffed-it the bunny. The little bunny is snuffed-it and I snuffed-it'd'd him.'

She takes a stiff, flattened, long-dead bunny out of the box and cradles it.

Eric lives with his mum and dad now. He'll be 32 this year, but he doesn't care what people think. His mum makes the best pasta and, anyway, it's his home.

She sings—

> Sleep
> Oh sleep
> My dearest boy
> I will cradle you
> I will guard you

Sleep, oh sleep
My love, my joy
Sleep, sleep and dream

You sat on my lap
We played together
The life-long day you lay
On my breast
You've always been
Close to my heart
Now you're tired
You can rest

Sleep, oh sleep
My love, my joy
Sleep, sleep
And dream

Dreams? I got 'em.

When I was only 17, I fell in love with a gypsy queen.

Well, with the idea of being a gypsy queen. Magic and powerful and close to the earth. My tribe around me. Dark, sullen, swearing men. Silent, smoking-like-a-chimney women. Savage shouting packs of children harassing little animals.

My gypsy blood swells rawest/reddest at night. This ditzy dispossessed woman-thing you see by day—come night, she surges.

Daytime is for panic. Idiot-making time. But blacktime, my brain is straight. That dicey day feeling? Gone. Now is me. Gypsy energy. It's like the guts of me roll right up my chest; the freaked out mess mutates, transforms. Power runs up my belly and the juice is magic, man. Magic.

And you just lie there, sleep-sweat glistening, soft flatulent noises shlupping out your nose, but your power is gnat's piss next to mine. Sure, daytime you're the together one, me the manic mess—but dead-time, I unfold my might. Night-might. And I do not soul-share. I sit right up, bolt up, eyeing your sweat lump, and I swear fire screams out my eyes. And you can't even feel this. This force. Don't know even the quarter of me. Dreams? Yeah, I got 'em. So many it'd shock you staring awake if you knew. Night—it be crazy time. But day squashes my brain. Morning, I'm stuck in your nutty, nutty network. My deep red blood down the plughole. Day patterns drain me and leave me trying, just bloody trying, to connect.

The gypsy queen is full of stories and brilliant ideas. She has a husband for children and a man for sex.

The man is called her 'coaxer'. He's trained up from childhood to give the queen pleasure without ever taking his dick out of his pants. The women of the tribe teach him what words to say, and where the places are that make you melt.

He comes to the queen when she wants him, and he does his work until she's teetering on the edge, a hand-grenade touch away from orgasm. So then the useless husband can come in and load children into her like sardines into a tin.

And the poor old coaxer has to stand outside in the cold, listening, watching her caravan bounce on its axles and feeling his balls turn blue.

Not a bad system, I reckon.

Specially the coaxer.

Every woman should have one of them.

She uses a comb and paper for a kazoo and sings—

> Coax me, baby
> Coax me all night long
> Coax me, baby
> Coax me up until dawn
> Do everything to me, baby
> But keep your trousers on
> With your face like a hatchet, your tongue like a frog
> When I get that feeling, you can be my little lap-dog

Coax me, baby
Coax me till I burn
Coax me, baby
Until I toss and turn
Do everything to me baby
But you can keep your sperm
Don't want to see your willy, don't want to see your
  dick
Don't want you inside of me, just come back and
  coax me quick
Coax me, baby
Coax me all night long
Play me baby
Play me like a song
Long as you remember in the morning
You'll be going home with your hard-on

The gypsy queen tells my past. Just cross her wrists with slivers and she opens those veins of history.

I was born because a dog bit my father on the nose.

In later years, he exaggerated the size and the fierceness of the dog, but in a fit of blind honesty once admitted it was a snappish terrier he put in a high cupboard as a joke. When he opened the cupboard door, however, the terrier got the last laugh. It seemed for a little while that my father would be wearing a dog on his face for the rest of his life as a sort of fashion accoutrement. But in its own good doggy time, the terrier let go and vanished into history.

My father's nose was so severely crushed that they had to remove the bones from it. He was 21 at the time, and he remained without a nose to speak of, or speak through, until he had an operation at 24.

In the intervening three years, he just had a big hole in his face. And that's the reason he fell in love with my mother—because she was Jewish and had a honker big enough to knock a buzzard off a shit-cart. So every time they kissed, her nose went into the hole in his face and he felt—complete.

I've got my dad's nose. It's around here somewhere.

Of course I would have preferred it if he'd left me his house or his car or stonking great wads of cash—but it just wasn't that sort of relationship, you know? He never knew quite what to do, face-to-face with a small, screaming, angry girl who kicked and kicked and never stopped kicking as if she missed having a womb to stretch.

Unfortunately, as hard as she kicked and as dirty as she got, her father never thought she was capable of doing little boy things like fishing and football. Instead he used to take all the local lads and leave her behind. When she couldn't get what she wanted, she would scream not just for hours, but days and days. Sometimes she would go into a sulk, which was at least peaceful, but after a week or so it became worrying as she refused to eat and would be found wandering around at night.

One time she broke a thermometer and saw all the wonderful silver balls you get on cake decorations—so she swallowed a few and had to go to hospital, where they tried to take her temperature but she bit the end off their thermometer cos now she'd got the taste for it.

Hospitals. Cold lino. Warm urine bottles. The heels of the nurses' sensible shoes ticking off the night hours.

Like that time I had the accident with my knee. And they made me go cold-turkey off pills. I was so scared I'd never sleep again.

Sometimes I think it's starting all over.

The only thing that made my fear of hospital bearable was that I was everybody's darling there—propped up like a battered beauty queen in the best bed in the ward, right opposite the nurses' station.

That, and the fact that I was so much more terrified of everything outside.

I felt like I was in the white, warm, sterile eye of the storm. Night-nurse followed day-nurse. Everything was routine. Monotonous. People suffered and died, but all it came down to was a squeaking of rubber wheels just before six in the morning.

I couldn't walk out of there.

I couldn't make myself move.

But nothing lasts forever. Not even paralysis.

One day they brought in this pathetic old lady who'd gone one better than me and got herself run over by a truck. And they gave her my spot! My best prime-viewing, freak-watching possie.

I rebelled. 'No way, I'm not moving from here.'

But you know nurses—all smiles from the waist up while their feet are busy knocking your bed-brake off. 'Don't worry—she's not expected to last the night.'

Tomato soup for dinner. Cool, I like 'matie soup. I take one sip and the truck lady vomits blood into her oxygen mask. What was going on here? I didn't want to watch this!

They gave her the last rites at two in the morning. But even that didn't stop her.

Heave. Cough. Choke. Groan.

And then to top it off, what'd she do? She lived! Sucked on to life like a limpet and the next morning lay there, smug as you like, in my spot as if she cheated death each and every night and survived to celebrate the dawn.

I could see right away she'd be the chirpy darling of all the nurses. I'd forfeited my Queen-of-Orthopaedics crown and if I didn't like it, I knew what I'd have to do—get up on the crutch they'd brought me a week before and walk.

Walk out.

And get run over by a train!

Yeah, who's the most seriously injured now?

So I get up on the crutch and I put my foot to the floor for the first time in four months and find out those bastard surgeons have left a scalpel inside my knee. Well, that's what it feels like.

But I keep going, step after step.

After all, I've got a train to meet. I've got to get so horribly crippled that I get my popularity back. 'Pardon me, boy, is this the amputation station? Boop-boop!'

Then I hear this whisper, this faded croak, coming from the truck lady.

She's watching me, and she's kind of curling the fingers on her mashed-up arm. 'Dear . . . dear . . .'

Oh no—I don't want to know. But of course I'm hobbling the couple of steps and bending down to the whispery voice. Down, down to the point where, in all the splatter movies, she suddenly jumps up with the power of a superhuman zombie and bites your face off! Rrrrgghhhrrrghhh!!!

It flitted across my mind that her teeth were in the drawer by her bed and, while she was reaching for them, I could always club her with the crutch.

But all that happened was she whispered, 'I think you're . . . so brave.'

Pause.

Well, fuck me!

So brave?

Me?

With all my fears and phobias and panics, the rubbish of my lousy relationships, secret sweet dreams and night-terrors, so afraid of everything in the world that I'd have to live in a plastic bubble if I didn't get claustrophobia.

Me?

Blind old bat.

Wise woman.

Panic artist.

Gypsy queen.

The sun's coming up and you've survived another night.

All this rubbish you've had out on the corner of your life all your life, and for what? In the hope that, someday, someone would come by and pick it up for you.

And all that happened was the pile got bigger. And you grew more attached to it.

Well, tomorrow's another night. And maybe it's not getting your rubbish taken out that counts—it's what you do with it while you wait.

Frankie has been steadily packing her rubbish and pulling the boxes in towards her bed. Now, as she lifts the sail into position and steps into the bow, the lights grow on the shape of the rubbish-boat she has created. She begins to beat out a rhythm, singing a rising song as the sun comes up.

> While you wait . . . while you wait . . .
> to rise
> to rise
> feel the sun up in my eyes
> see the dark cut down to size.
> Now panic falls behind
> it still curls asleep inside my mind
> as I know it always will
> But though the vampires of my fears awake
> in my heart there's more at stake
> they cannot have my soul to take
> I can hang on until
> I rise
> I rise
> someday I'll break these binding ties
> what a surprise
> what a surprise
> when I rise

She climbs into the bed, and magically melts into the bulge already

there. After a moment, she turns over and stretches to turn off the
tulip-lights before settling down to sleep.

Lights fade to blackout.

The End

Panic! Outtake:
Leap Year

One of our earlier sequences, which Petra later added back into the show when performing Panic! in the UK.

After Eric I married a bike boy. I thought life with him would be a warm breeze in my hair and a powerful throbbing between my thighs. Instead all I got was the warm breeze from between his thighs and a powerful throbbing in my head.

Pick-up 52. That's what my Pan, my rowdy pots and pans man, liked to play. Up he'd throw them in a storm, a rush-hour of cards, a flock of hearts and a clatter of spades, diamonds cutting my throat and clubs on my head, shattering, scattering, splattering on the floor. Then he'd look at me. Such looks. Turn me to pudding. 'Pick 'em up' he'd say. And I'd have to go scrabbling all over on my knees, picking them up. Counting to make sure. While he stood looking. Fifty-one. 'Fifty-one? Can't play Pick-up 52 with only 51.' Honest, I can't find it. I've looked everywhere. 'You must be blind. Eyesight like yours, you need to get closer. You need to get right down on your belly.' Friction smell of carpet, elbows raw. 'Scuse Pan, 'scuse Pan, lift your foot? 'Not till you find that card.'

Trouble was, they weren't just cards down there on the floor. They were the weeks of all my years. Pick-up 52. One by one. Make them all neat and tidy. So he could throw them up in the air again.

So I got out. I waited for leap year. And I leapt.

Tell you how it happened. He had this trailbike, see, that he loved. Loved. And this winter he brings it inside. Right inside on the carpet. Reckons he's going to strip it down and rebuild it. In between me and the telly. And, sure enough, it goes all to pieces. Dirty, oily, gutty looking things on bits of newspaper that he's always stopping to read. Springs and things coming out of other things and everything getting smaller and smaller—like one of those dinosaur digs where it looks like they've got totally bugger-all, but you know it'll come together in the end. I had to watch the telly through the back wheel all that winter. Every now and then he'd give it a spin—because he knew what that did to my head. Blink blink blink. Make you feel like you're going to have a fit.

Anyway, as the weather changes, so does this motorbike. It starts to pull itself together. And on the very first day of spring he bolts the final ratchet up the gadget and he stands back with a look on his face that I've never seen before. And if it's not love, then you'd need a big dictionary to find out what else it was. 'Now,' he says, 'the moment of truth.' And he throws his leg across that bike, flicks the stand up and sits there for a moment, back straight, foot poised on the kickstart, looking out, not at the telly or the wallpaper like a skin disease or the dirty old newspapers he's read a thousand times, but at the road he sees stretching out ahead of him. And then, like a man from a film who knows just what he wants, he kicks straight down. And the sleeping, cosseted, love-taking, telly blocking beast comes to life, greeting the spring with a scream.

She holds up a small mechanical piece.

And he's left this bit out so it's stuck in gear.

Straight into the telly. Luckily the acceleration was so great by that point that he was pulling a wheelstand, so he just sort of used the telly as a launch pad for going up the wall. Damn near reached the ceiling too. Well, those tyres are made for off-road. Anyway he describes this sort of half-circle on the wall, comes back down and goes head-on into the floor, falls over on his side and starts doing wheelies round and round because he still can't turn it off and he's sort of trapped underneath. Round and round he goes with him shouting out all the time for me to do something. Luckily in the end the back wheel gets a bit of traction on the couch, and the whole thing with him still hanging on shoots straight across the room and into the fishtank. And then it sort of chokes a bit and dies. Somehow all the water and the fish and the blood and the petrol puts it out.

Then, of course, the ambulance comes and off he goes on a stretcher. Leaving me to clean up. I get a toilet roll and blot up all the petrol and the neons and the guppies and chuck it down the toilet. Doesn't make much of an impression: the whole place still looks and smells like a four-car collision in a fish market. Back he comes, all gouged and stiff and stitched, limping on a crutch. 'What are we going to do about all this?' I say. 'Shut up,' he says, totally disgusted. Then in he goes, sits on the toilet, lights a cigarette and drops the match in the bowl. Where I've put all the paper soaked in petrol.

Well, this time when the ambulance comes back, they have to carry him out on the stretcher lying on his stomach, with his bum all blown up and his jeans in shreds, and a river running through the house from where our toilet was. 'What happened, mate?' says the ambulance men who're getting on first-name terms with him. So he's telling them. And they're laughing so hard that they drop him down the front steps and he breaks his wrist.

And his broken wrist must have set wrong or something. Because he couldn't grip properly after that. Not with that hand. And that was his throttle hand. So I knew he wouldn't be able to catch me no more. And that's how it came to be leap year.

Illustrations